You MUST Have Done SOMETHING

You MUST Have Done SOMETHING

David Graves

Whirlwind Publishing

This book is dedicated to all children of divorce, especially Katie.

Acknowledgements

First, I would like to thank my mother who taught me the value of family. Her tireless efforts made me realize the importance of family, above all.

My friends, Ronnie, Karen, Lou, and Nikki for standing by me through the darkest of times, as I don't think I could have made it to this point without you.

Thank you Brian Lee for showing me that there are groups of people fighting the same cause and that I was never fighting alone.

Thank you Dr. Michael Rathjens for giving me tools to withstand a judgmental society.

Thank you to my editor, Veronica Tuggle, whose support and expertise included telling me that this is a story that needs to be told.

The many parents who have, are, and will battle the family court system that erases them in the sole interest of monetary gain.

Katie, none of this was, is, or will ever be your fault.

Introduction: The Revenue Machine

Have you ever heard the phrase "Kids are resilient"? I suppose that may be true, but I ask, what other choice do they have? Child abuse, human trafficking, slave labor, and in this and many other cases, losing a parent to the higher bidder. Children are not resilient. Children are helpless, stifled, and even brainwashed. The more momentum picked up from a parent bad mouthing the other parent, the more easily a child can become estranged. The family courts fail to punish perjury, whether by spoken testimony, written affidavits, or false police reports; this allows an unscrupulous parent to gain an edge by exploiting the blind eye of the court. All too often, false charges are dismissed with no reprimand for fabricating charges and wasting the court's time. The lack of consequences for lying encourages the unscrupulous parent to create more of these allegations. A corrupt court recognizes this as a way to fill the docket, which in turn fills the pockets of each participating professional.

It's been reported that divorce is a $50 billion a year industry. It is also widely understood that the family court system is broken. However, I believe it is operating just as it was intended. Judges, lawyers, guardians ad litem, therapists (mine, yours, ours, and theirs), child protective services, mediators, police, social workers, court clerks, and so on all pull a paycheck from the revenue-generating machine known as family court.

This book is my story of "In the Fifteenth Circuit of Palm Beach County, Florida" Case #200910788 that currently has 46 pages, totaling 1226 docket entries to date. My intention is to show what the court enabled over the thirteen years that this case has been active, while continuing to profess having my child's best interest. The court allowed my former wife to spend 13 years and over $2 million to achieve her desired result: estrangement between our daughter and me.

This book is for the people who are about to enter into the proverbial knothole of the family court system, are already in it, or have already been pulled through. It is also for the adult children of divorce to help them understand what might have been going on while they were busy being "resilient." If this book causes one person to reconsider using family court for retaliation or calms the hatred for an ex-spouse, which could subsequently provide some peace for a child, I will consider this book to be a success.

CHAPTER 1

The Divorce Trial

" *A divorce is like an amputation:*
you survive it, but there's less of you. "
Margaret Atwood

Day 1 (June 3, 2010)

Case number 200910788 of the Fifteenth Judicial Circuit Court of Palm Beach County, Florida commenced on June 3, 2010. My attorney, Eric Cheshire, walked with me to the end of the hall to pray before the trial commenced, as he also did during breaks. He assured me that he knew the judge, the Honorable Judge Catherine Brunson, because they went to the same church. He later revealed they were only acquainted and that they only saw each other occasionally when they picked up child relatives at the church after daycare. My decision to file for divorce in the State of Florida could not be changed back to my current residence in the State of New Jersey, where my family and I knew the judges personally through politics. Eric had previously arranged for my wife Maureen and me to be evaluated by the court psychologist because he wanted to expose Maureen's severe co-dependency issues. He later said he regretted this choice. He felt it was this decision that rendered an unfavorable outcome in the divorce trial.

I had been in court every week for motions that I filed and motions Maureen's attorney filed—sometimes more than just once a week. I also had to go to the court clerk's office to file those motions, to report to court psychology in preparation for some of the motions I was filing, and to set up the details for the Social Comprehensive investigation I was trying to get off the ground. The Palm Beach County courthouse was only ten minutes from my work, but the time spent inside the courthouse routinely made me late returning from my half-hour lunch. Although my employer understood my situation, it was a place of business, and all the lost time was wearing thin. I knew my days were numbered because there certainly wasn't any relief in sight from courthouse visits. Eventually, my employer nicely asked that I leave the company. The company was nice enough to arrange my termination so I could collect unemployment insurance.

With the lawyers in place and all the motion hearings out of the way, both attorneys were ready to dig into any dirt they could possibly bring in. I composed a witness list for the trial, and all had been subpoenaed. Maureen involved the police during our child exchange meetings and used difficult behavior and dramatics to try to push me into frustration in front of the police and our daughter. Her tactics did not work, but they did make the exchanges more stressful for everyone, including our daughter.

On the first day of the trial, Eric's opening argument told the judge that Maureen and I married in 1999, had a child in 2006, and moved to Rhode Island in 2008. We separated in 2008, just months after we moved to Rhode Island. Eric told the judge that after the separation, I continued to see my daughter until Maureen moved to Florida in the middle of the night in September of 2009 and immediately filed for an order of no contact with the court in Florida, which was denied by Judge

Brunson for lack of evidence. Eric further stated that Maureen had "set a course to do everything she could to keep this little girl from her dad" and "witnesses have observed the father with his child and stated that he is perfectly appropriate to parent and to be with his child." He stated unequivocally that I had never committed any improper behavior as a father to my daughter. Eric continued his statement by pointing out, "This case is about a mother who will not comply with the public policy of this state and with Florida Statute 61.13 that each parent should have frequent contact with their minor children and that each parent should promote the relationship with the other parent and the minor child."

Eric then told the judge that Maureen had taken all of the marital assets, including tangible items, bank accounts, and contents of the safe deposit box and that I was entitled to an equitable distribution of those assets.

This divorce trial was changed to a custody trial in the first ten minutes and never left that course. Equitable distribution was rarely mentioned again. Next, it was Maureen's attorney, Greg Burdick's turn at an opening.

The first topic out of Mr. Burdick's mouth was about my anger. I *was* angry. It seemed then—and still seems—perfectly reasonable to feel angry when your spouse suddenly takes everything *and your daughter* on a midnight express to a destination 1200 miles away. However, Burdick implied that my anger was not reasonable as he tried to paint a picture of a person who should not have a relationship with his child. Greg Burdick went on to accuse me, unjustly and without evidence, of breaking into his home and drawing tombstones on his wall. The blatant lies he told during his statements are a disgrace to any form of a just system. This is one of the ways family court appears to be purposely using corruption to generate revenue. The expense I would be forced to incur in order to combat his lies would be paid in hours billed to him and my lawyer and also paid to the judge for additional hearing hours. When you cannot afford to hire an investigator to dispute opposing counsel's lies, you are forced to endure having those lies embedded in the permanent record.

Then Burdick laid the groundwork for money that I was awarded from my previous employer due to a contract dispute. He stated that my forthcoming award was part of the marital assets, and his client was due her share. Mr. Burdick then told the judge that I refused to pay child support. He refrained from mentioning that I was out of work because of the constant need to be in court; that fact did not play into his narrative.

My first witness as the plaintiff in the trial was Maureen's and my former neighbor, Tina Bigiotti. Tina testified to knowing our whole family. She described our daughter Katie as a "happy, vivacious, typical child." She testified that she never saw any inappropriate acts between Katie and me. She said, "...in fact, she [Katie] expressed remorse when she'd have to leave her dad to go back with her mom." My attorney, Eric, asked, "Do you have an opinion as to whether this man loves this child and if this child loves her daddy?" Tina said, "Oh absolutely. They both love each other tremendously." Eric then attempted to enter into evidence a letter that Tina wrote that gave a more detailed account of her experiences with our family. The exhibit was objected to on the grounds that it mirrored Tina's testimony. The objection was sustained, and the letter was not permitted into evidence. Mr. Burdick's cross-examination had no remarkable issues, and Eric's redirect was a few sentences for formality. Witness number one was to substantiate my being a good dad because that's what this case was about.

The next witness was Ron Coursol, a former coworker of mine. Ron testified to knowing me over ten years and that we socialized outside of work. He told stories about Katie and me visiting him and how much Katie enjoyed feeding the fish in his large, backyard tilapia farm. Eric asked Ron about the inter-action between Katie and I. Ron answered, that Katie and I interacted very well together, "He's a great father." Eric asked about any anger outbursts, Ron answered that not only did I not exhibit any anger in front of my daughter, but that in all the years we worked together, he never saw any anger from me at work either. He also testified that he had three daughters of his own and was comfortable having me over for dinner on a regular basis. There was no cross-examination from Mr. Burdick.

The next witness took an interesting turn at cross-exam-ination. Ann Lewis was a parishioner at my church. She was also a pediatric nurse practitioner. She had recently obtained qualifications to apply for an internship and eventually get her license. She had agreed to counsel me for a small fee. It helped me to discuss the issues of the divorce and custody issues, but her testimony was riddled with objections from opposing counsel regarding her qualifications as a counselor. The judge decided that her testimony could not to be considered expert testimony; however, she was permitted to testify about our sessions in her minor capacity as a counselor.

Mr. Burdick preempted a question to Ann Lewis by stating out of turn that I was physically abused as a child, which was another lie because I was not an abused child. He then raised the question whether Ann Lewis knew that people who have been abused as children were likely to be abusive themselves. It was obvious that Mr. Burdick's goal was to have the judge hear that question of abuse, even though it wasn't true. He knew that once you hear something like that, you can't unhear it. Ann Lewis told the court that she didn't believe that I was a threat to my daughter. Eric had no redirect questions for Ann Lewis. While her testimony was favorable to me, opposing counsel brought doubt to anything she said by focusing on her lack of profes-sional counseling credentials.

The next witness Eric called was Reverend Dr. Margaret L. Bellows. Dr. Bellows was also a parishioner from my church. Using fellow parishioners from church was an economical way to get people who had seen Katie and me together in both a social and structured setting. Dr. Bellows observed Katie and me in a play setting at her home. What made this session easy was that Katie knew Dr. Bellows from church, so she didn't see it as the professional observation that it was. Under direct questioning, Dr. Bellows told the court that she earned her doctorate in worship studies—which is similar to a doctorate in ministry—from the Robert E. Weber Institute for Worship Studies in Jacksonville, Florida. She had been an ordained minister of the Methodist Church for thirteen years. She continued her education and earned a master's degree in counseling and psychology from Palm Beach Atlantic University, specializing in school counseling, substance abuse, marriage and family counseling, and mental health. Eric asked Dr. Bellows if her marriage and family counseling training included issues in domestic violence, and Dr. Bellows affirmed that it did. She also stated to the court that her training included her qualifications to be a guardian ad litem for the Fifteenth Circuit Court of Palm Beach County and had been so to eight children.

Dr. Bellows testified on the observation that she did at her home of Katie and me. Eric asked Dr. Bellows if Katie acted strange or different, as if she had been abused by her father. "Absolutely not," she said. "She seemed very natural, very comfortable, and very at ease. I didn't see any red flags that would normally be found in an abused child." Eric asked how I behaved around Katie, and Dr. Bellows replied, "He enjoyed her, and she enjoyed him. He was very patient with her. He was able to get down to her level, both physically and emotionally to communicate with her in ways she was able to grasp and understand. What I saw was a very normal father-daughter relationship for a child that age." Lastly, Eric asked Dr. Bellows if she would have any reservations about me being around her own children. She replied, "No, nor my grandchildren either."

After Dr. Bellows's honest and expert testimony, Mr. Burdick had nothing as a line of cross-examination. He asked her to repeat her name and asked how Katie and I got in her yard, as if he didn't absorb that it was a formally contracted professional observation by a qualified volunteer guardian ad litem of the Fifteenth Circuit Court of Palm Beach County. His cross-examination was baffling but not harmful.

The next witness we called was Palm Beach County Sheriff's Deputy Brian Fitch. Deputy Fitch was the officer who had been dispatched after Maureen called for police presence at a child exchange at the Sprint phone store in West Palm Beach. At the time of the exchange, no police officer was present. I stayed behind in the parking lot after dropping Katie off to her mother, looking at messages on my phone. As I sat in my car, a police cruiser pulled up, and Deputy Fitch got out. He walked up to my car and asked about the exchange and where the other party was. I told him that the exchange was over. He immediately questioned why the exchange would occur without police presence with an active order of no contact. I told him that there was no order of no contact. Deputy Fitch became very irritated and told me that a call came from dispatch stating a woman needed police presence because there was a no-contact order. When Deputy Fitch realized Maureen had lied, he asked if he could please be a witness in court to testify that my ex-wife had lied to the police.

Deputy Fitch showed up in court in full tactical uniform, including a well-equipped vest. He was over six feet tall with red hair cut in a military style. He was quite a notable presence in the courtroom. My lawyer, Eric, had neglected to notify opposing counsel of Deputy Fitch as a witness, and as this massive man sat on the stand waiting to tell the court of Maureen's dishonesty, Mr. Burdick objected to this witness. Despite Eric's explanation to Judge Brunson of pretrial stipulations, the objection was sustained, and Deputy Fitch was excused without being allowed to testify.

The remaining three witnesses that we called were a facilitator of a divorce group at a local church, named Martin McKenna; a Sunday school teacher from my church, Vonnel Kutzman; and my longtime friend from New Jersey, Gary Weincyzk. They each testified to knowing me and to seeing Katie and me interact with no issues. All testified they would be comfortable having me around their own children. For this round of witnesses, Eric utilized people who knew us personally, professionally, or both and were willing to appear in court to give their favorable accounts of Katie's and my relationship to the court. After this round of witnesses, I was to be called next.

My direct questioning and cross-examination was recorded on seventy-five pages of transcript. Eric started with the basic questions about when I moved to Florida (1996), when Maureen and I started dating (1997), when we were married (1999), how many children we have, and if I felt our marriage was irretrievably broken. Eric prompted me with questions about Katie being the result of in-vitro fertilization and why Maureen and I went to such trouble and expense to have a child. Mr. Burdick objected on relevance, so Eric explained that it was "extremely relevant" that "this woman knew this man for almost ten years before they decided to go to such great lengths to have a child together." Judge Brunson allowed Eric to continue, neither sustaining nor overruling the objection. Eric began to ask me questions about my parenting Katie. I remembered thinking how having my daughter made me feel I found my true calling in life. I talked about how Katie and I used to watch *The Wiggles* on TV. I recounted the way we would jump up and down while watching their rendition of

"Tie Me Kangaroo Down." Mr. Burdick's objection to relevance was overruled by Judge Brunson. I continued with stories about our fun with *Hello Kitty*, *Dora the Explorer*, and *Barney*.

Eric changed the line of questioning to Maureen's and my separation. He asked me about what led to the separation. I told the court about the intrusive interference of Maureen's parents in Florida prior to our moving to Rhode Island. Then I talked about how Maureen obtained a temporary restraining order against me from the state of Rhode Island, but that the order also included joint custody of Katie. Despite that restraining order, Maureen and I were together at my newly rented apartment a half a mile from the marital home. Eric entered into evidence a stack of pictures of Maureen at my apartment and at my mother's home in New Jersey during the time of the temporary restraining order. He showed Judge Brunson that Maureen was using the restraining order for dramatic purposes only. In fact, he pointed out, when the temporary order from Rhode Island was domesticated to Florida, the hearing for the permanent order was heard by our divorce judge, Judge Brunson, who was now officially reminded that she denied the permanent injunction just nine months earlier for insufficient evidence.

It was finally time to recess for lunch. When we came back, Eric resumed going through the stack of pictures. One of the first pictures shown and described was of Maureen, Katie, and I at a picnic on Labor Day weekend, 2009. Eric asked, "So [this photo] is actually from the same month that your wife came into this court and asked Judge Brunson for the restraining order?" "Yes," I replied. He then showed photos of parties, picnics, and group shots from multiple events across multiple states, each with Maureen smiling for the camera. He pointed out the photographic evidence that she was sleeping under the same roof with me during the time she held the temporary restraining order against me.

Eric then posed questions that prompted me to testify that despite the current court order, Maureen had refused to give me a copy of Katie's medical insurance card, to put me on the emergency contact list at her preschool where Maureen was working, or to inform me of Katie being sick, her doctors, events, accomplishments, and progress of any kind. Eric continued to enter exhibits into evidence that included emails and holiday cards from Maureen to me that were full of praise about what a great father I was. In all, we submitted eighteen exhibits into evidence. There were no further direct questions from Eric to me.

Just prior to Mr. Burdick's cross-examination, he clarified with the court that we had not done cross-examination and direct questioning from one period of questioning by either attorney. This was an ingenious move that later came back to hurt us on Day 3 of the divorce trial because we never called Maureen to the stand for direct questioning.

Mr. Burdick's first question was for me to read the actual length of time the State of Rhode Island awarded me for visitation with Katie. The days were Tuesday, Wednesday, Friday, and Saturday with no overnight visitation. I added that his client owed me 700 hours of timesharing when she removed our daughter from the State of Rhode Island. I know it may seem trifling, but I wanted the judge to hear it and be aware. Mr. Burdick then addressed property that had been left in the marital home for me and alluded that his client had left some marital property behind. He then asked if I would relinquish ownership of Maureen's vehicle, which was in my name. I agreed, even though we still owed two more payments. Since my name was on the loan, no one seemed to think it was important to have Maureen make those last payments.

Mr. Burdick then asked about an alleged incident at Katie's preschool, where Maureen also worked. It was the day I brought the court papers in to show the director of the school why I should be put on the emergency contact list with the school. He then switched tactics to ask me about liquidating my mutual fund accounts in 2006. I replied that Maureen and I were still together in 2006, and I used the money to save our home from foreclosure. Eric objected three times during this line of questioning, and all objections were sustained. Mr. Burdick was clearly trying to imply that I had taken money from the marital assets, which was not true. After his line of questioning was shot down, he took all the documents back and ended his cross-examination. When asked if he wanted to redirect, Eric replied, "Dad rests."

Mr. Burdick then called Yoelmy Santana, director of Noah's Ark Academy Preschool. Mr. Burdick established that Katie went to the school and that Maureen was an employee. Ms. Santana was asked if she knew me and if there were any negative incidents with me at the school. She testified that I had shown up on a non-visitation day and hugged Katie, that on another day I pointed to my watch when Katie was not ready to leave when I arrived, and that she once saw me take pictures of an overflowing dumpster in the parking lot. Eric threw off the rhythm of her testimony by objecting to hearsay questions and testimony; most of his objections were either sustained or needed to be rephrased by Mr. Burdick. Ms. Santana ended up being a non-influential witness of any regard.

Mr. Burdick then addressed the court, asking to recess for the day so he could have the remainder of his direct and closing statements in one day. He asked the court for three hours to conclude. Eric contended that we shouldn't need three hours, and we could keep going. Judge Brunson asked the two attorneys to submit their Notices of Unavailability and recessed for the day at 3:15 P.M.

Day 2 (July 19, 2010)

Dr. Michaelanne Marie, who is later brought up in the "Therapists" section of this story, is from the Court Psychology

Division of the Fifteenth Circuit and was Mr. Burdick's first witness. Dr. Marie's involvement came from Eric's early request to the court to have both parents evaluated in order to feature Maureen's co-dependency issues as a mental illness. This strategy backfired when Dr. Marie's testimony completely negated her own evaluations, in which she reported to Eric and me that she saw no issue with my having joint custody of Katie, including out of state travel.

Dr. Marie was sworn in. Eric confirmed that Dr. Marie should be considered an expert witness as Mr. Burdick addressed the court to establish her credentials for the record. He also confirmed that the Office of Court Psychology was appointed to the case. Dr. Marie testified that she determined that I suffered from depression and anger. She testified that she believed domestic abuse would perpetuate from my conditions and that she would be concerned if I were to have unsupervised visitation with my daughter. She speculated that any treatment I had previously undergone was merely "seat time," by which she meant that I did not do the work; I merely sat through the sessions without gaining any of the benefits. Mr. Burdick asked Dr. Marie if there should be a restraining order. Eric's objection that the question was outside of the scope of the witness's expertise was sustained. It was also divulged by Mr. Burdick that Dr. Marie wrote a memorandum to Judge Brunson recommending that all child exchanges occur at a police station. Dr. Marie recommended a year of anger management, and Mr. Burdick followed up with the question of whether or not Dr. Marie recommended a re-evaluation before I ever spend time with Katie unsupervised. Dr. Marie added, unprompted, that I should also be required to submit to regular drug screens. Mr. Burdick's direct questioning was over. Eric cross-examined Dr. Marie, clearly surprised by her testimony.

Eric's first question was, "Dr. Marie, didn't you and I meet in your office and discuss Mr. Graves seeing his child out of state?"

Dr. Marie:	Yes
Eric:	And you had no objection to that, am I correct?
Dr. Marie:	At the time, what I had was no objection to his having contact with her.

That was a lie. I was there when Dr. Marie specifically said to Eric that she "found no issue with joint custody or out of state travel." This was after her testing and evaluations, but prior to her reports.

Eric:	(continuing) It's your opinion that his contact with Katie be supervised?
Dr. Marie:	Yes, it is.
Eric:	Has there ever been a history of Katie being harmed around her father or by her father?
Dr. Marie:	Not that I'm aware of.
Eric:	At any time in her five-year life, is that correct?
Dr. Marie:	Not that I'm aware of, correct.
Eric:	So why would you say now that there should be supervised visitation when there's been five years of no problems at all between dad and his child?
Dr. Marie:	Because when they were together, it seems like it was a short period of time. They haven't been together alone for long periods of time. I can't say that they lived together with no problems. According to legal records, there was exposure to domestic violence. I have copies of police reports.
Eric:	Copies of hearsay police reports provided by Mrs. Graves?
Dr. Marie:	Yes.
Eric:	Are you aware that Judge Brunson [points to judge] looked at those police reports in a restraining order hearing last September of 2009?

Dr. Marie: I knew there was a hearing.

Eric: And you know that in August of 2008, twenty-three months ago, [my client] was charged with slapping his wife in the State of Rhode Island, am I correct?

Dr. Marie: From the records, yes.

Eric: (starting to rapid-fire questions) Can you show me where? While you're looking for that, are you aware that Mrs. Graves tried to get a restraining order in the State of New Jersey, and it was denied?

Dr. Marie: I didn't know if it was denied or not.

Eric: Are you aware that Mrs. Graves twice has tried to get restraining orders, and they were denied?

Dr. Marie: No.

Eric: But you *are* aware that the only thing in this man's forty-eight years of life that he's guilty of is slapping his wife twenty-three months ago?

Dr. Marie: Correct. Here's the violation of a [temporary] no-contact order from Rhode Island dated 11-9-08.

Eric: Is that when his wife came and visited him and spent the weekend with him in New Jersey?

Dr. Marie: No, this took place in Rhode Island.

Eric's rapid-fire questions confused her, and she answered incorrectly.

Mr. Burdick: Objection, that's not the question why she said supervised visitation.

Judge Brunson: I'm going to overrule the objection.

Eric: And that's what you have relied on in deciding there should be supervised visitation?

Dr. Marie: He was very explosive in my office.

Eric: Let's talk about that. He was angry in your office?

Dr. Marie: Explosive.

Eric: Did he scream? Did he throw any objects?

Dr. Marie: Never directed at me. No.

Eric: Is there any reason for this to come up—or do you have any other reason that he has to be angry *except that his wife won't let him see his child or have a normal relationship with her?*

Dr. Marie: You would have to ask him that.

Eric: Any other evidence that this man has ever committed any violence around his child? Let me backup. The slap, we have no evidence that he slapped his wife in front of their little girl, do we?

Dr. Marie: I'm not aware of that.

Eric: So as you sit here today, you actually have no evidence that you can present to Judge Brunson that this man has ever been violent in the presence of his little girl; am I correct?

Dr. Marie: All I can do is present a review of information that I've gathered.

Eric went on in great detail, dissecting Dr. Marie's report on me, citing pages for her to explain herself, and comparing her testimony now with her earlier assurances that there would be no issue with joint custody. He brought up specific portions of her report and kept reverting back to ask how she determined supervised visitation was her recommendation. He was showing the court that even though Dr. Marie flip-flopped, that even though what she did say was damaging, there simply wasn't cause for supervised visitation, and I felt he did a good job of it.

Dr. Marie: Mr. Graves actually has above average intellect that could keep him from services.

Eric: ...on page 8, in the third paragraph you state, this is your quote, his abuse scale is within normal limits.

Dr. Marie: Correct.

Eric: And he attempted to present himself in a positive manner. Doesn't everybody attempt to present themselves in a positive manner, and if not, doesn't that suggest that maybe that person has psychological issues?

Dr. Marie: That's a little too literal.... We expect that, and we hope that in dependency proceedings.

Eric: Well, you did determine, according to your testing, quote 'His abusive scale score is within normal limits,' end quote, and I look down a little bit further into the last paragraph, quote, 'The results from the Parenting Stress Index, the PSI, indicate Mr. Graves responded in a positive manner.' So you have no indication in your testing that this man faked any of his testing to you, and according to your own opinion, Doctor, his abuse scale is within normal limits. Would it be reasonable, Doctor, that any parent being accused of child abuse would respond in a defensive manner if it was false or even if it were true, wouldn't that be normal?

Dr. Marie: I'm not aware that he was being accused of child abuse.

Eric: Well, you think he should have supervised visitation?

Dr. Marie: Again, I'm not aware that he was being accused of child abuse.

Eric: Do you want him to have supervised visitation?

Dr. Marie: I can't address visitation. It's about having unsupervised contact with his daughter.

Eric: Did you receive any information from Mrs. Graves concerning her husband?

Dr. Marie: Yes I did.

Eric: Let's look a little bit at her background. She and her mother had issues, and she separated herself from her mother; is that true?

Dr. Marie: Correct.

Eric: And she was abusing alcohol by the age of fifteen, is that correct?

Dr. Marie: Correct.

Eric: And the alcohol then progressed into marijuana and cocaine use, am I right?

Dr. Marie: Definitely I'm seeing marijuana and yes, cocaine once at age fifteen. I wrote this down. (This sounded like stumbling while minimalizing).

Eric asked Dr. Marie about speaking to any other "so-called therapists" and asked her who she spoke to.

Dr. Marie: I believe it was Dr. Veronica Ricci I spoke to.

Eric: Looking at a September 17th record, Mrs. Graves was diagnosed with the following: post-traumatic stress disorder, sexual abuse as a child, victimization during childhood, and physical abuse by an adult. Did she tell you she was sexually molested by her father?

Dr. Marie: No, she didn't.

Eric: Can you tell us what kind of effect that can have on a woman, specifically a mother, who's been sexually abused by her father?

Dr. Marie: It can make her very nervous and overprotective of her child.

Eric: It could cause her to keep her children away from a male figure in her life because she's projecting her abuser onto her husband; am I right?

Dr. Marie:	It's possible.
Eric:	And she has major depression?
Dr. Marie:	That was the diagnosis in '07.
Eric:	Do people with major depression sometimes commit suicide?
Dr. Marie:	It's a possibility. It is a risk.
Eric:	Do you know how many handguns Mrs. Graves has?
Dr. Marie:	I don't know.
Eric:	You don't know?
Dr. Marie:	No.
Eric:	Now the medical history on page 3, you said it was unremarkable. Did she tell you she had genital herpes?
Dr. Marie:	No, she did not.
Eric:	Would you consider that to be unremarkable medical history?
Dr. Marie:	I wouldn't consider it unremarkable.
Eric:	Now her psychiatric history. How long ago do you think the drug abuse was?
Dr. Marie:	I believe I was under the impression that all illegal drug use had stopped prior to the birth of their daughter.

I really believed that Eric had composed a great mosaic depiction of Maureen's mental instability. The absence of her truths was a deceptive tactic for Dr. Marie to shift focus onto me.

Eric:	And there was no supervised visitation at all out of the Rhode Island court, is that correct?
Dr. Marie:	Yes.

Eric brought his questioning to an end once he brought up Maureen's drug use, low self-esteem, the possibility that she was continuing to use drugs and her defensiveness during the evaluation. He had Dr. Marie admit that she recommended long-term psychotherapy for Maureen, and then he asked Dr. Marie why she did not recommend drug treatment for Mrs. Graves. Dr. Marie replied, "No. The first step would be negative drug screens," which was not in her official report.

Eric: I have no further questions, Your Honor.

When Doctor Marie walked past our table, she leaned over to Eric and told him what a good job he did, as if it were all some kind of contest. I thought that was one the most deplorable exhibitions I had ever seen, but this was all new to me. It certainly wasn't the last deplorable character exhibition I saw during this ordeal.

I was the next witness to be called by Mr. Burdick for his direct questioning.

Mr. Burdick began by bringing up monies that were from a lawsuit against my former employer for breach of contract. Most of the mediation agreement was under a gag order that included a stipulation that I not discuss details of the litigation or mediation about the case. I received some money that Mr. Burdick was trying to get on the record for the judge to rule on for equitable distribution. Eric perpetually objected under attorney/client privilege as well as the gag order itself. It took a long time for Mr. Burdick to get any information out of me to the court because of all the objections. It seemed to come in very small dribs and drabs. Ultimately, he muddled through it and made the point for the court to consider the money awarded in the litigation against my former employer for equitable distribution. He then made an effort to get the court to think I overspent within the household. Specifically for my hobbies of playing guitar, attending Rolling

Stones concerts, and buying baseball equipment. He also brought up every relationship Maureen knew about from the time I graduated high school until I married Maureen, including the very first girl I ever dated and my first wife. This was very difficult for me. I was directed by Judge Brunson multiple times to wait before answering, and I often lost my place and answered with another question pending. It was nerve wracking. I was not relaxed up there, and it showed. Looking back, I see that despite Eric's good job in his cross-examination, having me follow the damaging testimony by Dr. Marie fared very well tactically for Burdick.

In cross-examination, Eric asked me about the times that Maureen came to my place in Rhode Island and to my mother's in New Jersey during her temporary no-contact order against me. He asked about the time Maureen threw two loaded handguns at me when she was angry. Burdick objected to that question, and the judge overruled the objection. Eric asked me about the suit against my former employer, my church, and Maureen's place of worship, and that was pretty much the extent of cross-examination. In redirect, Mr. Burdick asked me if I had ever said to Maureen that I thought the Unity School of Christianity was a cult; I answered yes. Burdick then called Maureen as his next witness.

The first thing Burdick did was establish that the sole sexual abuse Maureen endured as a child was when she witnessed a flasher with his pants down, holding his penis. He then asked about marital assets, her mutual funds, and her expenses, and he verified that she earned only $8.50 an hour and paid over $400 a month for medical insurance. When asked a child support question, Maureen went into a narrative about the temporary no contact order and lied about the judge allowing her to leave Rhode Island. Subsequent to Eric's objection for hearsay, Burdick said, "I agree with that; I agree with that." Her narrative and his comments were stricken from the record.

Maureen told stories about my "enormous" spending for baseball, concerts, and musical equipment, that I had physically and emotionally abused her, and that I took Valium and told her to kill me.

Eric interrupted her testimony to say, "I've got to object. I think the witness is reading from something." The court determined that Maureen was reading notes as her testimony, so Eric's objection was sustained. Eric then asked the judge that all of her testimony be stricken, and that motion was denied.

It was late in the day, and the judge asked both attorneys how much longer they felt the trial would take. It was estimated for another hour. Eric asked the judge for a ruling on an objection regarding Burdick "leading this witness who had these cheat notes." The judge overruled the objection. Eric gave further argument for a change on the ruling. The judge repeated herself, overruling.

Maureen then continued her story of abuse and stated that she never threw loaded handguns at me. She also said that I repeatedly violated her temporary no-contact order. Eric objected to Burdick's method of leading the witness, then, when an objection was sustained, asking Maureen the same question in the proper format so she could repeat the desired answer. That objection was sustained, and the judge announced that the matter would not conclude today. Mr. Burdick said that his witness would be able to wrap things up with her testimony. Eric said, "Well that's generally what I like witnesses to do, Judge, rather than reading their script. I would like for the witness to testify from her memory, not a document."

Mr. Burdick then asked for three more hours. Maureen addressed the court out of turn and said, "This has gone on too long." I said, "Twenty-three months." The judge recessed for the day.

Day 3 (October 1, 2010)

The first matter of the day was Mr. Burdick bringing to the judge's attention that I tampered with evidence. What happened was that Burdick gave Eric some documents to review and never asked for them back. Subsequently, when we recessed at the end of the day, Eric handed them to me, and I put them in my briefcase. Eric and I laughed about it down the hall that Burdick couldn't keep track of his document, a printout of a text message in which I called Unity a cult. Burdick accused me of stealing it, but I just did what Eric prompted me to do. I thought it was funny at the time, but now, at the next hearing, it didn't sound good.

The next issue Burdick brought up was Eric's nine new rebuttal witnesses called since the recess. Burdick objected, and Eric prevailed. Eric responded that he wanted his time on this last day of the trial, which seemed unlikely to me with nine new witnesses. Eric said he was only using one of the witnesses and wanted an hour and a half of the remaining three hours. The judge agreed.

Maureen's first answer to the first question, as she took out her crib notes, was, "Give me a moment to catch my breath." Eric, again, objected to Maureen reading from documents as her testimony. The objection was overruled.

Maureen spoke of her thinking that I was having her followed after she left Rhode Island in the middle of the night. The truth was that I sent Katie a phone and used the GPS to know Katie's location, not Maureen's. Maureen kept the phone, so subsequently I knew where Maureen was, not Katie. Maureen told the court the reason she violated her own no-contact order was that I had been begging to see Katie. Maureen turned the visit into an opportunity for more embellishment that included her and Katie leaving and her asking a New Jersey judge for a no-contact order that was denied.

Maureen's testimony was objected to for hearsay a number

of times, and she said, "I'm a little confused on hearsay." Judge Brunson suggested to Burdick, "Mr. Burdick, perhaps you can help her and ask some questions." Maureen interrupted the judge and said, "We only have an hour and a half and I'm just trying to...."

Mr. Burdick: Mrs. Graves, Mrs. Graves, excuse me. Just tell the court what happened.

Maureen spoke about me coming to the preschool to see Katie, calling on the phone, referring to Unity as a cult "several times," and that Katie "didn't want to see her dad." Eric objected to hearsay, and the judge sustained the objection.

Eric had obviously had more than enough of the reading of a script and said, "Judge, this whole testimony has all been a narrative with his witness reading."

Judge Brunson: So your objection is to it being a narrative?

Eric: Yes.

Judge Brunson: I'll sustain the objection.

Mr. Burdick: Ok.

Eric: That's all it's been.

Apparently, all Eric had to do was say the word "narrative" for the perpetual objection to be sustained. Maureen managed to read a printed script that could very easily have been proof-read, critiqued, and revised by Burdick prior to its use in court as testimony. If I'd had the finances to back it, I would have asked for a mistrial.

Burdick then questioned Maureen about her low self-esteem and codependency issues. Maureen confirmed those two diagnoses, and when Eric objected on relevance, Burdick then gave the argument to the judge that because Maureen had these two mental conditions, I would take advantage of her. Objection was overruled.

Maureen then testified that she wanted me to be "healthy" and for "Katie to have a healthy father." This was the key to keeping me from her now. She also wanted me to be evaluated prior to ever seeing Katie.

Mr. Burdick: Ok, cross.

Eric: Ms. Graves, actually, you're the one that has the history of mental illness treatment as reported by Dr. Marie, am I correct?

Maureen: I have private counseling. I've had several private counseling and marital counseling.

Eric: You've read the report on you, correct?

Maureen: Yes.

Eric: And do you remember her reporting to Judge Brunson about your history of mental illness treatment?

Maureen: I don't remember those exact words.

Eric: Let me show it to you. On page 3 of 9: Mrs. Graves reported a history of mental health treatment. Do you remember that?

Maureen: I'm reading it.

Eric: Can you read the first sentence out loud into the record?

Maureen: Mrs. Graves reported a history of mental health treatment. She said that she was receiving individual therapy.

Eric: And you also reported that you had been sexually abused as a child, correct?

Maureen: I never reported that.

Eric: Well, let's look on page 6 of 9.

Maureen: Um, what...the last time we were in court...

Eric: I want you to read it.

Maureen: I said...

Eric: I want you to read it to me. That's my question to you.

Maureen: And I explained that the last time we were in court, and I can explain it again. That would be fine.

Eric: That's not my question, ma'am. I want you to read that note, what she said right there (points to document).

Maureen: (Reading) "A note dated 9/17/08 indicates Ms. Graves was diagnosed with the following: Post traumatic stress disorder, sexual abuse of a child, victimization during childhood."

Eric: Okay?!

Maureen: (Continues reading) "...and physical abuse by an adult."

Eric: And also your diagnosis was major depressive disorder, am I correct?

Maureen: I was just beaten up by my husband after a really, really long day, so, yes, I was probably depressed?

Eric: (Reading) "Diagnosed her as having major depressive disorder, recurrent, correct?"

Maureen: Yes.

Eric: Now you were asked questions by your lawyer about being up in New Jersey and you signed paperwork. Do you remember signing that paperwork September 8th, 2009...

Maureen: Yes.

Eric: ...in New Jersey?

Maureen: Yes.

Eric: And you tried to get a restraining order, didn't you?

Maureen: Yes, I did.

Eric: And did you succeed?

Maureen: No.

Eric: You did not succeed?

Maureen: New Jersey told me to come back and handle it in Florida because I was already at a hotel on my way back to Florida, and I wasn't in danger in New Jersey anymore because I was leaving the state of New Jersey.

Eric: That's what they told you?

Maureen: That's what they told me, and that's what the report says at the bottom.

Eric: Let's see what the report says at the bottom. Would you read that out loud to us?

Maureen: (Reading) "Reasons for denial: Not in fear of her safety; no immediate danger of personal injury or property damage; motivation for Temporary Restraining Order is custody [in] Florida."

Eric: So you were denied the restraining order up in New Jersey, that you just now told us you were so fearful of, because the judge up there determined that your motive was custody, right?

Maureen: I wasn't asking for custody.

Eric: That was dated September 8th of 2009, am I correct?

Maureen: Wasn't there a...

Eric: That wasn't my question, ma'am. Was that dated September 8th, 2009 by Judge Richard Andronici?

Maureen: Yes.

Eric: And then you came to Florida the next day, according to that paperwork. When you got here in Florida on September 10th, you came to this courthouse and petitioned this court for a restraining order, correct?

Maureen: Correct.

Mr. Burdick: This is outside the scope of direct. This is not cross.

At this point, Eric was repeatedly objected to a large number of times, which I felt really hurt his momentum. I thought he needed to ask the court to introduce Maureen as a rebuttal witness. Eric even leaned over to me to ask if he previously called Maureen as a witness for his direct questioning. Burdick brought it to the attention of the court, and it looked as if Eric wasn't in touch with the proceedings. I thought he looked bad at that moment. He resumed after a lengthy argument from both sides that lasted over thirty minutes. Judge Brunson was becoming frustrated. The court now recognized Maureen as a rebuttal witness, and the proceedings finally continued after that extremely long delay with Eric now on direct questioning of Maureen.

Eric: I want to get back to Husband's [evidence] Number 20. Isn't it true ma'am—and these are your words—"David has always been a loving, responsible, hands-on, involved father." Is that correct?

Maureen: That's what that says.

Eric: Is that your email?

Maureen: Yes.

Eric: Also in your email, quote, I would like to encourage a close, healthy father/daughter relationship, [end quote]. Is that correct?

Maureen: Sounds familiar.

Eric: Right here (points to document).

Maureen: Yes.

Eric: And if you go down to the next paragraph, you state, "While I painfully listen to my daughter ask for her daddy because I knew I wasn't ready, and I still needed my space." It was you who wasn't ready. "I was not ready and needed my space." Not Katie. Not your little girl. This has to do with you and your emotional state and your depression.

Eric: I want to show you Husband's [evidence] Number 21, which is your injunction that you filed against Mr. Graves on September 10th 2009. Do you remember that petition?

Maureen: Yes.

Eric: And this is two days, exactly two days, after the judge in New Jersey had denied your temporary restraining order because it was the judge's opinion that you were not in fear for your safety, and you were merely doing the restraining order up in New Jersey for custody purposes. Do you remember that?

Maureen: I don't remember asking for custody.

Eric: This is your petition, right?

Maureen: That's my petition.

Eric: Even though you asked the judge in New Jersey for custody, the judge made the determination, based on your testimony...

Burdick: Objection speculation.

Judge Brunson: Sustain the objection.

Eric: Now on the 10th of September, September 10th, two days later, you come to Florida. You come down here in front of Judge Brunson (points to judge), and I want you to specifically look at section 5 of your petition, Paragraph D, and read that sentence to us.

Maureen: (Reading) "Petitioner requests that the court prohibits time sharing with respondent with the minor child because petitioner fears the respondent will abuse, remove, or hide the minor child from the petitioner."

Eric: And now you're doing it again today for a third time; in a courtroom you are coming and asking a judge to restrict this man (points to me) from his little girl for the third time. Am I correct?

Maureen: Correct.

Eric introduces another Exhibit...a greeting card.

Eric: Would you agree ma'am, that's a card that you made for David on Happy Valentine's Day as a new daddy? Do you see that?

Maureen: (No response)

Eric: Do you recognize that? You made the card, didn't you?

Maureen: This is what, 15 days after Katie was born?

Eric: Right. What a loving...I think you made this card, didn't you?

Maureen: I don't recall.

Eric: And you said he was a wonderful, loving, and giving husband, correct?

Maureen: That's what it says.

Eric: And that's the card...you identified that card, correct, as you created it?

Maureen: I can't say...but, I mean, you know, I'm not saying that I didn't.

The card is admitted into evidence.

Eric: Let me show you ma'am, what's marked as

	Husband's Number 23 and ask you if you recognize that document. Do you remember making that card?
Maureen:	Her first Valentine's 15 days after she was born, do I remember making it? I don't remember making it.
Eric:	Does that say "Happy First Valentine's Day?"
Maureen:	Says "Happy First Valentine's Day." "She was born January 27th, so that would mean she...it was like 20 days after she was born.
Eric:	So apparently your husband wasn't a bad guy then, was he, with his little girl, according to you, correct?
Maureen:	She was 20 days old, and they didn't have a whole lot of time alone together, as it was. She was 20 days old or something.

The card is admitted into evidence.

Eric:	Let me show you what's been marked as Husband's Number 24 and ask you if you recognize that document. You guys were celebrating a new life in your life, right, parenthood?
Maureen:	Must have been her first Easter. She was just a couple months old. It says "Our new beginning parenthood." I'm assuming that's what it is. I don't know. There's no...
Eric:	Let me show you what's marked as Husband's Number 25. This was actually in your handwriting. "Daddy, this is my first Easter, wishing you a Happy Easter celebrating a new life together, correct?"
Maureen:	That's what it says.
Eric:	That's what you wrote. You created this card, didn't you?
Maureen:	I don't actually... don't remember creating the card,

but...

Eric: That's your handwriting?

Maureen: It looks like it.

Eric: That's your handwriting, correct?

Maureen: Okay!

Eric: Right?

Maureen: Right what?

Eric: That's your handwriting?

Maureen: Yes.

The card is admitted into evidence.

Eric: Let me show you Number 26. Did Katie write this or did you?

Maureen: Well, I don't think she could write yet, so that looks like I probably held her hand, and we wrote it together.

Eric: And there's no date on that; that's just a happy birthday card, right?

Maureen: That's what it says.

Eric: Whose birthday?

Maureen: This is David's birthday. This is a card from Katie wishing her daddy a happy birthday. "I'm so lucky to have..."

Eric: Your Honor, I'd like to offer what's marked as Husband's Number 26 into evidence. (Eric wasn't even waiting for Maureen to finish reading anymore. He regained the momentum he had earlier.)

Eric: Do you recognize that card?

Maureen: "First Christmas as My Daddy. A Special Christmas Poem from Katie." It's a card from...I'm guessing I made it. "My Daddy is My Hero, Love Katie."

Eric: There's no way Katie could come up with these words because she wasn't speaking, right?

Maureen: No, I'm not looking at originals, but I'm going to assume. I don't actually....

Eric: Actually you drafted this card.

Maureen: Well, yeah, these look like something...well, I don't know. You know, there's probably premade cards on the internet, you know. I don't know?

Eric: And these are your words? "My Daddy is My Hero. He's Caring and Strong. He Makes Me Feel Better When Something Goes Wrong."

Maureen: Okay, yes. Sure.

Eric: ...to dad, right?

Maureen: Yes.

Eric: I'd like to ask you if you recognize what's been marked as Husband's Number 29, dated May 2nd?

Maureen: (Reading) "Court order says for you to drop off Katie on Sundays at Burger King in Royal Palm Beach. I am not coming to your church in Wellington to pick her up anymore, this Sunday and every Sunday thereafter. Be sure to have Katie to Burger King at 10:30."

Eric: So you unilaterally decided you were going to change Judge Brunson's order that required you to pick up Katie at church, and you wanted it at Burger King, and you told your husband I'm not going to do that anymore? Tell me where you're supposed to pick up Katie.

Maureen went into a whole dissertation to explain why she made a change.

Eric: Move to strike?

Judge Brunson: Grant the motion to strike for failure to respond.

Eric: Just listen to my question. Do you recognize Judge Brunson's order?

Maureen: Yes.

Eric: So you told your husband that you're no longer going to obey this order. Is this the order that is in effect as we sit here today?

Maureen: Yes.

Eric: The bottom line is ma'am....

Maureen: I made a mistake.

Eric: Do you remember about an hour ago telling Judge Brunson that you were in fear for your safety?

Maureen: Yes.

Eric: Let me show you what's been marked as Husband's Number 30. Ma'am, you wrote this email, correct? Invited your husband over to your house to play with Katie and to take her? Those are your words, aren't they? Do you see that in that paragraph? Is that your email, ma'am, to your husband?

Burdick: I think she's trying to read it, counselor.

Eric: Judge, I didn't ask her to read the whole email. I asked her to identify it.

Judge Brunson: Objection overruled. Ma'am, answer the specific question.

Maureen: If this is my email?

Eric: Yes.

Maureen: Yes.

Eric continued to bring in exhibit after exhibit, most of which were composed in writing by Maureen, contradicting false claims, including written reports of her lying to police. He hammered her with questions related to each one. I felt the fact that Judge Catherine Brunson was our presiding judge and the judge in every one of Maureen's attempts at getting no-contact orders, the judge would easily see the false scenario Maureen was trying to convey to the court.

Eric made two mistakes in his handling of the case. His first mistake was when he involved the Office of Court Psychology. After Dr. Michaelanne Marie told Eric and me that shared custody would not be a problem with the findings in her examinations, something happened to change that. I asked Eric "What happened?" in court as it related to Dr. Marie's testimony. His answer was, "Something happened." The real point is that I will never know what happened there. The judge's ruling on the divorce was minimal time with Katie because of Dr. Marie's testimony. Every one of her recommendations was listed in the divorce judgment. Eric's second mistake was much more trivial. He lost his momentum during his cross-examination of Maureen, and Burdick threw his client a life preserver when he objected to Eric's line of questioning not being in the style of cross-examination, which was sustained by Judge Brunson. Eric got it back on track, but not before a 30-minute delay distracted his objective during questioning of Maureen.

CHAPTER 2

Courtship, Marriage, Separated

66 *Sensual pleasures have the fleeting brilliance of a comet;*
a happy marriage has the tranquility of a lovely sunset. 99
Ann Landers

I moved from being a lifelong resident of New Jersey to a Florida transplant of Palm Beach County in November of 1996. My best friend Al had lived in Florida less than a year before he invited me to stay with him and his girlfriend to help them get on their feet in their new life and to start my own new life in Florida. I found a job as a bellman at The Breakers, a hotel and resort in Palm Beach, and ventured out to find some nightlife entertainment and make new friends. The bar and grill called The Back Alley was close to Al and Karen's home. The place had live music and was three and four people deep from the bar on weekends. That was where I met Maureen.

Maureen was petite and attractive, yet there was a very distinct slump about her, kind of introverted, lonely, unhappy, unsure of herself, and sagging a bit in the shoulders. I know those weren't qualities that attracted me to her, but I perused her nevertheless. I learned later that she was living with a man and trying to find a way out of that relationship. Ultimately, I was provided the opportunity to be her next roommate. Initially, Maureen was opposed and denied my advances, but as she muddled through her personal situation, I made it a point to be there for her, and she eventually found me to be a sincere, willing person for her to confide in. Our relationship didn't proceed without incident; one night, for example, while we were out having dinner, her live-in boyfriend confronted us. He said, "You're jumping in my grave, and I'm not even dead."

Our first date was June of 1997. We saw *Mission Impossible* at the movies. Maureen and I saw each other every night for ten straight months before missing one day.

Maureen's previous boyfriend moved out, and I moved in. She had a Rottweiler that she kept in one of the two bedrooms in her third floor apartment. The room was filthy with dog feces and carpet that had been ripped up by the bored animal. This huge dog was cooped up in this one room with no company for hours every day. A short time after moving in, I suggested that we rent a house with a yard so the dog would have more space, which we could also use. After we paid for the extensive damage to the apartment, we moved to a house in Delray Beach, Florida, about 20 miles south from Palm Beach.

The city of Delray Beach is a great place for courting a new relationship. Atlantic Avenue has live music, restaurants, indoor and outdoor venues, craft shows, and the beach at the eastern end. We were close enough to ride our new bicycles to Atlantic Avenue if we chose to, or we could take the car, park, and walk The Avenue without spending a fortune. On the nights we stayed home, we would dine (at our new table), dance, and drink. We fell in love during this courtship. It was a wonderful time for us.

Our rental home had no central air conditioning and no heat. It was an older house built in the 60's. It was an okay neighborhood, just old. We had great times doing things like putting an inflatable swimming pool on the flat roof and lounging all

day, but some of the circumstances were wearing thin with us. We decided to upgrade. Upgrade a lot. We rented a much more modern home in Boynton Beach, about seven miles north from Delray.

In 1999, shortly after we moved to Boynton Beach, we got married. I had since taken a job as an outside salesperson for construction materials. It wasn't long before that career took off, and I was earning a six-figure income. We purchased a nice, modest, 1100 square foot, four-year-old home in quiet, rural Loxahatchee, Florida, about 30 miles northwest from Boynton, on an acre-and-a-quarter lot with fruit trees, a dirt road in front, and a canal in the back. By now, we had two cats and two dogs. We went camping together, went to craft shows, spent weekends away, etc. I brought her flowers every Friday night. I also spent every moment I could spare sitting in my home office bidding jobs for potential new customers and carefully maintaining my current builder accounts.

We tried for five years to have a child. Between Maureen's endometriosis and my age, which caused a low sperm count, we were unsuccessful. We invested in the in vitro fertilization procedure three times. The in vitro process is quite intense, and a couple has to *really* want a child to endure this painstaking process. One of the worst parts was the twice-daily progesterone injections into the upper outer quadrants of the hips. I had to administer these injections; the needle was about four inches long and had to be all the way in due to the oily consistency of the medication. Some would shoot out of the injection spot like a geyser when I pulled the needle out. I recall almost fainting sometimes after I administered the hormone just thinking of the discomfort that she must be going through. One attempt produced a pregnancy that resulted in a miscarriage. I will never forget when the nurse turned off the ultrasound screen after she confirmed that there was no heartbeat; I held Maureen as we cried together. I

made up my mind that I would do anything I could to see the next pregnancy to the birth. I decided that I too would carry this child. I rented a wheelchair for Maureen for the full term of the pregnancy. Maureen barely took a step out of the house before I had the wheelchair ready for her and the little girl she carried inside. I coddled her like a Swarovski crystal tchotchke. Maureen sometimes cried about the miscarriage, and I always reassured her, "We're going to do it this time!"—and we did!

Maureen and I worked together to help support my career. She was great with numbers and did the quotes, while I did the technical aspects to meet local and state building codes. We both came from the proverbial "broken home." We shared our stories over the course of our relationship together prior to our own home "breaking." The main difference I noticed between her childhood and mine was that neither of her parents really wanted her or her two brothers around much. As children, they were sent back and forth between Boston, Massachusetts, where the father lived, and Ft. Lauderdale, Florida, where the mother lived. In between, they were shipped off to boarding schools. They were never taught how to prepare a meal for themselves. They never played Little League baseball, or joined Cub Scouts or Brownies. They didn't even have any hobbies, until her two brothers took up gambling, drug use, and strip clubs.

My own situation was no picnic, and as I grew older, I had wished that I had a father figure in my life. I did, however, have my grandfather and my uncle, and they were great men in my life. My mother went to every one of my Little League and Babe Ruth baseball games. I was a member of Den 2, Pack 3 in Cub Scouts, and whittled my pinewood derby car every year. So, while my own childhood wasn't perfect, it sure beat Maureen's and her brothers' situation; I found a whole new level of appreciation for everything my mother did and sacrificed for my brother and me.

Maureen's parents were still not much a part of her life 10

years into our relationship. She often referred to them as "those people" or as "Mommy Dearest," "Dude," and "Leon," instead of Mom, Dad, and Grandpop. I knew that it was really her broken heart crying out through her remarks. I couldn't stand her family either. They were nasty and not liked by many people. Maureen always felt that she was in the way of her mother's romantic relationships. Her father was busy with a business, and her mother was busy with men. She told me these were the biggest reasons that she was shipped off to boarding school. While both her brothers got jobs (for a very short time) with their father's textile business, Maureen was never given the same opportunities. Her father's and grandfather's reasons for excluding her were identical. They said, "Women get pregnant" and "You can't count on women to be at work. They're a liability." When I asked my father-in-law for his reasons myself, he repeated, verbatim, what she told me. He did not see anything wrong with that standpoint.

Maureen came home from having dinner with her father and stepmother totally despondent over the news that her father and his wife were planning to adopt a Chinese baby. "He abandoned three of his own children and wants to adopt a Chinese baby?" Her father never did follow through with the adoption of the Chinese baby. It was just a trendy thing to consider in Boca Raton at the time. I believe that today there is a Chinese teenager somewhere who can sleep soundly and doesn't even know why.

The Florida building industry continued to skyrocket, which was great for my business, right up until it wasn't. The whole country had built itself into a large surplus of unoccupied residences, and the economy went down the toilet because of the mortgages banks were handing out like a soup kitchen line. This was our first real family crisis. I lost 85% of my income and suddenly couldn't even gross $30,000 a year. We had a mortgage and a one-year-old daughter, and mine was the only income. Now, my career was literally at a stop. It seemed to happen

overnight. I rode it out for a while, along with the builders. As I watched my colleagues disappear into unemployment and my clients' half-built construction sites start to grow vines, I looked into the option of selling directly to homeowners who wanted to fix up the homes they already had. So, I took a position with a company focused on high-end homeowners with estates. Those folks seemed to have the money to spend in this awful economy. It was hard starting out again, but I remained optimistic, at least for a little while. My strategy was to research Google maps the night before to find a name and address of a resident inside a gated community that I could give to the gatekeepers to gain access. Once inside, I would look around for any house within that might need my services. I took out ads in the high-end community newspapers. Generating new clients was slow work, which made it hard for me to maintain our standard of living. This, along with Maureen working as a stay-at-home-mom, we were sinking and falling behind on our bills, most importantly, our mortgage.

Just as our proverbial ship was sinking, Maureen's grandmother died. Until then, Maureen's mother was living about an hour away from us, closer to her own mother, and we would see her about once a month. Now there was no need for her to live so far away, so she bought a home five miles away from us. Meanwhile, Maureen's father, who owned a textile business in Boston, decided to sell the building to a developer because of the textile industry's demise in the United States. He and his fourth wife decided to move to Boca Raton, Florida and live a mere thirty minutes from us. Maureen was ecstatic. She was looking forward to having her mother and father so close to her. They'd had little time for her through the course of her life, and Maureen could finally have the void from her childhood filled in. The rejection from both her mother and father was now being reversed.

The timing couldn't have been worse. We were three months behind on our mortgage, and I was worried the bank was about to padlock our house with all our stuff still inside. We turned off the home fax line, stopped cable TV, and stopped eating out; we ate a lot of grilled cheese sandwiches. We contacted a real estate office and listed our house for sale while we still had a little equity and decent credit. We thought we'd downsize to a condominium in the area because builders were selling new properties nearly at cost just to minimize inventory. Nobody even looked at our own house though. People were afraid and just didn't want to take a chance on the country's uncertain economy.

Maureen started taking a course to get her license for a babysitting business in our home. She worked on it at a feverish pace hoping to somehow supplement the loss of our household income. It just wasn't to be though. With course schedules and certification testing dates so far off, we decided she should continue with it but not count on it to help save us right then. Maureen was invested in the dream of being a stay-at-home mom, raising our daughter. She has a degree in accounting and a long, steady career history, and we talked about the possibility of her going back into her accounting career, even if only for a short time. She just wasn't having any part of it. Maureen was depressed with the situation and contacted her father.

Well, the long-lost father stood in our home and scolded us for taking a vacation two years earlier. He flailed his arms with discontent and opposed Maureen even thinking about working outside the home. He gave orders about what we were *not* to do and did not have any constructive ideas of what we *should* do. He found a lot of blame and gave a real blow to Maureen's heart. After he finally left, Maureen and I looked again to each other for a solution.

Maureen and I went into therapy to address the possibility of losing everything and to discuss our options as husband and wife.

We were stressed and scared. We did this in the presence of a therapist so we could get feedback on our thoughts and feelings.

Much of what came out of the sessions was enlightening to me and helped me understand Maureen a little better. I felt sorry for what she had endured throughout her life. I was surprised to realize that she had no idea how much I really loved her. I think it actually scared her. She was scared in a way that made her unable to accept or return love. I recall one of the questions to me was, "On a scale of 1 to 10, what is the importance of Maureen's looks to you?" I said "3." I followed up with, "If she bathes and brushes her teeth (which Maureen did), I think that would cover it. She's my wife and the mother of our child; I love her." I looked back at Maureen. Her face was white as a sheet. I really didn't understand the puzzled look on her face, and I don't think she ever understood what I was saying. She had told me before that she never felt she was ever truly loved by her parents or in any prior relationship.

Since California's and Florida's real estate markets were the first in the country to be hit, my networking contacts of over 15 years were suffering the same economical demise. So, I decided to reach out to former contacts in the waste industry. I found one who was previously the northeastern regional manager at Waste Management, Inc. He directed me on a path that landed an opportunity in the New England area. Maureen and I discussed it, and we decided to look into relocating. I traveled back and forth to Massachusetts twice and landed a position with Allied Waste Services selling construction and commercial service. It offered a reasonable salary with commission and bonus opportunities. The table was set for what I thought was a way out of this mess.

Meanwhile, our relocation plan didn't sit well with Maureen's parents who had finally chosen to have time to be parents after forty years of not bothering—at least, they wanted to try with

Maureen, the only one of their three children who would even speak to them. Their opposition did not make any sense to me. Maureen's family was from Massachusetts, and her grandfather and one of her brothers still lived there along with her best childhood friend from one of her boarding schools. Her father still owned a home there and could easily jump on a plane to visit. Her mother didn't work either. But the idea of us relocating and somehow spoiling their opportunity to be forgiven and included in our everyday lives was more important to them than our own family's survival.

So we arranged for our new life in Warren, Rhode Island, a beautiful New England suburb. I drove out first with a couple of bags and what my car could carry. When the moving truck arrived, I staged the previously viewed, newly rented house for the movers. Maureen and Katie soon arrived by plane. The neighbors gave us a warm welcome, complete with an apple pie. I found out later from Tina, our neighbor in Florida, who was helping clean out the abandoned marital home that was still on the market for sale, that Maureen's mother, Mabel was furious about our moving. She told Tina that she will do whatever it takes to get "them" back to Florida. I was unaware of the statement or the plan to break up my family until years later. Regarding the in vitro fertilization, I did hear Mabel say to Maureen at Katie's second birthday party during the piñata portion: "See, you didn't even need a man to have a baby."

I officially started my position at Allied Waste on April 14, 2008. My sales manager, Ray, was an easy going guy. I liked his approach toward helping his people meet goals. He was new to the company as well, so of course there were veterans who were not receptive to change. Still, he respected his sales team, and he mostly got their respect, in return. I was trained by the top salesman at our branch who was also the top salesperson nationwide. I knew I was in good hands within the company. If

I failed, which was not an option, I would have no one to look to other than myself. So, I was determined to make this opportunity successful for my family and myself. I pounded the pavement, generated leads, and got signed accounts. The pay system was set up to "ramp" you into straight commission earnings but initially paid a salary equivalent to $40,000 a year. The salaried pay decreased over time as my accounts increased, and I earned a percentage from every account I brought in. I thought I could easily bring this to a $100,000 a year career within two years.

I set up an office in the basement of our new home. It was a finished basement, but it was damp down there. I bought a dehumidifier on Craigslist for twenty dollars and emptied it daily. The main floor of the one-story residence had three bedrooms, a large main bathroom, and a small master bathroom with a shower stall, a one car garage, a huge living room, and a room off the kitchen that we used as a playroom for Katie with all her toys and a TV. We used the door in the playroom as our entry door. It was just off the driveway. I suggested we set up Maureen's office in the bedroom next to Katie's bedroom because I would sometimes work late at night, and I didn't want to wake Katie up by working. Maureen started watching two children from a family across the street and another child from a newfound friend in the area during the week in addition to Katie. She made a decent income doing this, with the added bonus that she was able to continue being a stay-at-home-mom. We seemed to be adjusting ok.

Mother's Day came, and Maureen's mother, Mabel, flew up from Florida to visit and stay with us. We went to a Mother's Day buffet brunch at the Ramada Inn in Seekonk, Massachusetts. The place was packed, and even with reservations, we waited almost an hour for a table. Mabel was awful. She complained about everything up to and including the way the plates were removed from the table. After sharing with our table that she doesn't like or drink orange juice, she went to the buffet table, picked up an empty orange juice pitcher, walked it over to a waitress, and shoved it into her chest—all without saying a word. She was like a train wreck. This was really nothing new with her though. She makes sure she is noticed by being obnoxious. She is a vexation to anyone's spirit. I once looked up the symptoms of a sociopath. Except for the need to hurt animals, from what I have seen of her behavior, she fits the profile. However, with determination and a lot of deflecting, I managed to maintain a family holiday attitude throughout her stay.

The town of Bristol, Rhode Island holds the most widely known Fourth of July celebration in the area. Personally, I have never seen a community come out with such enthusiasm and pride. The surrounding towns come out in droves to attend this event. We attended, and Maureen said to me that she had never been to a parade in her life. It was a parade such as I had never seen before or since. I was proud to have been a spectator and to have shared it with my family. We visited Block Island with the Cranston Chamber of Commerce, which I saw as an opportunity in business as well as a new and beautiful place. With Katie, I took Maureen to her old school classmate's home in Attleboro, Massachusetts. She was married and had three children and a beautiful home in a very nice community. They had barbeques at their home and invited us often. The summer of 2008 was borderline storybook. We were earning a living. Everyone seemed to have what they needed and wanted. I was supporting my family again. Maureen was a stay-at-home mother and generating income with her small at-home daycare. Katie had friends. And we were all part of a tight-knit little community.

Maureen and Katie went to Florida in July to visit Maureen's parents and friends. I could not go because I had only been at my new job for three months and could not take off time so soon. Maureen packed enough toys for Katie to last a month, and I drove them to Logan Airport in Boston for their direct flight. I took the opportunity to accept an invitation from my boss, Ray, to go to a Brockton Rox minor league baseball game. The Brockton Rox was a big customer of ours, and Allied Waste had a box at the facility. It was a good opportunity to spend some quality business time with my boss and one of our biggest customers while watching some baseball.

Maureen and Katie returned from Florida. I do not know what exactly happened during their four days of visiting; some things we are never meant to know, but whatever it was started with methodical planning. I didn't know it at the time, but while she was in Florida, Maureen emptied our safe deposit box, even though both signatures were required for the box to be closed.

I picked Maureen and Katie up at the airport and started the hour-long drive home. Katie fell asleep in the car seat, and I tried to make conversation in spite of the mysterious tension in the car during the ride home. I asked about the trip. Maureen barely said a word. I noticed that there was less luggage than when they left. I asked Maureen where the rest of the luggage was, and she said that her mother was going to send the rest of Katie's toys in the mail. I eventually gave up because she gave barely more than one-word answers at a time.

Katie woke up when we got home and saw that I had bought an old-fashioned spring-type rocking horse for her from a yard sale. She and I played with it until late. When it was time for Katie to go to bed, I went into her room for story time, as I did every night. Maureen read *Ten Apples up on Top* (my favorite). Katie and I listened. I wish I had known that this would be the last time I would put my little girl to sleep in her own bed under the same roof as a family.

I went down to my home office in the basement. A short time later, Maureen shouted down at me from upstairs, "Katie and I are going to Florida for a week every sixty days. This is not negotiable." I thought, "What's going on? Something big is going on here. What the fuck?"

I went upstairs and asked her, "What?"

She repeated her statement.

"Who are you to tell me that it's not negotiable?! Who is going to pay for all this? You have a responsibility to these people whose children you are watching! You mean to tell me that your father can't get on a plane and visit here? Who wants to go to Florida in the summer and who wants to go to Rhode Island in the winter?" I was livid. I held open the door in the playroom and told her, "If you want to go to Florida, walk!"

With that, Maureen walked towards the door. As she got to the doorframe, she dropped down onto the floor as if she collapsed. It was August. All of the windows were open, including the door that I was holding open. She began to yell, "Somebody help me! Somebody help me!" She sat up against the sofa arm, looking at me and again yelled, "Somebody help me!"

Instead of leaving, I slapped her with my right hand across her left cheek. Then, I sat down on the sofa and spoke. I don't even remember what I said. Finally, I got up and went into the bedroom. I heard the car door shut and her pull out of the driveway. I lay down on the bed and couldn't believe what had happened. She was gone for what seemed to be hours. I think I fell asleep, but I can't be sure. I heard a car door shut again. I was awake when she came in, but it wasn't her. It was two police officers.

I was taken to the police station. Booked, finger printed, released after hours of being locked up in a cell all night. I was supposed to be at work. I called out sick from a pay phone. I had no shoes, no cell phone, no clothes except what I was wearing, and no money, and I was not allowed to return to my home because now there was a temporary protection order. I didn't even have keys to my car.

I went back to the police station after sitting in front of the Bristol library most of the late morning. The police agreed to call Maureen and have some things put out front: my brief-case, wallet (minus my ATM card), keys, a pair of shoes, and a couple of work shirts and pants. Not one red cent and I hadn't eaten for almost a day. I went to our bank and got a blank check that I cashed for money enough to get some food and go to the Holiday Inn in Swansea, Massachusetts, just a short distance from Warren, Rhode Island.

Have you ever tried to check into a hotel with no credit or debit card? I had to tell the manager the whole story to get them to let me check in. I wondered if my story was common for this front desk. I checked in and showered. I wondered what my little girl was saying about my absence when she woke up, and that's when I cried. That was the first of crying that lasted years, and I did not yet understand that I had just begun a long, miserable fight against ego, money, and entitlement, and that was just the in-laws.

Maureen had begun her journey to losing her identity. She has since been clinically diagnosed as co-dependent and an abused child. When I met her, she desperately wanted a child of her own. Her office cubicle was an Anne Geddes gallery. She was also desperately looking for a man to love her. She was the perpetual victim of one boyfriend after another. Many of her relationships actually overlapped in order for her to jump seam-lessly from one to another. I actually fell in love with her. I think that when she finally found the love she had been searching for, she didn't know how to return it. Ultimately, she just wanted a baby, and at 36 years old, her clock was ticking. Well, $27,000 of in vitro fertilization later, she had one.

CHAPTER 3

A Legal Kidnapping

> " *I've always been fascinated with the stealing of innocence.*
> *It's the most heinous crime,*
> *and certainly a capital crime if there ever was one.* "
>
> Clint Eastwood

The newspaper for the local township of Warren, RI had a police blotter, and my domestic incident made it to print. The whole paper was maybe fifteen pages long, and my two lines of fame were right after the report of "a dog barking loudly on Child Street." The news reached my office, and the women in the office marched in on my sales manager, Ray, who later called me into the office. I told him about the incident, which had yet to get in the way of my job. He was satisfied with my commitment to the company and offered his condolences. He shared some stories of his own marriage, which had ended in divorce with children involved as well. He assured me that he would set the record straight within the office. He was never able to stem the outrage from the women in the office. They continued to treat me as if I were Ted Bundy.

I stayed at the Holiday Inn for about a week and showered at public swimming pools. Thank God it was still summer, I thought. I found a third floor room that I rented for $100 a week until I found something a little more "mine" to move into—a small one-bedroom apartment for $450 a month. The apartment was exactly a half a mile away from the Rhode Island marital home. With the protection order in effect, I was the proverbial "so close, yet so far." It was hard. We were well on our way to being into the system.

When it came time for the protection order hearing, my boss set me up with the company attorney to represent me because I didn't have the money to retain an attorney on my own. I had applied for a public defender, but after speaking with him, it felt as though I was going to shoot myself in the foot by being represented by a man wearing a blue denim suit and hat.

Maureen came to the first family court hearing with the children she watched during the day. One of the parents later told me that Maureen had never said anything to them about taking the kids to the Providence courthouse. I still don't know who was watching those kids while she was inside the courtroom. My little girl was there, too, and I could see her from the other end of the hall. My attorney told me to just stay put. I hadn't seen, talked to, or held Katie in three weeks.

In court that day, I was granted visitation with Katie on almost every day of the week, but no overnights. Maureen claimed that we were going to "take baby steps" (a term she used for years to come). I asked the judge to let me see my daughter immediately after the hearing. He said that we could get together in the supervised visitation area and that the clerk would arrange it. At the very end of the hearing, Maureen raised the concern that I might flee with our daughter. The judge called a meeting in his chambers. He looked at me and said that if I were to "scoop up the child, there would be an Amber alert." He asked me if I understood. I said that I did, and nothing more was said. I don't remember that judge's name, but I wish that he had been the one who continued to hear our case. The visit in the court's facility was supervised by a young man who was very nice. He sat with us and held a clipboard, which he used to take notes of his observations. Katie took a poop, and I had no diapers. The man got one from the back that was a little small, but it worked. I guess I probably passed the diaper-changing test according to the system.

I watched my rabbit ear television, and thankfully, the Phillies were in the World Series. I threw myself into watching my hometown Phils play the Tampa Bay Rays in the Fall Classic. It was funny how I felt when the Phillies won. With the last out of the game, I was pleased that they won, but I was disappointed that the series was over. Looking back and wondering, the game must have been on Fox, because if it was on TBS, I wouldn't have been able to watch it with rabbit ears.

My neighbor, Mr. Dan from across the hall heard Katie and me playing and started being friendly. I had seen him around enough to speak and say hello to. Katie called him Mr. Dan, so that was how I referred to him, too. He was a quiet guy until you got to know him. He had a dry sense of humor and was a huge fan of Rod Stewart's band, Faces. Mr. Dan managed the frozen foods department at a grocery chain in the area. We shared stories, and he was a great friend to me. He was divorced with a 12-year-old daughter. He hated the institution of marriage and worked to convince me that my marriage was already over. He speculated, accurately as it turned out, that my wife had planned this separation in advance and was probably planning to take Katie and run back to her parents in Florida.

Mr. Dan used to knock on my door and take me out of the

house. "C'mon, let's go." He taught me how to eat "The Dollar Menu Diet." He pointed out that two cheeseburgers, a dollar French fries, and a dollar drink was as much food as a #3 meal and almost half the cost. He introduced me to the world of better reception antennas that were quite a few steps above the old rabbit ears I had been using. He took the time to write out different scenarios from his own divorce and custody battle. It was not out of the ordinary for me to come home from work and find anything from pages of Mr. Dan notes to a wrapped present for Katie from him.

As the winter came on, I was thankful to be indoors and have a friend like Mr. Dan. The void of not having my family was taking its toll, though. I found myself on the side of the road crying when I was supposed to be in a business office selling myself and sharing the details about why their business should trust my service, dedication, and commitment. While my new career was now bouncing like the Wright Brothers plane taking off, I still managed to sign some new accounts here and there. However, I was not living up to the expectations of my boss. Ray was aware that I was in the middle of the court turmoil, and I knew I wasn't performing up to my own standards. On November 11, 2008, I went to my boss and told him more about what I was going through. He asked that I resign and wished me the best. I have no hard feelings towards him or the company. It is, after all, a business. I was just a shattered family man. I was able to collect unemployment compensation because my boss reported that he laid me off, and that helped me stay financially ok for the time being.

Katie loved Halloween almost as much as Christmas. From a child's perspective, I can understand why. People on their street all got together, and we all walked around together, including Maureen's new BFF's, who had the look and attitude of people trolling for marks. Katie and I had a great time, but Maureen seemed detached from the whole fanfare, including Katie. While Maureen chatted with her new friends, I taught Katie the whole trick-or-treat procedure; she was a seasoned professional by the fifth house. Maureen had asked me to be a part of Katie's Halloween and told me the theme. Katie was Snow White, Maureen was the Wicked Witch, and I had rented a Prince Charming costume…an interesting parallel of characters, I thought. Everyone within the group knew that Maureen and I were separated and that there was a protection order, including the Warren police officer two doors down, whose home we trick or treated. For the sake of being a part of Katie's Halloween and to enjoy it with her, I took my chances; it brought nothing but joy to her, and I'm glad I participated. This is one of those elements within the system that is totally out of whack. In the enforcement of an order of protection, police officers sometimes end up in the middle of what they know is a conflict to their duty to the law. Officers are human and well aware that protection orders are often used as a tool for one spouse to lay the groundwork to assassinate the character of the other spouse who doesn't deserve to be locked up. Often, loving fathers are invited to the house to spend time with their children or asked to come over to cut the grass, and the ex-wife will use that opportunity to call the police for a violation of the order. I hope that one day we will have legislation designed to punish people who abuse the protection order process in this way, and we will see less of this kind of abuse.

The first snowfall came in November and yielded a good accumulation of snow. Katie was almost three years old. Maureen called me to invite me to play with Katie in the snow. The three of us built a snowman in yard of the marital home. We took pictures, got warm in the car, and Maureen even invited me into the house to warm up. Katie was confused with the arrangement. As I mentioned, the neighbor two houses down was a Warren police officer. She came down to the house uniformed and on duty. I panicked and asked Maureen to hide me, fearing being arrested. Maureen instead grabbed Katie up and left me standing in the yard. The officer saw me, and I tried to act calm and collected. She asked me what I was doing, and I told her that I had been building a snowman with my daughter. Again, she had just seen me a couple of weeks earlier on Halloween knocking on her door with both of them. She did not arrest me but told me to leave the property because it was not my time to officially be there. So I did. It was noted on the visitation order that I was allowed to be with Katie at the property. This came at Maureen's request. I'm not sure why it was noted as such, but when I did visit Katie on the property, Maureen would get in her car, park about four or five houses down, and sit there watching Katie and me play in the yard with the door to the house locked. At the time, I believed she was staking us out from down the street to be sure that I didn't kidnap Katie. But this really did not make sense because I often had Katie at my apartment. Thinking back, I just suppose it was some kind of mind fuck; over time, it was similar to Chicken Little's, "The sky is falling" declarations.

Back in Florida, my former employer had decided that they were going to change our commission schedule on completed sales and make the new policy retroactive. They did this to compensate for their own losses caused by the failing construction market. This shorted my earnings by over $64,000. Prior to leaving Florida, I had retained an attorney who worked on a contingency basis, and he was certain we would win due to a breach of contract. We settled out of court, and I was awarded a "mutual agreement" without the case ever reaching a courtroom.

The amount was a far cry from what they actually owed me, but Maureen and I had decided earlier that we would settle and perhaps have that money for our new start in Rhode Island. Now we had a new kind of new start, so I had my attorney send her $7,100 from the settlement to keep up the rent and to pay bills. The judge also awarded Maureen the entire $3,185 from a joint account with Fidelity Investments to "maintain the marital home." One of the notations of the protection order was that Maureen and I could communicate if it was regarding "the minor child." I talked to her about the money that the judge and I gave her and how she should be using it to maintain the Rhode Island residence. She said that she was saving that money to put in her retirement accounts. She told me that there was no way that she was going to use that money for bills. I started getting a clearer picture that perhaps she was stashing cash and planning to bolt back to Florida. Mr. Dan referred me to his divorce attorney, Jaqueline Grasso, whose husband coincidentally happened to be the county prosecutor in my domestic charge. While my attorney, Grasso couldn't represent me on the criminal charge, she could still represent me in family court. I found it ethically questionable that money was going into their household from both sides of the same divorce.

Maureen now had an attorney paid for by her father. She petitioned the family court to leave the state of Rhode Island. Magistrate O'Brien neither granted nor denied her request, citing no jurisdiction since we hadn't lived in Rhode Island for a year. The law states that the state of Rhode Island *does* have jurisdiction over a minor child after six months of residency. We went into the Magistrate O'Brien's chambers. The arteries in his face had ruptured internally, and the skin on his nose was mangled from alcohol deterioration; these features indicated to me that he was obviously a big and steady drinker. I sat right next to him in his chambers. He stank of liquor. I began to cry as I realized my daughter was on her way to being legally kidnapped. Then Maureen pointed at me and said, as we got up from the table, "Isn't he coming too?" She looked around as if someone misunderstood. It was clear that she was the one who misunderstood what was going on. Maureen's father duped her by directly giving the lawyer his instructions to clear the way to get them back to Florida, and this was my first indication that this whole thing was being orchestrated by him. The alcoholic judge failed to realize that the State of Rhode Island had jurisdiction of the child and that Maureen taking Katie out of the state would be a violation of the Uniform Child Custody Act; in fact, he stated otherwise in complete and utter violation of the law.

The criminal hearing came up. On the advice of my corporate attorney, I pleaded no contest and received a year's probation and enrollment in a batterers' group as my sentence for the criminal charge of slapping Maureen. I pleaded with her not to leave, to not take Katie away from me as she promised, Especially because Christmas was coming.

I was rehearsing with the Methodist church choir for the upcoming Christmas cantata. Meanwhile, Maureen's mother had joined the Unity School of Christianity and convinced her to become a member. At first I thought, "Well, at least it's something, instead of the complete absence of any spirituality at all." Then, I looked into this organization and found that it was started by a lady by the name of Mertile Fillmore and her husband. The organization met in Newport, Rhode Island in the Scientologist facility. Mabel was attending services back in West Palm Beach, Florida where Maureen and I attended some services prior to moving. I thought it was at least a start for her and that perhaps she would get some knowledge of religion. It turns out that the Unity School of Christianity doesn't seek God, the Father through Jesus Christ, the Son. They claim that we are all capable of Christ's miracles, and we are all one with God,

as Jesus is. They believe that Jesus was Moses, among others, by reincarnation. They do not believe that there is a heaven and hell. Basically, I found it to be an abomination of Christianity. Maureen was suddenly opposed to Katie going to the Methodist church with me and was able to stop me because Sundays were not a regular visitation day. This was particularly hurtful to me because I was baptized Methodist in 1962 at the age of one. Being Methodist is part of my identity, and I wanted to share it with my daughter as a spiritual foundation.

Katie and I went Christmas shopping for some decorations at Wal-Mart. She saw a 6-foot, pink Christmas tree and ran over to it. "Daddy, can we get it?" There was no way I wasn't getting that tree for my little girl. Into the cart it went. Katie picked out purple glass Christmas balls and other assorted ornaments she liked to go on the tree. I thought this variety of looks was not a great choice for a Christmas tree, but much to my amazement, the tree looked great. We had a pink tree with purple balls! Katie loved it, and so did I.

Around the same time, I stopped by the local animal shelter. I thought that having a cat would be good company for me. It was a good idea. I found an orange tabby kitten that was sick along with the rest of that litter of kittens. I had to wait for the shelter to clear his health status before they released him for adoption. I took him to my apartment, and Katie named him Milo after Milo and Otis fame. She had been watching the movie in her current rotation of videos. Milo was Katie's and my new buddy. She looked forward to coming over to my apartment even more to play with Milo. He was gentle and had a great demeanor for a three-year-old carrying him around. I taught her how to hold him, and she did her best to see that she didn't make him uncomfortable. The three of us had a blast together.

Maureen also came over to my apartment regularly. I'm sure she was curious about my living arrangements in the beginning, and because I had nothing to hide, I didn't see any reason to be a jerk about letting her in, despite her having a no-contact order. In fact, the funny thing is that the protection order is still in effect against me. In the order, Maureen claimed that she was terrified of me. Yet, she came into my apartment and ate meals with Katie and me. I usually had a camera around; Maureen and I took a lot of pictures throughout our lives together, this time of our lives was no exception. My lawyers and I have an endless supply of pictures of the "terrified" wife hanging out at the "crazy" husband's residence and eating, playing, smiling, laughing, and whatever. It was almost as though we were living as a family and capturing ongoing family memories. I didn't object to it. I frequently hoped she would forgive me for the August incident so we could be a family again, and I longed to tuck my daughter into bed. Those pictures were later used as my evidence when Maureen became more contradictive of her claim of terror.

Maureen had told me that she would never take me out of our child's life. She said that she knew how close we were and that she supported a healthy relationship between us. Katie used to hold onto my briefcase as I walked through the door as if to assist me getting in the house so we could get to the serious business of playing together. She and I were inseparable from the time I got home until it was time for her to go to bed. I loved (and still do) playing with her. It felt as though I shed 40 years off my life when we were jumping in place to the Wiggles playing "Tie Me Kangaroo Down" for example. One incident that really bothered me happened when I went to pick Katie up one day from the former marital home. I got down on one knee as Katie ran into my arms. We threw our arms around each other, and I gave her a kiss on the lips, as I had done countless times before. Maureen said, "Stop that!" I asked, "What?" She said, "That's borderline child molestation! Kissing her on the lips, knock it off!" I was so appalled, I stood up and told her to take that back. She didn't say a word. She has never taken it back. I called my good friend, Gary, who has been part of my life since we were kids. He too has a daughter who was now an adult in her mid-twenties. Gary knew Maureen and Katie too. He attended our wedding, we visited each other's homes many times, and we all vacationed together over the years. He remains a great friend to me to this day. I asked him what he thought about the remark Maureen made about kissing Katie on the lips because I was starting to doubt my own behavior and feelings. Gary said, "Dave, she's losing it." I believe that Gary was absolutely right. Maureen was all caught up in her divorced parents' orchestration of relocating them back to Florida. Maureen had to be so muddy in the head from the whole situation; everything was out of her hands and being methodically planned, mostly by her wealthy father who simply sat in his lair, clicking a mouse and writing checks. Then it happened...

Mabel had been staying with Maureen since a few days before Christmas. On Christmas Day, Maureen and Katie spent the entire day at my apartment while we all opened presents. I usually only had Katie for eight hours or so at a time, but Maureen dropped Katie off at my apartment for fourteen hours on Friday, December 26th and sixteen hours on Saturday, December 27th. She even delivered a Christmas-style dinner to me on Friday night. Maureen insisted on picking Katie up at my place and used her mother's visit as the reason for me not to drop Katie off or for Maureen not to come inside my apartment. I wondered why Maureen let Katie stay with me for such long periods of time, but I wasn't going to question it

Three days after Christmas, on December 28, 2008, I was on my way to church. I was driving on Child Street and looked down the next block where they lived. When I saw a moving van in front of the house, I turned down the next street and came around the block. I saw a police cruiser parked behind the moving van, and movers were loading the truck. It felt like my whole torso split open. Obviously, the police car was there to keep me away.

This was the answer to my unasked questions about Maureen's generosity with Katie's time over the Christmas weekend. Maureen and her mother had been using me as a babysitter while they packed the house. The system allowed Maureen to legally kidnap our daughter.

I went back to my apartment, frenzied, despondent. I called people. I don't even remember who now. I was on the phone crying for hours. I paced my building's parking lot and cried on the phone while the snow fell and accumulated around me. It was the single worst feeling I have ever felt, and I can't even describe it to its reality. My little girl, who I absolutely built my entire world around, was leaving my life a half a mile down the road while a pink and purple Christmas tree stood with her opened presents still under it just inside the door in front of me.

I truly cannot say what I did for the following hours. The next thing I remember was the next day. I was outside their empty house, standing over their live Christmas tree that had been discarded on the side of the street, its tinsel blowing in the wind. I watched my tears fall directly from my eyes to the ground. I heard them hitting the snow. When they hit the snow, they sounded so loud to me, and it felt as if they shook the ground on impact.

I didn't have a key to the house, but I looked in the windows. What I saw looked like the result of a small tornado. Dropped or thrown about the room were pieces of toys and games, papers, boxes, bags, packing tape, cords, paper drink glasses, and whatever else one may leave behind in a rush.

I called Jackie, my attorney. She filed an emergency motion to have "the minor child" immediately returned to the State of

Rhode Island. We were in court the next morning in front of Judge Lipski. Maureen's lawyer was present in the courtroom as well. The judge ordered the immediate return of the minor child if she in fact had been taken across state lines under the Uniform Child Custody Jurisdiction and Enforcement Act. Jackie called me later that evening and said that she had heard from Maureen's attorney. She told me that all hell broke loose in Florida when deputies knocked on Maureen's mother's door. According to Jackie, he said that Maureen was freaking out, and he chuckled about her condition. I called the Palm Beach County Sheriff's Department and spoke to the sergeant regarding the incident. The sergeant asked me if they should proceed with force if necessary to take them to the airport. I thought at the time that it was a bit of a strange question to ask me. If they had a court order, wouldn't they know what procedure to follow? I answered "No." Looking back, I wonder what would have happened had I answered "Yes." Nine days passed, and we were headed back to court. Maureen had gone silent. No calls answered by her, and none made from her to me. My attorney and I arrived for the follow-up hearing from my emergency motion. Maureen's lawyer was there but no Maureen. The Magistrate O'Brien, the one from earlier who had neither denied nor granted Maureen's request to leave, arrived rather than Judge Lipski. Magistrate O'Brien sat with so much egg on his face that he called a meeting in his chambers with the attorneys only. They left the courtroom full of people for 20 minutes. My attorney was the first to return from chambers back to the courtroom, and she looked completely disgusted. The judge sat at the bench and said, "My longtime friend and colleague, Judge Lipski ordered the return of the minor child. As I am sure he had reason to do so, and to the disappointment of counsel, I am going to rule to just let Florida handle this since the wife is already there." The motherfucker totally ignored the law, and because he fucked up to begin with, he pushed it off his desk like a piece of junk mail and didn't even have the balls to let my attorney argue the law on court record.

Mike, the owner of the rented house, called me. He asked me what was going on. He knew that Maureen and I separated, but he had just been informed by a neighbor that the electric company had shut off the power to the house. Maureen hadn't paid December's rent and now had the electricity shut off without telling anyone. The heat in the house was electric, and since it was the beginning of January in Rhode Island, the temperature was already below freezing. Mike couldn't get the power turned back on until the following day and asked me, rhetorically, if I knew what happens to pipes when they freeze. He further assured me that if the pipes froze, Maureen and I would be responsible for any damage. Meanwhile, Maureen had already filed for bankruptcy in Florida, so she would *not* be responsible for any financial obligations, including this one. If Mike had followed through with going after damage costs or the remainder of the lease agreement, Maureen would not have been liable. This was all part of the methodically orchestrated scheme.

I met Mike at the house the next day. I hadn't been inside because I didn't have a key. What a mess! She left all the food in the refrigerator and freezer. All of the frozen food melted, and there was a huge pool of blue Popsicle syrup on the floor around the refrigerator. Mike had a friend come over the night before to shut off the water. Now that the electricity was back on, he turned the water back on, and we checked the pipes thoroughly for leaks. We didn't find any, and I began to clean the house, starting with the refrigerator. Mike said all the things I expected to hear, gave me a key, and left.

I stopped working for a bit and started to look around at

things that had been left behind. I found so many things that I thought were overlooked that seemed worth saving like the birth announcement sign that was staked in our front yard with the stork holding the white cloth with Katie's name, weight, length, etc. I found the Fisher Price crib aquarium that Katie had learned to turn on by herself to watch the fish go around while music played. I realized that I just couldn't do this job by myself. The mess left behind was overwhelming, and as I looked around the house, I saw too many painful discoveries. I called Reverend Nancy Barr from the Methodist church. She told me she would coordinate with a helper and be there the next morning. I went back to just cleaning the refrigerator and quit for the day after finishing that one simple, yet daunting task.

I am so thankful to Reverend Nancy and the Bristol United Methodist church for having come into my life. I was attending services there just before Maureen and I separated. I joined the choir and had just performed in the Christmas cantata. I had gotten to know some of the members through the rehearsals, suppers, Bible readings, etc. Reverend Nancy invited me to have lunch with her on occasion to talk about my separation and how to cope with the splitting of my family. I enjoy and absorb scripture much better when it's associated with everyday living and not just readings from the Bible. Figuratively speaking, her church services were gift-wrapped and put right into my lap. She was a kind, soft-spoken, knowledgeable, teaching, caring, wonderful human being. God truly works through her.

Reverend Nancy and Robert, another church member, were at the house the next morning as promised at 9AM. I rented a U-Haul truck to move things to the basement of my apartment building, which I had arranged with the owners of the apartment building the previous day. We worked all day and into the evening, cleaning, packing, loading, and unloading. When Reverend Nancy opened the closet full of Maureen's clothes, my first thought was to throw them out; Reverend Nancy had a better idea, though. She boxed them and made me promise to send them to Maureen, which I did. Mr. Dan showed up in the afternoon, unasked, to help, and he came with boxes from the grocery store and lots of back muscle. Robert, Mr. Dan, and I packed the truck while Reverend Nancy packed boxes and cleaned. Maureen left the master bedroom set. I know she would have taken it, but when I drove by the house while the moving van was being loaded, I could see the van was packed full to the back end. She later told the judge that she left it for me to show her "fairness" of sharing the marital property. She also left the workout gym, the refrigerator, washer and dryer, my office furniture, a stereo receiver (no speakers), some of her overlooked clothes, all of my clothes, a hodgepodge of unwanted items, the movers' ten-page itemized list of the items loaded, and of course, a mess. We all went the half-mile to my apartment building where we unloaded the truck into the basement.

This was the third time of moving in a three-year, perpetual, unwanted life of moving.

CHAPTER 4

Getting Out of Rhode Island

" *Let him that would move the world first move himself.* "
Socrates

The only people I knew in Rhode Island were my cat Milo, my probation officer, my friend Mr. Dan, and the people I befriended at the Methodist church. Where does one go or what does one do when Mr. Dan is busy and the church isn't having any functions? I spent a lot of time shoveling snow around the apartment building, cleaning off my neighbors' cars, and throwing down ice melt in the walkways. I began to study for the test to gain designation as a Leadership in Energy and Environmental Design, Accredited Professional (LEED AP). I also spent time illegally going back and forth to New Jersey, mostly to help my mother, whose health was declining, but also to connect with my birth family and old friends there. Mr. Dan fed Milo for me when I went to New Jersey. I only stayed away for a couple of days at a time in order to not wear thin on Mr. Dan. It was illegal for me to make these trips because I was on probation and wasn't allowed to leave Rhode Island. I began to drink alcohol to numb my pain.

When I learned that I could get travel passes to go back and forth to New Jersey, I began asking Ken, my probation officer, for them every week. He wrote them for me with no objection until his supervisor, Nancy Hallman, overheard me getting one. She stormed over, picked up my file, and said, "There will be no more travel permits! This is ridiculous!" I was granted that particular April 2009 travel permit with the understanding it would be the last one.

When I got back to Rhode Island after that trip, I went on a crusade to get my probation transferred to New Jersey. I spoke with my probation officer regarding the transfer. He spoke with his supervisor, who completely opposed doing anything to cooperate. I immediately went to my apartment, typed a letter to her, and sent it certified mail that same day, even though the post office was right next door to the probation office. I also mailed copies Ken, my probation officer, the Rhode Island Assistant Administrator of Probation and Parole, the Director of the Rhode Island Dept. of Corrections, the Adult Supervision Services Chief of the State of New Jersey, the Chief Probation Officer of the State of New Jersey, the Honorable Governor Jon Corzine of the State of New Jersey, and the Honorable Governor Donald Carcieri of the State of Rhode Island.

See now the "power of the pen" to East Bay Probation and Parole Supervisor, Ms. Nancy Hallman: I received a phone call from Ken the next day at 11am. He asked if I could come in because he wanted to speak to me about something and didn't want to discuss it over the phone. I got in my car and headed right over. He sat down behind his desk and told me he wanted to start the paperwork to transfer my probation to New Jersey. He got back up and left the room. I noticed an opened envelope upside down on his desk. I picked it up, and saw that it was the copy of the letter I had sent to him and everyone else. His supervisor never emerged from her office.

I could not officially transfer my probation to New Jersey

until I completed my twenty-week batterer's intervention program (BIP). Since I was already at week nineteen, this was not a burden. The transfer was official within two weeks.

I had started the BIP group in November, went every Thursday, and never missed a week. I was able to find an alternate location and attend on a different day for the weeks of Christmas, New Year's, and Thanksgiving, but my main group was in Bristol, Rhode Island. Gail, the facilitator, was an awesome lady who seemed to look down on the system she represented while heading this group. I don't know if this was a particular "method to her madness," but she acted like a member of the group who just happened to be in charge. She was knowledgeable and kept the group and the content interesting, even while she put down the system she worked for. She sometimes had her hands full. We're talking about a court-ordered program here; disruptions would often arise from some know-it-all, adversarial participants, who were then asked to leave. One time, Gail had to be escorted by police to her car after the group session for fear of an earlier ejected loudmouth. Make no mistake about Gail though; she could ruin you with one phone call to your probation officer. I participated in the group with hopes of learning something about myself and others. I learned about the five types of abuse: verbal, physical, emotional, financial, and sexual. I also learned directly from Gail's mouth that men and women are not meant to live together. After twenty weeks, $500 in attendance fees, and a pat on the back from Gail for not missing a week, I received my "Certification of Completion."

I finally made contact with Maureen sometime in January 2009, weeks after she took off with Katie. One of the things I remember her saying was that she and her parents decided that since Katie wasn't going to see me anytime soon, they should tell her that I was in the army.

"The Army?"

"Yeah, the army," Maureen said. "Men go away in the army all the time and don't get to see their children."

I answered that with, "But I'm not in the army!"

I knew that Maureen's $2,000 IMac computer came with a video camera integrated into the top of the monitor. I had my laptop and suggested that I could see Katie via Skype video conferencing. Maureen agreed, as long as it didn't cost her anything. I sent Maureen the link to download Skype for Mac. I went online and bought a camera to attach to my laptop and another one for my mother in New Jersey. I downloaded Skype and installed the two cameras. It was bittersweet to see my daughter on a computer screen. She was confused, yet excited. I was happy to see her, yet angry about the fact that Maureen had taken her away from me and me away from her. I did the best I could with this new way to have some kind of communication with Katie.

Since we started these webcam calls, I have been trying to negotiate some kind of schedule to have these webcam calls with Katie on a regular basis. I even tried to have it included in my divorce decree proposal. I have yet to get any cooperation from either Maureen or the system. When I call, text, or email Maureen to ask to schedule a Skype call, what I usually get back is a text message, "Are you near the computer?" If I'm not in front of the computer at that moment, I get no call with Katie and no scheduling of a future call. My mother (Katie's grandmother) gets the exact same treatment.

When Katie was 4 years old, I bought her a cell phone so she could call me or her grandmother whenever she wanted. I preset my cell number on the number 2 and my mother's on number 3. I downloaded Snow White as the phone's screensaver. I sent the phone to Katie and went over the plan parameters with Maureen. My plan included "family finder." It was a service offered by Sprint to locate your children and give you their whereabouts. Maureen had refused to tell me which daycare Katie was going to, who was babysitting her, and for a while, even where our daughter was living. With the family finder, I was able to obtain all of this information for my own peace of mind.

With her phone, now Katie could call me on her own. I remember one time she called me from the grocery store to tell me that Mommy wouldn't let her get a bag of doughnuts. I told Katie that if she ate a bag of doughnuts, she might turn into a doughnut. She laughed and moved on to the next subject. Like magic, I was able to console my little girl even from 1300 miles away. When Maureen saw that Katie and I were able to remain somewhat close with the phone, she started opposing the arrangement. She took the phone away from Katie and started keeping it on her own person. I could tell the difference when the phone was not at daycare all day but was traveling about while Maureen went through her days. When Maureen took the phone away from Katie, I was again no longer able to see where my daughter was nor communicate with her as we had been.

A breakthrough had been reached when I was able to talk Maureen into bringing Katie to New Jersey for Easter and my mother's birthday on April 9, 2009. Of course, I had to pay for the travel expenses, and Maureen insisted on a direct flight both ways, I hadn't seen Katie in over three months.

When they arrived, Maureen cried, and I fought back tears, too. When I saw Maureen crying, I knew that she was sorry for taking Katie and I out of each other's lives. My mom took a really good picture of Maureen visibly crying as Katie ran into my arms.

Katie had seen Milo on our Skype calls, and she asked about him whenever we spoke. Maureen told me that she wanted to take Milo back to Florida for Katie to reunite with him and keep her as her own. I immediately started jumping through hoops to find an airline that allowed pets to fly on board with passengers. US Airways was the only carrier who offered "emotional support" animals on its flights. Then I had to get a doctor's note and pay for Milo's ticket on the return flight to West Palm Beach. Finally, I drove Milo to New Jersey and left him at my friend Karen's house; he was going to stay there until Katie and Maureen left on April 14th. I took Katie over to see him during her stay and let her know that Milo was going back to Florida with her. Literally three hours before the plane's departure, Maureen changed her mind and refused to take Milo. I pleaded with her not to do this to Katie, and my mother offered to pay for all of Milo's expenses throughout his life, if money was the issue. Maureen simply claimed that her father wouldn't approve, and she wasn't taking him.

Other than the Milo situation, the visit went very well. We celebrated GG's (short for Grandmom Graves) birthday, and I put together an Easter egg hunt within the common area of GG's property. Now again, the protection order was still in effect until November of 2009; Maureen had claimed she was in fear of her life in Rhode Island court. Less than two weeks before her arrival in New Jersey, on March 26, 2009, Maureen sent me an email that included, "I would also like to know…if I completely dropped the Temporary No Contact order, what would that do for you?" I ask you, Reader, does that sound like fear or more like manipulating the system to use as a bargaining tool? Later, in the divorce trial, Maureen claimed that she insisted I not sleep in my mother's house while she and Katie were there and that after I agreed to that, I slept there anyway. That was a flat out lie in court. Maureen's stories perpetually changed depending on what effect each situation would have. The court finally dismissed the protection order for lack of evidence.

I petitioned the court for permission to travel to Florida to see Katie. The motion was granted, and I was allowed to go to Florida six times during my remaining probation period. I had to report to my probation officer when my flight dates and times were and where I would be staying while there. I was permitted by the court to have Katie for six hours each day with no overnight visits, which was fine since I would be in a hotel anyway. More "baby steps," as Maureen earlier said. I bought plane tickets, rented a car, stayed in a hotel, ate every meal out, and entertained Katie. It cost a small fortune to do all this, but it was necessary for Katie and I to remain as close as possible under the circumstances. I took my guitar with me so Katie and I could resume singing together and to maintain our bond through our love for music. Maureen packed a bag of toys for us to play with, so I did get cooperation from her in that regard, but that was the only support she gave.

Maureen and I would meet in an agreed location to make the "child exchange," as the court calls it. She usually showed up late. She was late for everything, and this was certainly no exception. When I called her to confirm times or to speak with her regarding anything, she simply would not answer the phone. This made it difficult to coordinate a visit. It seemed that she just wanted my visits with Katie the most inconvenient and abrasive experience that she could. I began to get the impression that she was hoping I would simply give up on my little girl. Not a chance.

Of course, I was abstinent from "self-medicating" during my stays in Florida. My pain came from not being with my daughter, and as long as I knew she and I would have quality time together, my heart had joy. I did not want any numbing.

It was spring and time to get out of Rhode Island for good. By the end of April 2009, I had finished my BIP group, and my probation transfer to New Jersey was completed. I donated a lot of stuff to the Methodist church to downsize what I had to move. I left items in the church Sunday school, with Reverend Nancy's permission and appreciation. She said whatever they couldn't use, they would find someone who could. I saw Mr. Dan as he was coming and going throughout the day. I gave him my Fender Stratocaster guitar and my amplifier, in appreciation for his being such a great friend to me. I waited for him after we finished loading, but he didn't come back. I found a note from him on the seat of the U-Haul. Mr. Dan wrote that he didn't like good-byes, and he wouldn't see me again before I left. As quickly as he came into my life, he was out of it. I will always be thankful for Mr. Dan's friendship to both me and my daughter. He was a stranger who touched my life with his friendship in my time of great need. May God bless my friend, Mr. Dan.

My friend Bob kindly rode with me to Rhode Island, helped me load, and followed me back in my car to New Jersey. As I mentioned, I had been back and forth to New Jersey since Maureen left Rhode Island in December of 2008. I had rekindled lifelong friendships of some of the people—like Bob—who I had known my entire life but lost touch with after moving to Florida and starting a family. One of those friends told me, "You can't cry through Xanax." I saw that it was so and began to take Xanax to help me cope with my depression, anxiety, and sadness. I bought them off the street at first. After a while, I got a prescription from a doctor. The strange thing is that the doctor prescribed a higher dose than I was getting from the street. I could only take half a pill each day or I would sleep all day. They are strong.

I was moving back to the Township of Florence, New Jersey. To give a picture of this town, you should know that at one point, they had thirty liquor licenses within the town's 10.1 square miles. The town includes a dilapidated Superfund steel mill site at the one end in Roebling and a similarly abandoned ductile iron pipe foundry at the other. These are set against a centerpiece view of Tullytown, Pennsylvania's huge landfill, which is across from the once-beautiful yacht club's boat launching park. The landfill is complete with more seagulls than one could imagine. I had a lot of good reasons to leave Florence for Florida back in

1996, but now I was going back because it seemed the best choice at the time, especially considering my mother's declining health; she needed my help. So, I rented a storage garage, unloaded what was left of my belongings there, and moved into my mother's home, taking my clothes and a few personal items such as pictures. My mother was getting around using a cane. She lived in a second floor condominium, which was not a good thing because stairs were very difficult for her. We found a company that installed outdoor chairlifts, and that lifted the burden of getting outside. Since she could still drive a car, she was finally able to enjoy getting out and about again.

Back when I had been traveling back and forth from Rhode Island, I frequented an establishment called Dr. Lou's Place. Dr. Lou's Place was an old bar that was re-opened on December 18, 2008. The new format that Lou implemented was an open mic night every night. This was a great place for musicians to perform and an outlet for me to do the same. I practiced playing solo songs and stood in with other musicians. Going there to perform was a way to blow off steam in a constructive and creative way. I knew I would be spending a lot of nights there until I finished up my probation in November. As I got to be friends with Dr. Lou, he took an interest in my divorce and custody battle as he was in his own fight—at a much later stage of the game—that had been going on for many years.

Dr. Lou gave me a job cooking in the kitchen. I got to know many of the people who frequented the place, and some of them, through sharing their music and their own life experiences, helped me deal with my broken heart caused by no longer being an active, hands-on father to my daughter.

In addition to Dr. Lou, I connected with one other man there in particular, Ronnie. Ronnie played the bass guitar. He and I shared a love of listening to and performing classic rock music. He was a recovering alcoholic who left a life of abusing himself many years prior. He had a 20-year-old daughter who for many years—and even up to the present date—he had a hard time seeing because of dealing with his daughter's mother, especially when he picked his daughter up at the former marital home. Ronnie was a simple man, who enjoyed a simple life to its fullest. He thanks God every day for what he has. He is a confidant and friend to me. Ronnie would call me out of the blue just to see what I was doing or how I was feeling. When I would tornado, mentally and emotionally, after an upsetting call from Maureen, he would redirect. He would insist that "things aren't always going to be this way" and would show me a recent cell phone picture of his own daughter and say, "It's worth the fight, my brother." I went to him a couple of times regarding my own recent drinking, and he told me, "If you drink, that's your business; if you want to stop, I can make it my business." I had to at least try to stop the pills. I had been taking .05 mg a day of Xanax. It may not sound like much, but I knew that I was using them as a crutch. At some point every day, I felt the emotional need to cry. Each time I did, I would take half a Xanax. My body had grown accustomed to it, and I felt the chemical change fighting in my body when I didn't take it. I recall one time while working in Dr. Lou's kitchen; I deliberately left the pills at home. I began to tremble and perspire. I drank a Coke to try to get through the withdrawal symptoms quicker. That was really the wrong thing to do; by putting caffeine into an already distressed system craving a sedative, I made it worse. I was unsuccessful at stopping the Xanax at this point.

I spoke with a friend in Florida and asked him who his divorce and custody lawyer was. He gave me the name Eric Cheshire. Eric got my friend full custody of his two daughters. Later, I found out it was easy for him to do that since the ex-wife was abusing the children. For Eric, winning that case was like picking up a quarter off the sidewalk. When I called Eric, he told me, "What drives me in this business is when one parent won't allow the other parent to be a parent." I later learned that this translated into reality as, "What drives me in this business is the money generated for me when one parent won't allow the other parent to be a parent." For a $3,000 retainer and $300 an hour, I now had my representative in place.

Using the summer to my advantage, I decided to cut grass in the township for extra money. I picked up a cheap, used lawn mower, a weed whacker, and a leaf blower. I printed flyers and left them in the doors of all 2500+ Roebling residents. I drove around in a sedan with a lawn mower hanging out of the trunk. All I could think about was Katie as I mowed, weed whacked, chopped down trees, removed tree stumps, and did any other job I could muster up. I had to pay for this attorney in addition to my regular living expenses, including child support. Under the revised court order from Rhode Island, I continued to travel back and forth to Florida to see Katie in June, August, and September of 2009, spending over $4,000 in expenses to do so. All the time I was in Florida, Maureen continued to make things as rough and inconvenient as she possibly could for Katie and I to be together. Eric filed my divorce papers in September 2009.

CHAPTER 5

Organizing against the Campaign

"The key to organizing an alternative society is to organize people around what they can do, and more importantly what they want to do.

Abbie Hoffman

B ecause of moving out of Rhode Island, my unemployment was terminated in the state. Other than what I was able to earn by way of cooking in the kitchen at Dr. Lou's and cutting lawns, I barely made enough to put food in my stomach, let alone pay an attorney and send child support.

I hadn't paid any child support in five months. I wasn't able to file a motion in any court. No state had jurisdiction, or so they claimed. Rhode Island's Magistrate O'Brien already ruled that his court washed its hands of the case when he cited Florida was to handle it, and I was in New Jersey.

According to my attorney, all I could do was to wait until the upcoming divorce in Florida. He told me that I needed to get to Florida as soon as possible, even though he knew I couldn't leave New Jersey until November, 2009. Of course, getting to Florida after November was not the problem. The problems were: How would I get my things there? Where would I go once I got there?

I was fighting against Maureen's father, a rich man who was certainly buying his way with the courts and his own daughter thus far. I sent what I could to my attorney and visited Katie three times that summer. I had a cell phone bill of $40 a month, a storage bin of $100 a month, and car insurance. I did not have any money left over for any luxuries of any kind. I knew enough people in New Jersey to ask around for employment leads, but because of the still-lingering Bush economy debacle, I had to ask people to stick their necks out to help me find a short-term job within their network or with their employers. I just had to get through until November because I was leaving to be close to my daughter in the fall.

Looking for work in Florida via the internet was an ongoing project. I kept up with Indeed.com and contacted some of my former business associates in the construction industry, but not much had changed for the better in Florida.

Meanwhile, I traveled about my hometown going from Gary's, to Bob's, to Dr. Lou's, my high school friend, Lee, and to Karen's, looking to socialize within my small network of supportive friends to keep busy.

I had dated Karen back in 1983. We remained friends but lost touch after I left New Jersey for Florida in 1996 and started a family. Karen worked for thirty years at a company that provided insurance for collectible cars. Her daughter was now sixteen years old. She divorced and currently had a boyfriend who was unemployed due to the failing economy. Sometimes the two of them would come over to Dr. Lou's and watch bands perform and hang out with me. Karen usually had a big circle of friends and many times had small parties at her home. She is a soft spoken, kind-hearted person who usually was a great person to go to for clear-headed advice. We were growing closer during this time.

Subsequent to the breakup with her boyfriend, we talked

about me moving in with her, but I knew there was no room in my heart or my head for a relationship. Who would want to be involved with me anyway? I was a complete mess. She said that she understood that my child was what I was after, and she would never get in the way of that. She even laughed and let on how ridiculous it would be for her to try to compete with what I had on my emotional plate.

I began to look for residence options in Florida. I checked Craigslist and found a mobile home for a $3,000 asking price. I exchanged many emails and phone conversations with the owner of the mobile home, Steve, to arrange the sale and readiness of the home for my return.

As a back-up option, I decided to call the electric company and see if I could get the power turned on in the abandoned house in Florida. They told me that it would cost $395. I gave them a tentative date of November 10th and paid the deposit on their internet site.

Around this time, I ran into an old friend who I had known since we played little league baseball together. He worked for a national moving company, and we discussed the possibility of my things hitching a ride to Florida if there was a run with some room on it. This would be significantly less expensive and less trouble than renting a moving truck.

During that same summer, Maureen started to communicate with me via telephone and email. I was pleased to see that she was reaching out because Katie was and will always be our common denominator. Maureen and Katie had moved into her mother Mabel's rental property, which was in foreclosure. So Mabel was over there constantly. Maureen was not paying any rent to live there. The court records on the foreclosure seem to indicate that Mabel was simply letting the bank take the property and that Maureen and Katie were just staying on the property until the bank was ready to move in and seize it.

Maureen and I discussed the scenario of my probation being transferred to Florida to "co-parent Katie." Katie missed me and continuously asked me, "Daddy, when are you coming back to me?" To that end, Maureen wrote a letter to Richard DelFino, Assistant Administrator of Probation & Parole State of Rhode Island; Jenny Nimer, ICAOS Commissioner, in Tallahassee, Florida; and my New Jersey probation officer. Here is the actual letter with our names changed and the few typos corrected.

> I am Maureen Graves, wife of David Graves. David was placed on probation in Rhode Island for a Domestic Violence issue. David was so distraught and depressed over the outcome of his actions that has resulted in a separation of him from me and his 3-year-old daughter. Due to his behavior and my lack of financial and emotional support, I and our daughter moved back to Florida to gain that support from my family and my friends from my home state of 35 years and also to gain some distance from David, to get a break from him, and perhaps give David some time to find some acceptance that we are no longer a family living together.

> Although I know David still loves me and would like to reconcile, that is not an option on the table for discussion. I feel that David has realized that his daughter is more important to have without me than to not have at all. David has always been a loving, responsible, hands-on, and involved father. Katie misses her father and asks for him daily. My intentions when leaving David was not necessarily to also separate Katie from her daddy, however, with the emotions so high-strung at the time, there was no other choice. I would like to encourage a close, healthy father/daughter relationship.

> I know that David's probation is concluded on November 9th which is about 3-1/2 months away. To most people, that is not a long time to wait, but to a 3-year-old, it is a lifetime. I would not have made this request 3 months ago, even while

I painfully listened to my daughter ask for her daddy because I knew I was not ready and still needed my space. I feel that with the support system I have built around me, perhaps David and I can peacefully co-parent Katie from separate residences so that her home is not completely broken.

Please find this letter to respectfully request David Graves's probation to be relocated to Florida as soon as possible. There are already court orders placed in Rhode Island for a visitation schedule and child support that can be used as guidelines here in Florida until we replace those orders in Florida.

Thank you in advance for your consideration.

Respectfully,

Maureen Graves

The letter was later admitted into divorce court as husband's evidence. It showed that Maureen flip-flopped back and forth on her attitude toward me. I'm sure that despite knowing what was best for Katie, as the letter would indicate, Maureen's parents stepped in and forced her to do a complete 180-degree turn around. As I said, Maureen tried to get another restraining order in two states. When both attempts failed, she simply cut off all communications between her and me and between Katie and me. No phone calls, no emails, no Skype calls, nothing. I went the entire month of October 2009 not speaking with my daughter. This was when Maureen took the pink phone away from Katie so we couldn't call each other directly. It wasn't until I got to Florida that I was able to use mediation to resume my communication with Katie. It was a very difficult time. I often wonder what she said to our daughter; if she used the "Daddy's in the army" story, how did that go over?

I went about cutting lawns, cooking in Dr. Lou's kitchen, and playing music. I took the exam for the LEED AP certification, but I failed the test by seven points. I ran errands for my ailing mother and took her to doctor appointments, rehabilitation centers, cleaned her house, and moped around. I cried a lot. I continued to self-medicate to numb the pain.

Bob, who helped me move to New Jersey, and Sara, his wife, lived in the same condominium development as my mother, which is where I was staying. I frequently went to visit with them and spill my guts. Bob drank a thirty-can pack of Miller Lite each day. He was trying to get permanent disability from the state of New Jersey for a bad back and just sat home drinking and watching sports and pornography all day. Eventually Sara lost her job of ten years due to company cutbacks, and she started sitting at home drinking wine all day. One day, Sara tried to give me oral sex while Bob was passed out on the couch. She said that I needed it. My life seemed like a movie... something like "The Truman Show." Nothing felt real anymore.

I hated my existence. I knew that I just had to get through this and out of the situation, but it seemed that everywhere I went, the first words I'd hear were, "You want a beer?" I was tired and weary. I thought about Katie constantly, was losing hope, and was tired of hearing myself talk about it. My eyes no longer tingled when I started to cry; the initial feeling just prior to crying was pain in my tear ducts. My weight went up and down like a rollercoaster. I would lose ten pounds, then gain fifteen back. I was just in so much pain over my daughter that I kept numbing myself. I decided to find someone to talk to where there wasn't any alcohol...a mental health professional.

I went to see an LMHC named Tammy and told her of my situation. Based on what I told her, she said that Maureen certainly sounded co-dependent, and that she was probably being controlled by her parents. She also said that I was depressed. Tammy was convinced that my only focus was having a relationship with my daughter and that I needed to continue that path.

She also suggested that I continue therapy once a week. I think the funny thing about talking to someone in the mental health profession is that just about all of what they tell you, you already know yourself.

John Sweeny, a retired Superior Family Court Chief Judge has been a lifelong friend of my mother's. He is an extremely kind man who has an aura that demands respect just by being himself. My level of respect for the man is almost that of a fear level. He just has that way about him. I went to his home to tell him my story—leaving nothing out—and to ask his advice. I included the night I slapped Maureen. I knew that if I wasn't completely forthcoming with him, I could not get advice that would help me.

He sat in his recliner chair with a broken ankle and listened to every word without one interruption or question. When I completely finished, he told me that I first need to forgive myself for my own wrongdoing, or I would destroy myself. Then he told me that I would need to maintain representation of counsel, or my chances of getting any kind of desired results were slim. How accurate he was on both of his suggestions!

This was when it hit me: I should have filed for divorce in New Jersey where my extremely politically active family knew so many judges. This was and will always be my biggest regret of how I proceeded with my divorce. I had every right to file in New Jersey because I was now a permanent resident. At least I would have gotten a chance of something besides dismissal to a second-class citizen father in the eyes of family court.

Because I could sing, the mayor of the town asked me to

sing the National Anthem at the flag raising ceremony on the morning of the Fourth of July festivities in the township. Dr. Lou came and videotaped the ceremony to post on his website. My 89-year-old grandmother came to the ceremony because she lived right in the center of town—the ceremony was happening half a block away from her home. My grandmother was totally deaf. My grandfather had died six years earlier and I wanted to help her communicate with people. I decided to get her an email machine. It was called a "mailbug." She took to emailing like a seasoned professional. This 89-year-old woman got her friends' and relatives' (including Maureen's) email addresses, and she was connected like never before. This is how my grandmother became another victim of Maureen's mother Mabel via email. Mabel would upset my grandmother by sending her emails about how glad she was that Maureen and Katie were there in Florida with her. She wrote about all the fun they were having. All the time, my grandmother couldn't even speak with Katie on the phone due to her being deaf.

Mabel further upset my grandmother by saying that her son—Maureen's brother—and I were "out of the same mold." Mabel compared me with a man who hadn't had a job in at least fifteen years, except for fraud and working at a nursery that grew marijuana in Florida. He gambled, stole, and came from parents who never said they loved him. Mabel's son and I came from two completely different molds and were two completely different people. Mabel only said these things to upset my grandmother. This was actually no surprise to me. I truly believe the woman is a sociopath. She lives to upset people. After the baby shower for Maureen, Mabel took all of the guests' email addresses and filled those people's inboxes with religious messages, political propaganda, and chain letters until I was inundated with calls to get her to stop.

My other brother-in-law, David, was also a real shyster. He

would manipulate people like no one I had ever seen. When he was living in our house in Florida, I came home from work one evening and saw him convince 6-months-pregnant Maureen to sign up for the medical insurance he was selling—in spite of the fact that I had full medical coverage for my entire family through my employer! He told Maureen that after she bought the insurance, she could cancel it. He just needed to show sales. His reason for doing this was because he had to show sales results, but he didn't want to go out and try to sell it, as he was being paid to.

After Maureen emptied our safe deposit box (3 days prior to our separation), David sold my coin collection on eBay. Have you ever tried to call eBay on the phone? It's not an easy task. When I did finally get through to a human being, I was told that eBay is happy to cooperate with law enforcement to prosecute people selling stolen property on their site, but that is the extent of their involvement. Just imagine trying to find a cop who is willing to investigate such a thing…it isn't happening.

David's eBay ID was "TEENJOCKETTE." He usually sold Goodwill shirts and shorts that he paid one to three dollars apiece for. He told me the reason for his ID was so people would think he was a virgin teenager who played sports and sweated a lot. He said that no one would know for sure if he was a male or female, opening up a larger market for people who are interested in teen-used, sweat-in sports clothing…Shyster!

I called and told Maureen that I knew her brother was selling my coin collection. She told me that it never happened, but if it did, she had every right to do it since it was marital assets.

Funny thing is that she never sold any of her jewelry acquired over our years together or used the thousands of dollars that I gave her in Rhode Island after the separation. The only marital assets she was interested in selling were my coins that I collected over the years and my white gold necklace that she gave me the night before we were married.

I told her I had contacted eBay, and I was going to prosecute. I think that spooked her because, if you check eBay, you will see that the username is deleted. David sold—but never sent—the coins. He incurred a barrage of negative feedback for sending regular quarters to the winners of the gold coin auctions. He auctioned off the exact same gold coin multiple times, yet never sent the pictured gold coin. My gold coin.

In October, my friend from the moving company called me and said he had a truck going to Florida with room for what he saw in my storage garage. I met the movers at the storage facility; they loaded everything up and hauled it to their location in West Palm Beach for a mere $600. The going rate for a U-Haul at that time was $1,500, and I would have to load everything, drive, unload it myself, and pay gas and tolls.

I was gearing up to get to Florida to be with my daughter. My stuff was on its way. I had given a deposit on the mobile home I wanted to buy. I could see a light at the end of the tunnel. I hadn't spoken with Maureen or Katie despite my continued attempts. I truly believe Maureen thought I would give up on that child. My tenacity was going to outlast her father's money. It was a contest of unconditional love versus money.

To complete my departure out of New Jersey, I had to satisfy my probation sentence for slapping Maureen back in August of 2008 in Rhode Island. Andy, my probation officer in New Jersey, was an ok guy. He never broke my balls, and he told me I was one of his lesser concerns regarding my maintaining control. He and I had our jobs to do, and we did them. Mine was to simply stay out of any kind of trouble, and his was to verify that I was staying out of trouble. Part of that was that I had to submit to random drug screenings. I'm not sure why since my offense did not include any use of alcohol or drugs. Ironically, prior to my separation, I hadn't used alcohol for eight years, and the only drug I had ever used in my life was marijuana. Now that I had to take a drug test, I used both. I had to present my prescription paperwork to Andy for the Xanax, and I certainly didn't drink before going in to see him. I guess it must happen that people do go in drunk. I had to tell him in advance and get any travel to Florida permits approved. He gave me them with no problem. He knew all I wanted was to resume a relationship with my daughter.

Andy hinted from time to time that Maureen was contacting him, but he never went into any detail. I think she was trying to find out if I was in fact coming to Florida once the probation was over. At no time did I ever tell her anything other than I was. The one thing he did say to me as he looked me in the eyes was "there are cops down in Florida too" and to "be careful." Between what I said to him and whatever Maureen said to him, I think he surmised what was really going on.

Throughout the summer and while I was looking for short-term work in New Jersey, I had searched unsuccessfully for work in Florida. I must have put in 100 resumes. I think that a lot of the jobs posted either are gone in minutes or simply don't exist. I was on Indeed.com every day, so I knew which postings were new. For the first time, I was moving back to Florida with no job waiting for me when I got there. I decided that once I got there, I could meet with my former business associates in person and see what was happening. This would be a much less "faceless" way of selling myself to potential employers, and it seemed more likely to find success.

I rented a storage garage in Florida over the internet for my things that the moving company was storing at their facility in West Palm Beach. I gave my lawnmower, weed whacker, and blower to a friend. I said goodbye to friends, my mother, grand-mother, packed my car, and left on Saturday, November 7, 2009. I already had my release from probation the previous day (Friday), so I left two days earlier than Monday, the 9th. It spooked me a bit, so I left my cell phone off for the ride. I drove with intent, focus, and fear...intent on getting there, focus on my daughter, and fear of the unknown.

It's a twenty-hour drive, so I had a lot of time to think. I drove all day and night and made it as far as South Carolina by stopping minimal times to eat, stretch, or fuel up. I just knew that every mile that I drove, I was one more mile closer to Katie. I called no one until I called my mother after I woke up in South Carolina in a twenty-five dollar a night motel. I drove the second half of the trip and arrived in Florida on November 9th. The day that I was officially allowed to leave New Jersey, I was already in Florida. The moving company met me at the storage facility and unloaded my things into the garage.

As the truck was parking outside the garage, I called Maureen. She picked up the phone and I said, "I'm here, and I want to see Katie." She said that she would call me back in a little bit. I went back to helping unload, and my phone rang. It was my lawyer. He told me that he heard that I was in Florida because Maureen's lawyer called him and wanted to have media-tion as soon as possible. I wasn't in Palm Beach County, Florida for three hours and already had a court appointment. November 30th was the agreed date between the attorneys. Until then, there was no order in place in the State of Florida.

The family court bullshit started right away. When I picked up Katie, Maureen had me sign a piece of paper that said, "I, David Graves, agree to bring Katie back at 6 p.m." If I were kid-napping my daughter, would I be bringing my belongings in a moving truck to Florida? If I intended to kidnap her, wouldn't I sign the paper anyway?

I told Eric about it. He said that because there was no order in place, I could bring Katie back whatever time that I felt like it. He said that Maureen's attorney probably told her to have me sign the paper.

I asked Eric, "You mean if I wanted to take Katie to Disney World, I could?" He said, "Yes." I did think about it for a while, but of course, I decided not to. I wasn't there to cause trouble. Maureen was already doing that. I thought that the trouble would subside, but the money man, Maureen's father, kept insisting she keep the chaos going. After all, what else does a co-dependent do when the puppet master—daddy with the money—gives you your orders?

After the truck was unloaded into my storage unit, I went to our old house, which was in foreclosure. I had paid a deposit of $395 to get the electricity on, but the meter had been removed by the electric company. My key still worked in the back door, but the house had been broken into. Some of the walls had holes, phone books had been thrown around, and business cards of realtors sat on the counter and floor. The place smelled of animal feces as well.

I had planned on staying there. I didn't have any furniture, but if the utility company had come through, I would have had running water and air conditioning. However, I was screwed.

I went out to my car and unloaded some things anyway. I was picking Katie up in two hours, and I couldn't even wash my face. I walked around the empty house, went into every room, and just looked. I went into Katie's room and stared at the cartoon style, fairy-tale mural that I papered on one whole wall in her room. It showed a bridge over water, trees, and a swing on it. I sobbed thinking of the times that I played guitar to her as she swung in her swing. I walked through the rest of the house thinking of good times, work times, and watching my little girl run and play. I looked down at my wrist at one of the two pink rope wristbands a friend's daughter had made for both Katie and me. At that moment, I stopped, sat back on the floor, and cried.

I took Katie to a Royal Palm Beach sports complex. I had a soccer ball and we kicked it around. It was easy to impress my 4-year-old daughter by kicking the ball forty feet straight into the air. This prompted a "do it again" scenario. I ran into an acquaintance, Martin, who later testified in my divorce trial about his observation of Katie and my playing together. We also played on the playground equipment at the park. We had such a nice time. I was glad my feet were back in Florida, near my daughter.

That night, after I got back from my visit with Katie, I got a call from Frank, the driver from the moving company. He asked me if I was doing anything for the next couple of days because he needed help moving a house full of furniture from West Palm Beach to Tampa. I thankfully took the offer. The company paid for room and food for me for the next two days along with a train ticket from Tampa back to West Palm Beach. I parked my car at the West Palm Beach facility, and I was off to Tampa to make a few dollars and be indoors. I did take $500 dollars with me to Florida when I left New Jersey, and this moving job was certainly going to help. I was hoping for something with the moving company after this job, but this one job was all they needed from me to cover someone canceling on them at the last minute.

When I got back from Tampa, I had to find somewhere to reside. I couldn't stay in the foreclosed house. I went to Best Western at the airport and went into their business center. I went on Priceline and entered that I was willing to pay thirty-five dollars a night for a room. They sent me to the Crowne Plaza, half a block down from Best Western. For the next week, I bounced from one hotel to another using Priceline. I used the business centers at the hotels to print resumes for taking into businesses as I looked for a job.

I remembered an email that Maureen had sent to me while I was still in New Jersey. She'd said that our old neighbor, Tina, would let me stay in her guesthouse for fifty dollars a week while I was there to visit Katie. Here is a portion of Maureen's actual email from Thursday, Mar 26, 2009 at 10:53 P.M. Notice that it was ok for me to come into Maureen's home at this point. Her father hadn't given his orders yet for Maureen to be difficult about Katie and me spending time together.

> I spoke to Tina in Loxahatchee and she is happy to let you stay in the guest house and hang out there with Katie and play with toys and stuff if you wish. There is a daybed, refrigerator and shower there. I told her that you would give her fifty dollars for a week. In addition, you can come in here and play with her for about an hour and then she can pick out toys to take with her or I'll pack a bag or whatever. After the first or second day of her showing you stuff and you playing with her here, my guess is that after that you could probably just pick her up and go. If there is some place in particular that you wanted me to join you for a while, like the ball field or something, I would probably do something like that, but we can discuss that as it comes up.

I called Steve, the guy with the mobile home. He told me there was a problem with the dates that I could move in. He also told me that he had failed to tell me earlier about his contract with the mobile home's real estate agency. He had to pay them an additional $2,000 for them listing the property, in spite of the fact that I found it on Craigslist. If I was going to buy it, I was going to have to absorb the additional cost.

I drove over to Tina's worried about the new information. If it didn't work out for me to stay with Tina, I wasn't sure what I would do next.

I sat down with Tina, and we talked for hours. She had recently divorced and was having financial trouble herself. She told me I could stay there rent-free for a while until I could find a job. It gave me a home base to work from with my laptop, a place to shower, privacy, and some peace. Tina had a large, enclosed pool area with a high-top table and a view of my old house next door. I sat there with my wireless internet laptop, grabbed someone's signal, searched the internet for job leads, and made a course of action for every day. Occasionally, I saw someone cutting the grass next door at my old house. One day, I walked over to find that the service had been hired by the mortgage company.

My attorney, Eric, called me and wanted money. I hadn't been in Florida for two weeks, and he was threatening to withdraw if I didn't come up with another $1,500. He had been after me to get to Florida as soon as possible, I did what he suggested, and now he was threatening to bail on me. I convinced him to give me a little more time.

I found a job pressure-washing gas stations. I worked from 9 P.M. until I was finished sometime in the morning. It was something. I needed something. I sent Eric some money to hold him. I was able to give Tina her fifty dollars for rent, and I sent Maureen support for the first time in a while. The work was not hard, but it was tedious and of course, wet. My shoes were soaked within minutes. Rubber boots didn't do much good because I was washing overhead as well. Since the job was at night, I was still able to knock on potential employers' doors during the day. I went to old networks within the construction industry. Florida's economy was still in the toilet.

The pressure-washing job only lasted a month. The owner refused to pay me what he promised, and because it was a cash deal, there wasn't much that I could do about it.

November 30th was the deposition/mediation. Maureen's lawyer kept us there for six and a half hours. There were no marital assets left. She had already taken them all. The only thing to discuss was Katie. They knew I had limited funds, and they squeezed me that day for every minute they could.

My attorney had the idea to have Maureen and I each undergo a custody evaluation by court psychology. He knew of Maureen's instability and co-dependency. He asked me if I could pass the evaluation. I told him that I could. My depression was due to my situation of having my child taken away from me. Eric told me that under the circumstances that was to be expected and would be viewed as such by the evaluator.

I was granted visitation with Katie every Tuesday and Thursday from 3 P.M. to 6 P.M., every Saturday from 10:30 A.M. to 2 P.M., and every Sunday from 8 A.M. to 10:30 A.M.. It was written that on Tuesdays and Thursdays, I was to pick her up at her day care and not be late, on Saturdays, I was to pick her up at dance class, and on Sundays, pick her up at Burger King. I was to return her each trip to the Burger King.

It wasn't much, and I didn't want to sign it. Maureen used the term "baby steps" again at the mediation. My lawyer told me that we could be on "cruise control" for now and change things later at the divorce trial. So I signed it.

Prior to the new order, I had spoken to Noah's Arc Academy director, Yoelmy "Joy" Santana numerous times over the phone from New Jersey about different policies and practices at Katie's daycare. She had been cooperative about discussing them and sympathetic regarding the recent separation of Katie's parents. It's important to know that Maureen was now working at Noah's Ark as a teacher's helper of some sort.

After the new order, when I picked Katie up at the Noah's Arc Academy daycare, the director Ms. Santana came out with Katie and told me that for every minute that I was late in bringing

Katie back, I would have to pay one dollar. I really thought she was kidding at first, and then she assured me that was the policy for parents picking up their children in the evening. *But I'm not picking her up in the evening,* I thought. Plus, because Maureen has so much difficulty waking up in the mornings (and always had), she was the person who was the last to leave in the evening while parents picked up their children from the daycare.

I turned from the daycare with Katie holding my hand, and we left for our time together. One day, I was in the parking lot of the daycare reading a book because I had arrived ten minutes early. Ms. Santana walked past my car, and we exchanged hellos through my opened car window. My phone rang just as she was entering the building. It was my lawyer. He told me that Maureen called her attorney to tell him that I was early at the daycare. Her attorney called him and that I was not to leave until 3 P.M. It was 2:55. I told him that I was not leaving, and he is to not take any more of these petty calls from her attorney and for his secretary to take messages. They were simply harassing me and running up my legal costs.

Soon, Ms. Santana informed me that she would no longer discuss anything regarding Katie at the daycare. She told me I was not on the contact list, and it was the facility's policy not to discuss anything regarding the children who attend there with anyone who is not on the list.

Maureen had begun her official estrangement campaign and was alienating me from Katie.

CHAPTER 6

Making a Rope Out of Ashes

*" It's lack of faith that makes people afraid
of meeting challenges, and I believed in myself. "*
Muhammad Ali

When Katie was 3, she and I went to my friend Ron's for Thanksgiving. Ron had custody of his two girls. He used and recommended Eric to me for my divorce. Maureen held me to getting Katie at 3 P.M. and wanted me to bring her back at 6 P.M. per the agreed order. My phone rang at 6:05, and I hadn't left Ron's house yet. Maureen was irate because I didn't have Katie back at the Burger King exchange location on time. I had honestly lost track of time and had to whisk Katie off to Burger King without even the proper goodbyes and thank you.

As Christmas was coming, I asked Maureen for extra time for Katie and I to spend together on Christmas Day. Maureen told me that Christmas fell on a Saturday and that wasn't my day to see her. She said again that she would not deviate from the court order. Maureen was very difficult while we tried to come to some kind of agreement on this issue. The negotiating emails back and forth were incredibly exhausting—twenty-six emails in all, often arguing over as little as fifteen minutes of time. I managed to get her to agree to let me have a total of five hours with Katie on Christmas Day.

On our pre-Christmas visit, Katie and I went to Target. She picked out a two-necklace set as her Christmas gift for Maureen, which Katie later said that her mom never wore. Katie saw a piggy bank wearing high heels and just loved it. I went back after dropping her off to buy it, but it was already gone.

Katie and I wrapped Maureen's Christmas present from Katie at Starbucks with Maureen sitting inside watching.

I went back to my friend Ron's home as that was going to be the place where Katie and I would celebrate our Christmas the next day. Maureen showed up on time, and Katie was nervous. The poor thing was feeling like a victim of this divorce poison, and Maureen just didn't see it or didn't care.

On Christmas Day, I felt miserable all morning. It was the worst feeling that I could imagine. I was alone for Christmas. I sat on Barb's back porch, hoping the phone would ring. I could not stop thinking about what my little girl might be doing and how her eyes would light up as she found her gifts from Santa. I could hardly bear this. How could Eric not include holiday visitation in the agreement?

When Katie showed up for our visit, we spent some time opening presents and playing with them. We played with the Strawberry Shortcake dolls. I remember the Lemon Meringue doll was almost unobtainable—and I paid an exorbitant amount of money for it—but we had to have the whole gang. Katie also loved the Fisher Price Little People, and I got the Sara Lynn castle. Hello Kitty presents were also big items this particular Christmas. Particularly a Hello Kitty sticker book that kept us collecting stickers for months. She had barely enough time to take a decent ride on her new Dora bicycle, so I let her take the bike to Maureen's house and keep it there. After all, Katie didn't spend enough time with me to even have it feel like it was her bike.

After Christmas, I composed and mailed the Notice of Appeal of the divorce to Maureen and her attorney. The purpose of this appeal was to get a more reasonable court order for time with Katie. One attorney wanted $10,000 just to fill out the paperwork. I can see why; it was a daunting task. I couldn't believe that I actually filled out all the paperwork correctly on the first attempt. Later, my attorney, Chris Jette, negated the appeal, and I agreed to move forward with the stipulations written in the divorce order instead of the appeal. I regret that decision to this day.

Despite her earlier email about me playing with Katie in her home, and perhaps because of yet another unsuccessful attempt in getting a restraining order against me, Maureen now did not want me coming into her home. Burger King was the primary "exchange" location. The only variation was on Sundays, when Katie and I were done at Sunday school. Maureen picked her up at the Methodist church in Wellington and took her to the Unity School of Christianity in West Palm Beach. Then after they went to Unity, I picked Katie up at the Sprint phone store in West Palm Beach.

Maureen had no religious upbringing at all as a child. Nor did she have any religious beliefs as an adult. The meaning of Christmas to her was Santa Claus and eight tiny reindeer. Mabel found the Unity School of Christianity and convinced Maureen to attend. When I was trying to get Maureen to go to a "Trinity" church, Mabel told me that she was "too old to understand all that crap." Unity is like Roadhouse Grill: "No rules, just right." They claim that everyone is perfect just the way that they are. Oddly enough, when the Unity building was damaged by Hurricane Frances in 2004, they organized a clean-up team to help with the damage to the building, and Mabel was asked to leave and never return. I'm sure that her overbearing demeanor was just too much for them to endure any longer, but so much for the acceptance of all individuals. Mabel later went back to Unity after their spiritual leader was replaced.

The more I looked into it, the more I found the Unity School of Christianity to be an abomination of Christianity. It was formed by Myrtle and Charles Fillmore. The work of Unity officially began with the publication of the *Modern Thought* magazine in 1889. Unity believes that all of us are capable of anything that Christ did or can do. The Methodists, on the other hand, believe that Jesus did works that no one else in the history of mankind was able to do. He literally died on the cross, and He literally rose from the dead. Christ has no equal. It is arguable that the Unity School of Christianity is a cult.

Maureen and I had several disagreements about what I see as abominations of true Christianity. During the various motions throughout the divorce, she had it written into an agreed court order that I am not allowed to call Unity a cult. The irony of that is, the same First Amendment that protects an individual's freedom to religious beliefs, protects my freedom of speech.

Katie and I would use our three-hour visits on Wednesdays and Fridays to eat at Denny's or Friendly's. We would go across Friendly's parking lot to the movie theater and get stuff out of the quarter vending machines. It became something that we did often. We didn't have a lot of time to do anything substantial with only three hours of time together (and later only two hours). So going to the movie theater to "get some stuff" was fun for us. I could get five dollars' worth of quarters and have a great time with her. Obviously, going to an actual movie along with dinner wasn't an option with the time constraint of only three hours together. Maureen wouldn't "deviate from the agreement" to accommodate small changes, but Katie and I still found fun things to do with each other within those parameters.

While I was still in New Jersey, I signed Katie up for a T-Ball team in Florida and paid all the entry fees. I sent Maureen all the information, particularly that the games were literally played right across the street from her residence.

Maureen refused to take Katie to the games citing that she didn't want me to give her any responsibilities to have to take Katie anywhere. The truth is that Katie and I like baseball, but Maureen doesn't. So, she wasn't going to support any activity that I excelled in and that Katie enjoyed while being with me. She refused to understand that Katie enjoys it, and as her mother, she has a responsibility to support her.

When I got to Florida, I contacted the coach, apologized for Katie's absence, and told him the reason why Katie hadn't been there. He told me that he runs into this all too often and that he understood. He told me to bring her to the remaining games.

Katie's first game started at 6:45 P.M. Maureen worked only two miles from the field. She finished at 6 P.M. She wouldn't let me pick Katie up at the daycare, but she assured me she would have Katie at the game in plenty of time. I had Katie's uniform and would have to dress her in the car. The start of game time came and went. I called Maureen over and over, but she didn't answer. The coach knew what I was going through, and I could see the look of sympathy in his eyes when I told him that Katie would be there soon.

Maureen finally showed up at 7:15. Katie was so intimidated because the game had already started and because she had to get dressed in my car. While walking her to the dugout, I could tell she was scared. She said she wanted to leave, but I wanted her to have a chance to calm down, so we went to the bleachers and just watched.

When the game was over, the kids had juice and chips. Katie

wanted to be a part of the after-game festivities, so I took her back to have refreshments and meet her teammates.

This kind of thing happened over and over again. Maureen was hell-bent on making it as difficult as possible for Katie and I to have any shared activities or any time to bond together. She did everything she could to keep me from being a dad.

For the first two months that I was in Florida and able to see Katie, Maureen was late bringing Katie to me more often than she was on time. Of course, if I wasn't outside the Sunday school at exactly 10:30, Maureen would make a scene. One time, she came into the Sunday school class and demanded to know where Katie and I were. The teacher told her that we had already left. Somehow, she must have walked right past us on her way into the church.

I told my attorney, Eric, about Maureen's habitual tardiness. He advised me to call the police to be present at the exchanges to document it for court. It took only two days of police presence for Maureen to be miraculously able to arrive on time. Once she stopped being late, I stopped calling for police presence. Then Maureen started calling them to be present, claiming that she was in fear for her life.

The exchanges took on a whole new level of drama. Maureen called the police to be there up to a half an hour early or would keep them around after the exchange and chat them up. I knew this because I sometimes drove by the location early and would see them all out there. Katie and I would leave Dunkin Donuts, and they would still be there, or I would go to the gas station or grocery store after dropping Katie off, and there was Maureen, Katie, and the sheriff's deputies, still hanging out long after the exchange was over.

Maureen was throwing me under the bus with Katie standing there holding her hand. Most of the cops were eating this up with a spoon. It's sad that they would support this behavior while a three-year-old stood there listening while Maureen wove her web of lies.

The officers would approach me with questions such as, "Where did you get the money for a Lincoln Continental?" I answered that the car cost me $3,000 two years ago. Then he added, "Well, the gas must be expensive."

One deputy finally had enough of the situation when Maureen began screaming at the top of her lungs that Katie shouldn't have to go with me. I sat Katie on the trunk of my car; she was crying.

"That child will never trust me again!" Maureen added.

The deputy lost it, got in Maureen's face, and told her, "Excuse me, ma'am. This is your fault! You stood out here in front of your child, talking bad about her father. You're doing this! I think it's time for you to leave. Get in your vehicle and go."

The two deputies then helped me console Katie by talking to her. The one deputy used his police knife to open the Ariel doll from its packaging so I could hand the doll to her.

I had the entire dramatic scene videotaped by placing a camera in a tree prior to everyone's arrival. I told Maureen later that although her trust statement about Katie was for dramatic purposes, if she didn't knock it off, her statement about Katie never trusting her again could one day be true.

Maureen would usually sit with Katie in the car waiting for the police to get there to witness the exchange. If they were late, this had the added bonus of cutting into my time. At one of the exchanges, however, the police weren't there yet, but Maureen was in a rush and didn't wait for them to arrive. She was in a hurry, so she got out of her car, opened my door, and took Katie out. She wasn't afraid for her life if she was pressed for time. This happened on any occasion when she was in a hurry.

At least one of these times resulted in the story I mentioned in Chapter 1. I waited for the police to show up after Maureen left. The deputy pulled up, and I got out of the car. I explained to him the circumstances regarding Maureen's non-presence at the location. The deputy was forceful in his demeanor and said that with a protection order, I was in violation. He alluded to arresting me. I told him that there was no protection order. He went into his patrol car and called dispatch. Maureen had told the dispatch officer that there was a protection order against me to ensure police presence at the exchange. The deputy was furious that Maureen had lied to the police to ensure their presence. He finally asked to be subpoenaed for court.

As I mentioned before, I did subpoena the deputy for the divorce trial, but my attorney never put him on the witness list. Opposing counsel objected to his testimony, and the objection was sustained by the judge. The cop sat on the stand in full SWAT gear but had to get up and leave. He wanted to testify to the judge that Maureen lied to the police to get what she wanted but could not thanks to the negligence of my attorney, Eric Cheshire.

There were never any police officers Sunday at 10:30 at the Wellington church either. Maureen was in a hurry to get to Unity across town and didn't want to risk having the police not on time. Again, the urgency of claiming being "in fear for her life" was nonexistent when time was a factor.

Maureen would arrive at the exchange locations and move about the parking lots as if she were vying for position. I sometimes thought of it as Indians circling a westward bound wagon train before an attack. She would circle my vehicle and look for what appeared to be her "preferred" angle from a parking spot. I was in the Big Lots store watching it from afar one day as she did this. It looked ridiculous. It was actually that moment when I decided to write this story. She would also not get out of the car with Katie until the exact minute for the time of the exchange, just so I wouldn't get a couple of minutes extra. I can't imagine what Katie was thinking as she saw me standing next to my car, waiting to take her on our outing.

Katie asked me as we were pulling up for me to drop her off one time, "Daddy, why are the police always here?" I didn't expect that, and the only thing I could think to say was that she would have to ask her mommy.

Because I was living at Tina's, which was right next door to our former home, I was concerned that Katie would recognize it and say something. She hadn't for weeks, but one day, when we were feeding the horses down the street, she looked up at me and said, "Daddy, I used to have that house." My heart broke because it threw me off guard. I thought that she would have forgotten. After all, it had been over a year since we actually lived there, and Katie had just turned two when we left.

I told her, "Yes we did." She asked me if we could go in there. I told her that it wasn't a good idea because we don't have it anymore. She pleaded, so I said "OK." I still had the key, and in we went. Katie stood in the middle of the living room and looked around and said, "I like this house." It felt like my chest split open, and my heart fell to the floor.

Katie's birthday is in January. The only time that I could get with her was for the 3 hours on my usual day, which was Wednesday. On this year, her birthday just happened to fall on Wednesday. In preparation, I was going to bake a pig-shaped cake for her. She loves pigs. So I went to the grocery store to pick out the ingredients to make the cake.

I stood in front of the cake decorating display, and I began to cry. I felt as though I could just collapse on the floor in the aisle. I was so tired, sad, and despondent. I missed her so much. I missed watching her shows with her. I missed playing with her from the time that I got home until story time and bedtime. I missed coming into the front door to hear her call out, "Daddy!" as she ran to me and grabbed the handle of my briefcase to walk me into my office and "help me" put it on my desk.

All of these things were whirling around in my head with the memories of the short two years that she and I were on the planet together, living our lives together, and growing together.

I planned to take Katie to the South Florida Fair for her 4th birthday. This went so well that it became our yearly tradition until Judge Sarah Willis put a stop to it eight years later in 2019. On this birthday, though, Maureen refused to hold on to the cake so I wouldn't have to keep it in the car and take a chance on the frosting melting. She said it wouldn't be that hot. So, the frosting ran.

I picked Katie up at her daycare, and we went to the fair. I spread a blanket on the parking lot and laid out her presents as if we were having a picnic, just the two of us. I got her a pink Etch-a-Sketch, Hello Kitty jewelry box, a bicycle helmet that she had been wanting, and a few other things. I brought out the "pig" cake, and in spite of the melted icing, she loved it. She was still such a loving and appreciative little angel. People walked by and thought it was so cute that we were having a birthday picnic in the middle of a parking lot. It made me wish that I had wanted to do it this way instead of being forced into it. I had no better idea, none of her friends were there, and we had a three-hour time constraint. The people walking by and commenting made a difference to my feelings about the circumstances. They helped me to look at the bright side. They'll never know how much of an impact their words had on me.

We went on to the fair and rode the rides together, ate ice cream, and went to her favorite part of the day, *the pig races*! Now just having a party of two, it was difficult to take pictures of both of us on the rides, so I just held the camera at arm's length and snapped pictures. I occasionally asked another fairgoer to take a picture of Katie and me both. It turned out to be a great day full of smiles and fun for us, and I have the photo memories to remember it by.

Although the court enabled Maureen to conduct years of never-ending attempts to ruin Katie's and my time together, I managed to steadfastly counter those vicious efforts, even while I continuously pushed myself back up through the morass of despair. It indeed felt like I had to make a rope out of ashes for Katie and me to simply enjoy ourselves.

CHAPTER 7

Fighting Money with Tenacity

"Let me tell you the secret that has led me to my goal. My strength lies solely in my tenacity."
Louis Pasteur

On Sundays, I took Katie to Tina's house, where I was still staying in her in-laws' suite. Katie and I played waffle ball by the pool. She hit the balls into the pool, and we retrieved them with the pool skimmer. Katie played with Tina's two cats. We also baked cookies and played other games.

Katie loved Tina and remembered her from when we were next-door neighbors. In fact, Maureen had taken Katie to visit Tina when they first left Rhode Island and went back to Florida. However, after Tina took me in, Maureen started calling her, trying to gain information about me in regards to anything. Maureen also sent a few emails trying to scare Tina into not letting me stay there. Tina was no dummy though and could see exactly what Maureen was trying to do. When it became clear that Tina was not going to be on her side, Maureen dropped her like a hot potato. Then, of course, when Tina testified in my favor at the divorce trial about my parenting skills and my love for my daughter, Maureen hated her. Later, after the trial, Maureen's mother,

Mabel, called Tina twice and threatened her. Tina found the calls and emails humorous. I found it refreshing to see someone who was able to see through Maureen's manipulation attempts.

My attorney, Eric, withdrew from the case right before Christmas. He cited irreconcilable differences (sounds like a divorce itself). On the motion, he stated that he represented the Respondent. It's funny how it is assumed that the husband is usually the respondent when in this case I was the Petitioner—more of that "system" mentality. I just didn't have any more money to send him. I pleaded with him not to leave us, but he just said that he is a "hired gun."

I contacted father's rights organizations, free legal organizations including Legal Aid of Palm Beach County, and Christian legal organizations. I sent a letter to Senator Bill Nelson explaining my situation from Maureen's kidnapping of our daughter in Rhode Island to my inability to obtain legal counsel. His office replied with a letter signed by the senator that said he was sorry, but the legislative and judicial branches are two separate entities within the government; there was nothing his office could do to help. I emailed 56 people in the legal aid system, and other than a few "I'm sorry, good luck" replies and an irate phone call from a paralegal in the Palm Beach County Legal Aid offices asking where I got her email address, I got nothing.

I bought a book called *Represent Yourself in Court and Win*. I read it and knew that I spoke well enough and concisely enough to handle myself in a courtroom, so I gave it a shot. I filed for indigent status, filed motions, prepared in the self-help center at the courthouse, filled out motion packets, researched case law, etc. I was on my way to having—what Maureen's attorney called—my Google law degree. I even called a man who had been in the system for 14 years fighting for his children. He took the time to speak with me for an hour on the phone. He told me that as long as I stayed in my daughter's life (no matter how minimally the mother would allow), it will all work out; my daughter would see things as they truly were, and my child's mother would have to answer to our daughter for it one day. Many other people have told me that as well. The thing is that I don't really want our daughter to resent her mother for what she has been doing. Unfortunately, I do not have much control over that, and I will feel sorry for Maureen if that happens.

He also told me that representing myself in court would seem pompous to the judge, I won't be heard or taken seriously, and I should reconsider. The problem was that I just didn't have the money to reconsider.

As I entered into my "law practice" by being in the courtroom, I soon saw that he had a valid point. It didn't matter how well I spoke or carried myself; I was looked down upon for representing myself, and the judge barely looked at me, even when I addressed the court.

I lost the motion to stop the domestication of the Rhode Island order. I lost my motion to have the court impose a court overseen co-parenting program order. However, I did win a motion for a social comprehensive investigation. A "social" as the system refers to it, consists of interviews of your neighbors, looking through your home for child-friendly accommodations, looking into you and any caregiver's mental capabilities, etc. I gave the judge no choice. I stated to the court that if Mrs. Grant's allegations were true, one would think she would be screaming for the investigation by the court. The motion was granted. However, Maureen's attorney never checked the box that recognized my indigence status, and the investigation was going to then cost me $5,000 instead of $150. When I didn't pay the $5,000, her attorney filed a motion for non-compliance of the court order. First, he didn't want the investigation and then, after he sabotaged the paperwork, he demanded that the investigation commence.

Opposing counsel motioned the court for another mediation. It was granted by the judge. I attended the mediation, and Maureen complained that she couldn't get up in time to have Katie to me by 8:45 A.M. on Sunday morning for us to go to church. I told her that she could drop her off at 9:15 A.M., giving her another half hour. Maureen also didn't want me to pick Katie up at daycare at 3 P.M. and insisted that I get her at Burger King at 6:15 P.M. until 8:15 P.M. I thought 8:15 P.M. was too late for a 3-year-old to be out and that she should be bathed and getting ready for bed by that time, but I agreed to try to be flexible. I'm sorry that I did. It cut my time with Katie from three hours, down to two on Wednesdays and Fridays.

Maureen's attorney was confused about why Katie had to go to two churches every Sunday. His exact words were, "Why does the child have to go to two churches on Sunday? Isn't this a little much? Of course, I'm a Russian Jew, so don't go by me." He suggested Maureen and I could switch off Sundays so Katie could go to the Methodist church and the Unity School of Christianity every other week. Maureen refused. She insisted that we stick to the original agreement, with the time change to 9:15 A.M. instead of 8:45. After Unity, I would pick Katie back up at the Sprint store in West Palm Beach at 12:30 P.M. and return her to Burger King at 5:30 P.M. that evening. In other words, Maureen insisted on four exchanges in one day every single Sunday. This was basically a mind fuck and a total bullshit inconvenience for everyone. It's likely that her father told her to do it.

Tina needed to move out of her house and into her townhouse due to her home going into foreclosure. I put the trailer purchase near the top of my priority list. I wanted to move it to the top, but money was still the biggest issue.

One day, I was at my laptop on Tina's screened porch when she sat down at the table across from me and asked how everything was going. I told her that I was working out details and payment plans with the owners of the trailer so I could move in ASAP. Tina told me that her friends wanted to help and then handed me a check for $2,000. I began to cry with joy. Tina said that this was a "happy thing" and asked why I was crying. I told her I was emotional from happiness and surprise.

Now that I owned it, I started scrubbing the trailer. I bleached everything; the floor tile grout that was supposed to be white was black from dirt. I scrubbed the walls, ceiling, toilets, tubs—everything. Tina gave me paint from her garage. I bought cleaning and painting supplies from my new favorite stores, Family Dollar and Big Lots. I was determined to turn this 1973 Fleetwood mobile home into a home for Katie and me.

The trailer had two bedrooms, two bathrooms, kitchen with a dishwasher but minimal cabinets, and a laundry room that had room for a desk for a makeshift office. After the initial scrubbing and moving in of the furniture from the storage facility, I concentrated on the living areas and the bedroom that was going to be Katie's personal space/bedroom. When I took Katie there, she was so happy that I had the "house," as she called it. We talked about a color to paint her room, "PINK!" was all she said.

I went to my old house that was still in foreclosure and took the cabinets out to install in the mobile home. I thought "Fuck Citibank." The man who helped me take out the cabinets looked at the stove in the house. He told me that his stove was broken. "Well, here's a stove," I told him. "Want it?" I asked. I gave him the stove, dishwasher, and mounted microwave oven free of charge, "As long as you don't watch Fox News," I laughed.

As if it weren't imperative enough already, I had to find a job even more now than before. I had lot rent, property taxes, and a host of other new bills to pay, now that I owned my mobile home. Using the wireless modem in my laptop, which was still a relatively new technology in those days, I could receive an internet connection. The trouble was that it wasn't constant, so I sometimes lost the signal. That was not good when it took 45 minutes to fill out applications on a company website. I woke in the morning and surfed the internet for jobs, posted resumes, and filled out applications. I did go to the library sometimes, but those computers came with a time limit, which meant that I could be bumped off the system right in the middle of completing an application or researching a possible lead.

On some days, I went on field maneuvers, banging on doors to sell myself to potential employers. I had to land something fast.

I officially became a member of the Wellington Methodist church just after Christmas. The people there were wonderful to Katie and me. They had seen us on the grounds, attending Sunday school, and they took an interest in us. Of course, my faith was one of the only things that I had, and sometimes I felt as though it was truly being tested. Some days I became discouraged with God's plan for me, the condition of my life, and the strife that was beating me down.

One Sunday morning, I was in conversation with two women, Rachael and Rhonda, in the hallway of the fellowship hall. They asked me some personal questions about my situation, and I told them about my journey thus far and that I needed to get work soon. Rhonda gave me her husband's email address and told me to send him my resume. I did so, and he forwarded it to the men's group at the church. Within a week, I received a call from a man in the men's group who noticed my ceramic tile background. He hired me to tear out a section of his shower and replace the backing and tile. After that job was finished, I received a phone call from a company that sold toupees to salons across the country. I interviewed with the sales manager, Ray, and started with the company at twelve dollars an hour as a growth representative. I made phone calls to past, present, and potential customers in an attempt to increase business. The job included medical and dental benefits for both Katie and me.

The new trailer life was lonely, and I realized that I do not like to be alone. It's not that I don't like my own company; I just like to be around at least one other person. Of course, this did not help my depression. I found myself living an existence of waiting for my two hours with Katie on Wednesday and Friday and our big five hours together on Sunday. To combat the loneliness, I spent time on the phone with my friends, who were spread out along the eastern seaboard. Karen, Valerie, my mother, Gary, Lonnie, and Scott all spent time with me on the phone throughout this time that I was alone in the trailer.

I started watching rabbit-ear reception television again. I received only three channels. The thermostat for the heater required that I wake up in the middle of the night to reset it; that was a real pain in the ass. My bedroom ceiling was very low, and with a high bed, I felt like I was in a coffin. The ceiling seemed like it was inches from my nose as I lay in the bed. I ate food from Family Dollar and Big Lots.

One bright spot was my neighbors. My across-the-street neighbor went back up north every spring and summer; I came home from work one day to find that he had left bags of food on my porch for me. My next-door neighbors on my patio side were Dana—a forty-five-year-old guy—and his mother, Marge. Dana drank on their breezeway from 10 A.M. until he was ready for bed. He listened to music, mostly country and mostly at high volume. He had no driver's license; his mother went out for his beer. I remember the first time I went to the trailer after closing on it; some of the lyrics of the song I heard playing were, "I hate my job, I hate my wife, blah, blah, blah, I hate my life." I thought, "Oh great."

It turned out, though, that Marge was a nice lady, who'd had a tough life, which she told me about over time. Marge baked cakes for Katie and me. She had some toys over there that Katie and I played with (like Toss Across), and I made sure that I taught Katie to return them when we finished playing. Marge and Dana were decent neighbors, and Dana and I reached an understanding about the noise. He liked music, and I could play the guitar, so I was able to entertain him. He had another friend who also played guitar and came over on occasion. So I had a nice place to play some music—which is a good way for me to vent safely—and of course Dana and his friend made a couple of drinking partners, so I did not have to drink alone.

My rest was non-existent. I started having horrible night-mares. One recurring dream was that Katie had sand in her eyes, and I was unable to move to get to her. And no one else would help her. Other times, I woke up seething with anger at the in-laws who took her away from me. I can't get over the men-tality of those people that made them destroy the spirits of their own children only to do the same thing to mine by undermining her right to spend time with her father. I dreamed of their deaths. I dreamed of their judgment days. Sometimes when I woke up, I had to talk myself back to what the actual situation was. As if one day I would wake up and the whole horrible situation will have been a bad dream itself.

I painted Katie's room pink with a dark pink trim around the windows, baseboard, and door frames. I found a Hello Kitty border and put that along the top of the wall. Her room had a bathroom in it, and I painted the green bathroom white, refin-ished the harvest green toilet white, and put self-adhesive tiles on the bathroom floor. I assembled the bed that I bought for her when I was in Rhode Island, which she had yet to sleep in.

When I moved out of the trailer several months later, Katie still hadn't slept in that bed. Maureen consistently refused to let her stay over.

On Sundays, Katie and I would make homemade pizza and cookies, we'd run in the sprinkler, watch cartoons together, etc. I taught her to swim at the pool. We made the best of the time that we had together.

After I had been in the trailer for four months, I was finally past the fifty-degree nights, so my heater thermostat did not require the close attention that it did during the colder months. I was able to get a little more rest at night.

Easter was approaching. All of the Easter egg hunts were on Saturday, and I couldn't get Maureen to let me take Katie to one. What I could do was talk to Katie on Easter Sunday about the hunt that she went to the day before. Unfortunately, Katie had a bad time at the hunt that she went to. The kids were too rough, and she didn't get many eggs. My heart broke as she told me the story. I called Maureen, and she confirmed that it didn't go well for Katie. Luckily, I had planned an Easter egg hunt for Katie at my place, and she had a blast. I filled the eggs with Dora and Disney Princess rings, Hello Kitty stickers, hair ties, etc. We made homemade pizza. She was so proud of herself.

I had to get money together to get an attorney again. I started looking around for things to sell to get enough money to get my old attorney back. I had to settle for my old attorney because every new attorney I spoke with said I would have to pay an $8,000 retainer before they would take on a new case, and I would have to spend hours explaining the whole story all over again.

All that I had left to sell were my sports collectibles that I had been accumulating since I was 10 years old. I signed up for a new username on eBay: selling_everything_4_lawyer. I laid the items all over the floor, took pictures of them, and listed them on eBay. I sold autographed baseballs and bats, antique baseball gloves, jerseys, and jackets; I even listed my guitar. I sold almost everything except the guitar. I raised almost $1,500 in a matter of two weeks. I had to wait for all of the auctions to end and for payments to clear. This took another week or so.

Back in New Jersey, friends held a benefit at Dr. Lou's Place to raise money for my attorney as well. I went back to New Jersey to participate in the humbling experience. I took some collectibles to the affair and sold more there. The benefit raised another $800 for my lawyer. I included an additional week's pay in what I gave to Eric, and since he was a guitar player, he offered me $800 in time for my $1,500 Sienna Burst, Fender Stratocaster guitar. With all that, I managed to get him back to represent me. Remember my interpretation of his motivation? *"What drives me in this business is the money I make when one parent won't let another parent be a parent."*

CHAPTER 8

The Therapists

> 66 *I think politics comes out of psychology.* 99
> Bruce Springsteen

An important cog in the wheel of the "Family Court Industry Revenue Generating Machine" is the use of therapists. Some therapists are chosen by litigants to gain an edge, some by attorneys to present arguments in favor of their client, some by the court to influence their rulings and opinions. Some of these therapists are under contract with the court and are their "go to" (so-called) experts. This sector of the Family Court Industry is huge when it comes to having any one of these on your side, and of course, it is with absolution that money buys one's desired finding.

Dr. Michaelanne Marie was first involved after I told my attorney of my wife's severe co-dependency issues. My attorney thought that exposing those issues in preparation of the divorce trial would be helpful. So, he petitioned the court to have evaluations done by court psychology. Dr. Marie conducted evaluations on both Maureen and myself by using the MMPI-2 exam, among others. With the MMPI-2, you basically choose true or false if you agree or disagree with a particular statement. I recall one specific question on the examination was "I am fascinated by fire." I indeed am fascinated by fire. Its makeup of colors as they relate to the different temperatures and the way it requires oxygen to breathe are only two of the fascinating things about fire. When I told my attorney that I agreed with that statement, he lambasted me for answering this in such a literal, overthought, truthful manner and told me "They're looking for pyromaniacs." Also used in the evaluation were a substance abuse screening inventory (SASSI), a child abuse potential inventory (CAP), a parenting stress index (PSI), and the verbal interview assessments.

Nevertheless, after the examination was completed but before the reports were written, Dr. Marie told my attorney—with me sitting there—that there was no reason that I should have a problem with getting shared custody of my daughter. She also agreed to observe my daughter and me in a private session for an additional "side" fee, to be paid in advance by money order or cashier's check. Everything seemed to be going ok, aside from the circumstantial stress.

Prior to the observed private session between my daughter and me, the written evaluations were submitted to the court. In Maureen's report, Dr. Marie addressed only issues about Maureen that I brought up to her in the initial interview. Maureen's codependency, her brief use of cocaine, her smoking marijuana. The remainder of the ten pages was all about me in a negative light. Dr. Marie referenced two no contact order filings by Maureen. One attempt on 8/4/08 and one on 9/8/09. Dr. Marie did not mention that both filings were ultimately denied by a judge for lack of evidence. Dr. Marie referenced me negatively in Maureen's evaluation 58 times. Maureen's evaluation became an unfavorable piece of court evidence against me, and it wasn't even my evaluation. Dr. Marie had all the findings when she vowed a favorable outcome for shared custody to my attorney and me. What happened? I don't know what happened to that point, but I do know what happened next.

I went into the Office of Court Psychology with a five-hundred-dollar money order made out to Dr. Michaelanne Marie for her stated fee to observe my daughter and me together. Dr. Marie emerged from her back office, yelling that she would not do the observation. I was dumbfounded. I had the money order in my hand, looked at it, and could only think to say, "It's already made out." Sometimes we will never know the reasons for any particular outcome. This was merely one of the first of many such incidents, with a multitude of different participants to come.

Dr. Marie testified in the divorce trial. At one time, she referred to Katie as "Maureen's daughter" and quickly corrected herself by saying "their daughter." Despite her claim after the evaluations of previously having no issue with shared custody, Dr. Marie stated on the witness stand that she would "have a concern about any unsupervised contact" with me. Under further direct questioning by Maureen's attorney, Dr. Marie suggested one year of anger management, consecutive negative drug screens, and another evaluation to determine the need for psychotropic medication for me.

My attorney did a good job of bringing up Dr. Marie's assertion that shared custody would be no issue and the aborted observation session of dad and daughter. He asked Dr. Marie if she previously stated that there would be no issue. She didn't confirm it with a straight answer, and my attorney asked her if she was aware of any situations during my daughter's life that I had hurt or abused her in any way. Her testimony was "Not that I'm aware of." My attorney referenced three no contact order filings by Maureen and asked Dr. Marie if she was aware that attempts to ascertain restraining orders were denied (after all, she referenced two in Maureen's evaluation report). Dr. Marie replied that she didn't know that they were denied. My attorney then read from Dr. Marie's evaluation report:

...at the bottom of your report on page 7, you said these data do not suggest the presence of any cognitive impairment that would significantly impact upon his ability to parent or to learn new information relevant to parenting. So at the time you didn't feel like he needed supervised visitation? So after all the testing, everything you looked at, you changed your mind?

Dr. Marie answered no. She then said that my cognitive ability reflected my above-average intellect and that I could benefit from services. Paid services.

When Dr. Marie got down from the stand, as she made her way to the courtroom door, she leaned over to my attorney and said "Nice job." Personally, I thought so as well. I thought my attorney thwarted all of the recommendations Dr. Marie suggested in her expert opinion. He unequivocally made the points that Dr. Marie found no evidence of prior drug use or any history of abuse of my daughter whatsoever before she "changed her mind." Nevertheless, she testified that she recommended negative drug screens and supervised visitation.

A few years later, I petitioned the court for more timesharing with my daughter. Opposing counsel insisted on a re-evaluation by Dr. Marie. I told my new attorney, Chris Jette, that I learned that the office of court psychology was overseen by the County Commissioners and that one of the commissioners, Paulette Burdick, was Maureen's attorney's wife. I told Chris Jette that I wanted him to argue that it was a conflict of interest. He attempted to discourage this argument because he said it wouldn't work. When Mr. Burdick questioned me about it while I was on the stand, I used the opportunity to tell the court about my concerns regarding a conflict of interest. Mr. Burdick asked me if I thought his wife and he discussed cases before going to sleep at night. I told him I didn't know what happens in his home. Judge Charles Burton referenced my testimony in his order and ruled that while the court didn't necessarily agree that it was a conflict of interest, my concerns were valid. So, Dr. Marie was off the case, but not before her previous testimony at the divorce trial did its damage. The court gave me unsupervised timesharing, but no overnights with my daughter. Remember, Dr. Marie was from the Office of Court Psychology. More specifically, their website states, "The Forensic Psychology Services Office provides psychological assessments/evaluations as ordered by the courts of the 15th Judicial Circuit." It's pretty obvious that this office has a lot of influence, even with a good cross-examination.

Ashlee Comeau's name was first brought to my ears by my 6-year-old daughter, who was riding in my car, and she proceeded to tell me about "Miss Ashlee." She told me that her mother was taking her to see Miss Ashlee, and she didn't want to go. She said that Miss Ashlee "just wanted to know her business." I acknowledged Katie's concerns and told her I would talk with her mom about it. What I did do was look up child psychologists with the first name of Ashlee in the area. I quickly found Ashlee Comeau, located not even a mile from Maureen's home. I called Ashlee Comeau. We spoke for almost an hour. In that phone conversation, Ms. Comeau revealed that she was having difficulty connecting with Katie and that Katie didn't want to share much with her.

As a substitution for Ms. Comeau's sessions with Katie, she asked me if I would be open to sessions with Maureen. I agreed. Ms. Comeau got involved after the divorce was final (2012). I had little time with my daughter up to that point, but we made the best of the time we had together.

Maureen and my first session with Ashlee Comeau was Thursday, January 19th at 5:30 P.M. I must say that the most ground was gained going to Ms. Comeau's sessions. She convinced Maureen that Katie should spend more time with her dad, and I got overnight timesharing with our daughter after two years of not having any chances to put her to bed at night. I will also say that we had the best judge, even up to the current day, with Judge Thomas Barkdull III, but I will tell more about him later. Maureen and I went to Ms. Comeau's sessions for five months. It was actually the easiest time for all, subsequent to the divorce. We all seemed to be doing ok.

Maureen's parents were far from Ozzie and Harriet, and it came out in sessions that they had been extremely intrusive in our marriage. Additionally, Maureen told Ashlee stories about her childhood that were not flattering to Maureen's parents or a positive childhood for her. Maureen's parents divorced when she was 3 years old. It is also important to know that Maureen's multimillionaire father had financed all of the court proceedings of this case, and continued to do so to the current date, which has been twelve years so far. His financing has, so far, totaled over two million dollars, at a low-ball estimate. Maureen contended, under oath at a deposition, that he was loaning her the money, but I digress.

Ashlee decided that it was time to bring Maureen's parents, one at a time, into a session. That was our last session with Ashlee Comeau. On May 8, 2012, I received an email from Ashlee that she was sorry that we "have not been able to work together as planned for the well-being of Katie."

What chain of events took place to suddenly stop this therapy? Since it all happened behind the scenes, I could do no more than speculate. The one thing I knew was that I was dumbfounded at how suddenly therapy was stopped after the suggestion to bring in Maureen's parents.

A number of years later, just prior to the 2019 trial for *Former Wife's Petition for Modification*, I contacted Ashlee, asked her to prepare the files of our case, and told her that I planned to subpoena her to court to testify about our sessions. Ashlee told me that she wasn't in practice any longer and that she destroyed her files.

Dr. Michael Rathjens was and continues to be my therapist. I have been seeing him for a number of years. I trusted him at an early stage in our professional relationship. He listens to me until I am talked out and never interrupts me except for clarification or to better understand something. He only rarely offers advice before I am finished speaking.

I feel that therapists tell a reasonable, cognitive, person what they already know. For me, I guess I just like to hear it come back at me. Not what I want to hear, but what I know to be common sense, basically. When it comes to Dr. Rathjens, I mostly take his suggestions on how to endure the pain of this whole experience. I often remind myself that I am not the real victim here. The real victim is a child who has been in the middle of this ludicrous, ridiculous level of contempt that is driven solely by evil and money.

A lot of what Dr. Rathjens says to me, I also hear from close friends. The most common piece of advice I have heard from a multitude of people is that my daughter will know the truth. She actually already does. The problem is that she's currently a teenager; she's not fully developed intellectually and won't be for about another decade. She has been programmed to feel a lot of fear towards me, which likely causes other fears related to her inability to fully understand the situation. Dr. Rathjens suggests that I should just be there for her and wait it out, even as he recognizes that waiting is not easily done. As part of following his suggestion, I attend every one of my daughter's soccer games, and I use my trusty Nikon to take an average of 100 photos of each game, post those photos as a Shutterfly link for all the parents to see, video tape games for the coach, set up and take down the canvas bench shelter, and cheer like the fan that I am.

Dr. Rathjens and I did have a small falling out once. It was caused by the court-appointed guardian ad litem, Anne Alper. An upcoming chapter will give a much more in-depth story of this lying, court attorney who has made her living by destroying families for financial gain and has been doing so for decades.

Anne Alper asked me if she could contact Dr. Rathjens and ask him three questions. 1. Do I attend the sessions on a consistent basis, and when did I begin to use his services? 2. Does he think that I follow through with his recommendations? 3. Does he see any reason to believe that I am presently a danger to my daughter, emotionally or physically? Dr. Rathjens answered five years, but not consistently, yes, and no. All of which were the answers I expected him to give.

The questions were only a ruse. Anne Alper really called to have the opportunity to speak to Dr. Rathjens and simply lie about me. He told me she asked her questions, then spoke for forty minutes after stating, "I have concerns." Ms. Alper told him of atrocities that absolutely never occurred. I was actually able to prove one in particular as being a complete fabrication. Ms. Alper told Dr. Rathjens that when I took my daughter to Disney, I got her a Goofy balloon she wanted, and while we were eating breakfast in the Denny's, I told her that I was going to pop the balloon and hurt her mother if she didn't smile for a picture that I took of her holding her balloon. I showed Dr. Rathjens the picture, and he saw the genuine ear-to-ear smile. He seemed to come back to a realization that he was being duped by this hired gun. Other than having that picture, I had no way of defending any of the other issues that she brought up in those forty minutes of "her concerns." Dr. Rathjens and I are still having sessions. He's actually one of the only therapists I've trusted in these past twelve years.

Dr. Antonio Abad, a forensic psychiatrist, was brought into the case by my attorney. As I contended at the beginning of the chapter, each side gets their own favorable ruling depending upon who is writing the check to any given therapist. Dr. Abad was a strong presence. Dr. Abad's online biography states, "Dr. Abad has unique and extensive experience in Forensic Psychiatry with more than 10 years as an expert witness in Forensic Psychiatry for the City of New York, at the NYS NYC Combined Supreme Court. He has also served as an expert witness for Prosecuting and Defense attorneys in various states and in Spain." Dr. Abad was the person who found that I was not in need of any psychotropic medications. During our initial conversation that was basically to see if I was mentally unstable, he looked me in the eyes and said, "I am your advocate." His favorable report (no surprise, I was paying) was submitted to my attorney. Dr. Abad died shortly thereafter and never made a courtroom appearance in my case.

Dr. Kristin Tolbert was the replacement for Dr. Michaelanne Marie when Judge Charles Burton agreed with my testimony that her involvement was a conflict of interest. The judge chose Dr. Kristin Tolbert from the court's contracted evaluators and ordered that she was to perform an evaluation. The majority of all costs were to be incurred by my former wife.

Dr. Tolbert's business was called Psychological Center for Expert Evaluations, Inc. I met with her for the initial interview/evaluation on November 25, 2014. It was the first of six visits to her office for testing and one on one "evaluations." I hadn't researched Dr. Tolbert prior to meeting with her. It was the last time that I did not research any individual once they entered into our case. If I had, I would have seen her being referenced online as "The Blonde Monster," and I could not have more of a concurring opinion.

The actual sessions themselves really were not remarkable. What I did find to be of interest were the list of "collateral contacts interviewed" which included Maureen and Dr. Marie. On the other hand, collateral contacts not interviewed included every therapist that I had seen for the five favorable evaluations that I paid for. Remember the beginning paragraph of this chapter that money buys the favorable outcome. Maureen was in contact with Dr. Tolbert's office regularly. The only reason that I don't say "daily" is that I cannot unequivocally prove that to be true. After all, this was her big chance to keep me from getting any more time with our daughter.

After all of the evaluation sessions concluded on December 19, 2014, it took Dr. Tolbert until March 26, 2015 to email a rough draft copy of the evaluation to Maureen, her attorney, and me. Not even my attorney. The "rough draft" was filled with a plethora of erroneous mistakes, including my name, "Mr. Bean." Dr. Tolbert referenced text messages that Maureen sent to me and reported them as being sent in the reverse manner, me to her. It was a shit storm of inaccuracies. The "move" was to get the report out there and to have corrections made by my ex-wife, and that she did. Can you imagine the mess Dr. Tolbert's mistake-ridden report would have made of my ex-wife's desired results? The text messages that were incorrectly referenced to be from me disappeared from the final report. Obviously, my name was corrected as well. The final, manicured report was then submitted to all parties on April 4, 2015, just shy of five months after the sessions concluded. It was pretty clear when I did my research, after the extremely damaging report from Dr. Tolbert, that she was busy lying under oath in her own divorce.

Dr. Kristin Tolbert seemed to have quite a good thing going by being a contracted evaluator with the Fifteenth Circuit Court of Florida, Palm Beach County. However, that changed later down the road. Dr. Tolbert was sued for negligence Case # 50-2016-CC-006869-XXXX-NB, Palm Beach County, Florida. She was no longer a contracted evaluator for the court, she was dealing with her own divorce, she was facing eviction, her business, Psychological Center for Expert Evaluations, Inc., was no longer at its posh setting in Palm Beach Gardens, and I no longer saw her on the local news channel for projected, public evaluations during hurricanes. I called Dr. Tolbert and told her that I was enjoying watching both her personal and business lives spiral downward online. I felt I just had to let her know that I knew of her misfortune. She's even currently being sued by Capital One for credit card debt. Karma came down hard on her, and I am not even a little bit sorry.

Ultimately, Dr. Tolbert's report and testimony kept me from getting any additional time with my daughter, but it did not take away the time we had been given by the court. Dr. Tolbert made another appearance in 2019 at my ex-wife's *Petition for Modification* trial to remove all of my parental rights. Dr. Tolbert had the same four-year-old report, the same already-heard testimony, only a new, first year, rookie judge, Sarah Willis.

When Dr. Tolbert made her second appearance on our case, I was a pro se litigant, which means I was representing myself. I looked for ways to discredit her on the stand, and I already knew her to be dishonest. I read through some of her court papers that were public record. I did some research on her former husband who was a firefighter and paramedic, and who was the Lead Paramedic Instructor in Boynton Beach, Florida. The man is a real-time hero. Knowing what I did of his former wife, I thought he would know some negative things about her, possibly including dishonesty in court under oath. I was right. He told me that I would need to look no further than Kristin Tolbert's financial affidavit for their divorce and for me to be careful because she likes to sue people for internet stalking.

As the pro se litigant cross-examining Dr. Tolbert, I asked Dr. Tolbert if she had ever lied under oath. After her answer, I took my certified copy of her Family Law Financial Affidavit and attempted to enter it into evidence. The courtroom exploded with an objection from opposing counsel, and Dr. Tolbert spoke out in court that I had her personal information. I replied to her courtroom outburst in turn that it was a matter of public record, and a certified copy of that record showed that she, a forensic psychologist, had sworn that she only earned $833 a month and had a monthly deficit of $6,879 after expenses. It's obvious that she's much more than just bad with money. She's a flat-out liar. Unfortunately, opposing counsel's objection was sustained by Judge Sarah Willis. Dr. Tolbert stared at me while addressing the court that she wanted this stricken from the court transcriber's record.

My attorney told me to go and see **Dr. Martha Jacobson** in Broward County. She also was a child custody evaluator and an expert witness. She wanted $5,000.00 for a full custody evaluation. I did not have that kind of money, so I asked Dr. Jacobson if she would just do an MMPI-2 exam and report. She agreed but told me that there were many tests needed to conduct a full child custody evaluation. I could not find Dr. Jacobson's correspondence, but I did find my attorney's letter to her, confirming her stance on the MMPI-2:

> Thank you for scheduling an MMPI2 examination for Mr. Graves. I understand that the results of the MMPI2 examination are limited only within the parameters which test is capable of representing. I also understand that the examination results, and interpretation of said results, are only that, and not in any way a custody evaluation.

The results were of course favorable to me. I found that Dr. Jacobson did not have some fans out there. I found this on thelizlibrary.org:

> For years, Broward County Hollywood, Florida-based psychologist Martha Jacobson ("Marty") frequently has been hired in various capacities in the South Florida family courts to act as custody evaluator, parenting evaluator, parenting coordinator, or therapist. Without apparently any concern at all for the impact of her recommendations on the children involved, she has earned large fees coming up with

outrageous custody evaluations and recommendations that not infrequently are to separate perfectly normal primary caregiving mothers from their children for extended periods of time.

I did wish I had the $5,000, but it would be moot because I would never keep my daughter from her mother.

Dr. Phil Heller was another suggestion from my attorney. Dr. Heller came on board in May 2015 to thwart the unfavorable report from Dr. Tolbert. I sold my Rolling Stones autographed Fender Squire Guitar on eBay to pay Dr. Heller's cost. He requested all records from Dr. Tolbert. Copies of those records cost $52.66. Dr. Heller was $3,000. Dr. Heller spoke of how he and US Congressman Ted Deutch were responsible for getting legislation passed for some kind of protection of children. I heard Ted Deutch speak and take questions at a campaign for State Senator Maria Sachs. Congressman Deutch trumpeted his own horn about how he got tougher penalties for non-custodial parents who don't pay child support. When the congressman took questions, I asked him how he felt with regard to Social Security Act Title IV-D, in that it encourages anything but equal, shared parenting by paying federal funds to states for every dollar of child support collected as an incentive. That's not arrears, mind you. That's every dollar. I was the only man in the room of about forty women. Congressman Deutch answered with what he had done for domestic violence issues. Not one word of what he said answered my question.

During the time I was working with Dr. Heller, Katie was becoming extremely rude and disrespectful to people she would encounter. There was a lady who worked at our local supermarket and prepared food samples at her station. She just adored Katie and would offer her some of what she prepared while engaging in conversation with her. Katie was so mean to her and to a lady at a church function, our neighbors, on play dates, and it had been going on for weeks. I had spoken to her about it several times. At the family function at our church when Katie was very mean to the girl running an exhibit, I felt it was time to attempt to use a bit more disapproval to get through to her. I told her to go to the car because we were leaving. Just before we got to the passenger door that I opened, I gave her *one* spank on the butt. As I walked around the car, I thought of asking her how she thought she would change how she had been handling herself. When I got in the car, I instigated the conversation. After we talked it out, I asked her if she wanted to leave or stay and watch the events. She told me that she wanted to stay. She and I went back to the event. I got her a chair to sit in to watch me partic-ipate with two other adults in the "Pumpkin Slingshot" event. My partners, husband-and-wife, won the event. I walked back over to Katie, who was watching with others, and she asked me if she could play "Dunk the Pastor." From that point on, Katie had a great time at the festivities, and the disrespect for the peo-ple she encountered went away.

What happened next was a shit storm.

While I have no real proof, I am certain that whenever Katie returned to her mother after being with me, she encountered an interrogation. It certainly would explain why she was so quiet on the ride back. I think she was preparing. Another explanation I had is based on the professional opinion that when Katie went back to her mother, she would find acceptable things to talk about that would assure her mother that she was happier being with her. Katie used to offer information to me about things that went on in the other home. She asked me several times not to say any-thing. I told her that I would never, as long as it wasn't something that was harming her, and I kept that promise. I knew that if I betrayed her trust, she would never consult me as she grew older and peer pressure and harmful situations presented themselves.

Maureen had obviously ascertained the information of

the incident at the church function. She took Katie to a doctor, called child protective services, and filed for one of her no contact orders. There was a claim that there was a "red mark" on *her back* from the spank on the butt (through denim shorts). The statement Maureen filed with The Department of Children and Families stated I spanked her two times. Embellishment is important to the cause. The DCF investigation report stated that their findings were that Katie was in no danger while in my care. I did find that Maureen's mother's statement to the investigator that "these visits with her father need to stop" were quite remarkable. I had the DCF investigator served with a subpoena to testify in court. The report itself is hearsay unless the investigator testifies and is able to be cross-examined. The DCF investigator never showed up to court and suffered no consequences for ignoring the subpoena. The permanent no contact order was denied by the judge, as they all were.

When I told Dr. Heller of the incident, he did a one hundred and eighty degree turn and told me that spanking Katie was no way to get her attention after weeks of contemptuous behavior. He suggested the method he used when he walked into a class and people were talking; he "flicks the light on and off to get their attention." I asked him if he really thought that flicking the lights on and off was the way to get through to my daughter after weeks of trying to find ways to change her behavior. I didn't even wait for an answer. I told him that I thought he was completely off base with this comparison. Our professional relationship was severed and certainly with no refund.

Terry Trobaugh headed a place called Arts Therapy. He ran a six-week anger management course that met once a week. He laughed a little when he told me to just take the same six-week course eight times to get to the 52 weeks that the court ordered on Dr. Marie's recommendation; so that's what we did, and I ended up with a stack of these completion certificates from

Terry. I can tell you that I saw some court-ordered, angry people come through that place in my time with Terry. Some would lose their tempers and storm out and Terry would say after they left, "The court's not going to like that." I also saw him privately. I liked him. He gave me some grounding tools to use if I felt myself getting angry for any reason. He was soft-spoken and extremely insightful. He would sometimes go off-subject and tell me things about his own daily routines, like a special application that he used for avoiding traffic jams and other tools he used to deal with daily aggravations. Terry has since passed away.

Marion Stamm's name was given to me by Terry for the sole purpose of conducting another MMPI-2 exam. I paid her $500 to get an MMPI-2 evaluation to take back to the court, in an attempt to thwart Dr. Marie's interpretation of the results. While favorable, opposing counsel uncovered, unbeknownst to me, that as a LMHC therapist, Marion Stamm was not qualified to give the exam. How the hell was I supposed to know this? I've wondered if she continues to give these tests for $500.00. As for Terry's suggestion to go to her, he was just trying to help me by giving me her name. It just didn't work out.

Imagine for a moment that you earn between $50 and $60K per year at your job. You have a minor child on state-funded health insurance, as my former wife has had our daughter on for years and up to the present date of this writing. Despite numerous pleas to Judge Sarah Willis that my daughter was fraudulently on this state-funded, welfare insurance and for her to please order that she be put on my employer-provided coverage at my cost, those requests fell on deaf ears.

To qualify for these state funded *"Stay Well Kids"* or *"Healthy Kids"* benefits, there are a number of prerequisites. They are:

- Be between 5 and 18 years old
- Uninsured
- Not eligible for Medicaid or Children's Medical Services
- Either a U.S. Citizen or qualified Alien
- <u>Applicant child may not have access to employer-sponsored insurance; or if such access, then the cost exceeds 5% of the family's income.</u>
- Applicant child has not voluntarily lost employer coverage within six months of application

My ex-wife and I earn over $100,000 a year, collectively. And remember, my ex-wife has a legal team panel of involved professionals on this case who charge hundreds of dollars per hour. Here's one:

Dr. Michael O'Hara: Clinical Psychology Practice and Forensic Psychology in Family Law is the header of his webpage at drmichaelohara.com. There's no secret here. Dr. O'Hara advertises to anyone who visits his webpage that he specializes in courtroom testimony—essentially a hired gun for court. Dr. O'Hara accepts insurance and according to his website, he charges $200.00 per hour for "clinical" services and accepts cash, check, and credit cards. Rather than using her medical insurance with a closer therapist, Maureen chose instead to drive over 30 miles one way to take Katie to this expert family court witness, Dr. Michael O'Hara, and pay all expenses to him out-of-pocket, claiming only that our daughter needed a therapist.

Just prior to Maureen bringing on the expert witness, Dr. O'Hara, she filed a motion through her counsel to "Enjoin Former Husband from Interfering with Minor Child's Therapy and Attorney's Fees and Costs." This was granted despite the continuing court order that I have the parental right to be involved with all of Katie's medical records and information. Prohibiting me from asking Dr. O'Hara any questions kept me from ascertaining any information for any court testimony from Dr. O'Hara.

Dr. O'Hara did little in courtroom testimony as my attorney claimed his testimony was a violation of Katie's HIPAA rights. Opposing counsel told the court that his client waived those rights, but the judge found in favor of respecting those rights and did not allow Dr. O'Hara's testimony. Where Dr. O'Hara became useful to the parental alienation campaign was that he worked in unison with the paid guardian ad litem, who was allowed to give hearsay testimony per the court order. A free pass to lie in court without the threat of cross-examination is a nice perk to have, and the guardian ad litem was able to claim testimony reflected what Dr. O'Hara said at any given time, basically backing up the premise that "Dad is bad."

One issue that was averted by not having contact with Dr. O'Hara was that he was unable to have me in session. That could have been a pretty big issue if he had had the opportunity to diagnose me with the latest popular disorder. It was plastered all over in the Fall 2016 Issue of *Stephens' Squibs*, a publication by attorney Eddie Stephens. That Fall 2016 issue claims that 1 in 17 people have Antisocial Personality Disorder (ASPD) in family court (*https://eddiestephens.com/2016/12/05/1-in-17-anti-social-personality-disorder-aspd-in-family-court/*). The article was co-written with Dr. Michael O'Hara. As a precaution, just in case I was ever evaluated by Dr. O'Hara, I sent myself a let-ter that stated Dr. O'Hara will diagnose me with ASPD and left the postmarked envelope sealed to potentially be opened in court one day. I still have the letter unopened in a file.

Connie Ingram was the therapist who was found due to opposing counsel's insistence that a family therapist be agreed upon by him, the guardian ad litem, my former wife (who refused to attend), Dr. O'Hara, Dr. Rathjens, and myself. Connie Ingram was the *only* therapist that all but me knew of. Even Dr. Rathjens, who had never worked with her, had heard of her. I did a little research and found that Connie Ingram was Facebook friends with one of Katie's schoolteachers and that her Psychology Today résumé stated that she took my health insurance.

I decided to call Connie and give her a bit of a telephone interview. I got voicemail, and Connie called me back with a blocked number.

I introduced myself and the court order that brought us together for my reaching out to her. She told me that she was completely unaware of the situation. I knew this to be untrue, as opposing counsel had stated in court that he had already spoken to Connie Ingram in detail about the case and that she had already accepted the case. It makes sense because how could he commit to her involvement to the degree of a court order if he didn't know if she had the time or was even willing to take the case on? I let her slide and moved forward.

I then asked her about Katie's teacher, who was listed as her Facebook friend. She completely denied knowing the person. Lastly, I asked her about my health insurance. She replied that she did not accept any type of insurance for court-related matters.

I reported all of this to the court at the hearing on *Former Husband's Objection to Connie Ingram as Family Therapist and Motion to Present Family Therapist Candidates Directly to the Court for Consideration.* I printed out a document with every therapist in a fifteen-mile radius who was listed on the Psychology Today website as a provider who took my health insurance. I included Connie Ingram's page to prove that just because any particular therapist claimed to accept my insurance, it actually depended on the circumstances of court involvement. I observed that with opposing counsel, the guardian ad litem, Dr. O'Hara, and Maureen all calling and discouraging any potential candidate choosing a provider was an extremely challenging task. The ultimate family therapist, Laura Melvin, was not assigned until seven months later on August 21, 2019. During those seven months, I hadn't seen or spoken to my daughter, except at her soccer games.

Laura Melvin came about as I found that when I followed the court order and reported any candidate to all parties concerned, I ended up with a long list of therapists who would bail out subsequent to being contacted by the other involved parties. I decided to try a different approach and just not tell anyone I had chosen a therapist until the court hearing was set. The other parties all kicked and screamed in court and said I was trying to control the situation and that I was not in compliance with the court's order.

I had seen Laura Melvin three times as a person who was willing to testify on my behalf. She accepted my insurance for sessions but was up front that any court appearances to appear as an expert witness would render a port-to-port charge. In the three sessions I had with her, I told her of my challenges with finding a family therapist and what had transpired with all of the communication that came from the "collusive coercives," as I referred to them. She expressed astonishment over what I was telling her and asked if the judge was continuing to allow this sabotage. She offered to cease our one-on-one sessions and become the family therapist. She also agreed to stay under wraps and to be sequestered at the courthouse until I texted her to come into the hearing to be appointed as the family therapist.

When Laura Melvin entered the courtroom, she was sworn in and basically interviewed by opposing counsel and the guardian ad litem. I did this deliberately so that the judge and I could hear every word that was said by the "collusive coercives." Members of counsel had nothing they could say other than questioning Laura about her qualifications and agreed level of involvement in the case. It worked, and on August 21, 2019, I thought I finally had a therapist in place who could help. Remarkably, this was during this hearing that members of counsel insisted on the term "Reunification Therapist" as opposed to the term "Family Therapist."

In her testimony, Laura said that she insisted on "full

transparency" and that all parties needed to be informed of any session-related issues or progress. I liked that she said that because I often felt that there was much that the collusive coercives did behind the scenes to get favorable results from their hired guns.

On August 22nd, just one day after the hearing, I received a text from Laura Melvin that stated, "We meet tomorrow at 10 am. I have 30 minutes set aside for our meeting." The next text was, "Sorry wrong text above. I meet with GAL (guardian ad litem) tomorrow morning." I replied, "Under the full disclosure agreement of all at the hearing, I am entitled to be present."

I showed up for the meeting. Anne Alper, the guardian ad litem that was paid $100,000 over two years, sat in the waiting room with me. When Laura came out of her session room, Anne Alper demanded that I was not to be present at this meeting. I replied that under full disclosure and because I was a self-representing litigant, I was indeed entitled to be present. Furthermore, if nothing was to be said outside of the realms of the truth or coercion, there was certainly nothing to hide. It was a standoff that seemed to last minutes, but it was really more like fifteen seconds, and ended when I left. I returned immediately to my office because I now knew that I was dealing with a liar who was willing to be bought by the highest bidder. Not to disappoint, Anne Alper filed a report to the court that I was present, stalked her, and she needed to be escorted by security to her vehicle after her secret meeting with Laura Melvin.

Never in the history of flip-flopping had I ever seen a bigger change than the one that I saw in Laura Melvin. I can't help but wonder what Anne Alper could possibly have said that would change Laura Melvin's opinion so drastically. Furthermore, I was charged full costs for some sessions and 50% of the no-show sessions when those bills were supposed to be split after my insurance paid its share On December 19, 2019, after I made it clear in advance that I wanted to use that session to give Katie her Christmas gift, yet Laura Melvin insisted on discussing issues. My daughter left crying with her gift in hand as Laura Melvin persisted in a totally different objective than was agreed on for that session and caused great distress for all in the room.

That was the last session. After Katie left in tears, I told Laura Melvin that she was bought and that the meeting with the paid guardian ad litem turned her completely around in her objectives and actions. With my hand on my hip, imitating her as she lambasted me with the same pose, I told her to go fuck herself. That was not the last of Laura Melvin. Opposing counsel filed a motion, and a court date was set. Unfortunately, I was admitted to the hospital and was unable to attend. I did file a motion for a continuance, and I contacted the judge directly, in writing. Judge Sarah Willis denied my motion, and I was found to be in contempt. I later filed a motion for a rehearing. That motion was granted on May 27, 2020, yet it has not been heard to date, well over a year and a half later. Subsequently, the contempt finding against me sits in court cyberspace, and remains unenforced, as we continue to wait for the rehearing.

Jeff Ray came in subsequent to the court hearings for a "Reunification Therapist." Jeff was to speak with Laura Melvin about his sessions with me. Laura Melvin kept that information as a preparation reference for my sessions with Katie. I only saw Jeff for a short period of time, not because I didn't like him; I actually did like him, but I had my own, regular therapist, Dr. Rathjens, who didn't want to play the court's game and get caught up in all of the nonsense. I stopped seeing Jeff Ray about the time that I told Laura Melvin to go fuck herself, so there was no point in continuing to see him. It was not because of any actions on his part; Jeff was just part of the court's recipe to have all the therapists working in conjunction to feed the revenue machine collectively and rake in the money.

As I mentioned, the term Family Therapist was changed to

Reunification Therapist. This was because Maureen refused to go, so the guardian ad litem (paid for by Team Maureen) had the court change the description of the therapist as a passive reference in court. The court gave me eight days to find an alternative Family Therapist to Connie Ingram. Eight days! Do you know how difficult it is to find a therapist who is taking on new clients, will communicate with other therapists already involved in the case, *and* report to the court? I found a few who were willing to take the case on at first. Unfortunately, after the guardian ad litem, Dr. O'Hara, and opposing counsel were in touch with each of them, each therapist called me with a reason to not want to be involved. Again, keep in mind that prior to bringing any therapist candidate to the court, the collusive coercives had to be notified.

Lisa Abrotsky, 02/06/2019, New Reflections, originally took the case and later retracted after being contacted by the guardian ad litem.

Ashley Cooper, 02/06/2019, New Reflections, originally took the case and later retracted after being contacted by the guardian ad litem.

Ashna Wallace was a friend of a coworker of mine. She told me on the phone that she works with children and would be part of the court proceedings. After I notified the parties involved, she retracted that offer. She did not give me a reason. I later emailed her and asked for a reason to write in this book, but she did not reply.

Marilyn Mee made it all the way to a motion to appoint before she changed her mind.

Ordered by the Court on 02/14/2019

- The Former Husband stated at the hearing that his selection of Marilyn Mee is no longer an option since Ms. Mee informed the Former Husband that subsequent to being contacted by Dr. O'Hara, she is not willing to take on this matter. Therefore, the Former Husband's Motion to Appoint Marilyn Mee is hereby DENIED.

- The Former Husband's suggestion, through his filing of his Notice of Providing Family Therapist, of New Reflections Counseling was withdrawn by the Former Husband, subsequent to being contacted by the Guardian Ad Litem and is therefore no longer a consideration by this court as a selection for family therapist.

- The Former Wife's Motion to Appoint Connie Ingram was supported by both parties agreeing that Connie Ingram is and was selected by and suggested to the parties as the family therapist by both the Former Husband's therapist and the Minor Child's Therapist (Dr. O'Hara), however the Former Husband objects to the appointment of Connie Ingram primarily because his insurance does not cover the cost of Connie Ingram's therapy. Both parties agreed that Connie Ingram does not take insurance for family therapy.

So, we have gone through a plethora of different therapists during the course of this twelve-year custody hearing. In an ideal world, people would be motivated by integrity and a sincere desire to do the right thing. They would not be tempted to accept bribes to change their professional opinions. Out of all of those therapists, I truly believe all but Terry Trobaugh (deceased) and my current therapist, Dr. Michael Rathjens, were swayed by whoever was paying the bill. While he is indeed paid by me, Dr. Rathjens simply gives me the tools to help me deal with the heartache of the situation. He has never actually been involved in the litigation and unfortunately, I feel that seeing me in therapy for the amount of years that we have had sessions, he probably would bring the most to the table with testimony.

CHAPTER 9

The Attorneys

> *Lawyers are the only persons in whom ignorance of the law is not punished.*
> Jeremy Bentham

Eric Cheshire was my choice for a divorce attorney in Florida. When I hired him, I was residing in New Jersey, subsequent to leaving the marital state of Rhode Island. No state could claim jurisdiction since Maureen left Rhode Island in the middle of the night with Katie and neither one of us had residency in Florida. My biggest mistake was not filing for divorce in New Jersey. I had already claimed residency by changing my driver's license, vehicle registration, and voter registration. My family knew all the judges in Burlington County, New Jersey, including the recently retired John A. Sweeney, who went to high school with my mother and worked in politics with her for many years. John L. Call, Jr. was the presiding judge of the family division in Burlington County, New Jersey and a personal acquaintance of mine. The official announcement when Judge Call was appointed for the position came from the Honorable Judge Ronald Bookbinder, who my mother referred to as "Ronnie." Maureen knew of none of these personal family acquaintances, and I would have at least had a chance for justice in family court. For some reason, I didn't think it through and filed for divorce in Florida. Eric Cheshire told me, "When a parent won't allow another parent to be a parent, that's what drives me in this business." I bought the pitch.

As I look back now, by reading the over two thousand pages of divorce trial transcript, Eric didn't do a terrible job. He dropped the ball in some ways, like never calling Maureen to the witness stand for direct questioning; he tried calling her during cross-examination, which I thought was a ridiculous way of conducting himself as an attorney. Opposing counsel objected, and the judge agreed. Eric lost his momentum in his line of questioning, and it took many minutes to sort out in open court. He failed to list witness Palm Beach County Sheriff's Deputy Brian Fitch, who was anxious to testify at the divorce trial because Maureen had lied to the police to get assistance from them during child exchanges by telling the dispatcher that there was a no-contact order in effect. Six foot five inch Deputy Fitch was excused from the courtroom after opposing counsel objected to his testimony. He showed up in court wearing full tactical gear and a military-style flattop haircut that resembled Sargent Carter from Gomer Pyle.

Eric made one critical mistake in handling my case. Based on Maureen's severe co-dependency issues, he got the Office of Court Psychology involved. You've already read how Dr. Marie's flip-flopped findings were a surprise in her divorce trial testimony. Dr. Marie was later asked by Burdick to re-evaluate me to the judge, but I had since discovered that Burdick's wife, County Commissioner Paulette Burdick, effectively signs her paycheck. I claimed that having her involved was a conflict of interest with Judge Burton, who validated my concern with his ruling.

Greg Burdick was Maureen's second attorney after her first attorney listed herself as "Limited Appearance" back when Maureen filed her first motion in Florida, one of her many attempts at a no-contact order. Burdick had it pretty easy after the 180-degree turn of Dr. Marie at the divorce trial. Burdick had a method of attempting to push my buttons even when we weren't in front of a judge. I could take those buttons away while before a judge, but off the record opportunities were something different. He went on a lot of "fishing expeditions" while questioning me during depositions. For example, he once asked me in a deposition, "Tell me about the episode in the convenience store," which was a total stab in the dark, hoping that there was an issue at some time, somewhere and that his question would draw it out. In a mediation that had just concluded a segment, Burdick got up from the negotiations table to return to Maureen, who was in another room. In regards to one of Maureen's demands, I said to my attorney, "Is she for real?" Burdick answered with a snide remark about "*Two* healthy parents." I felt that was just another example of his unprofessional behavior by throwing a dart at me. He also called my attorney and accused me of breaking into his house and drawing tombstones with "Burdick" written on a wall. Evidently, someone out there disliked him more than me, if the incident even happened, for that matter. As I sit here writing it, I wonder now if I was charged with legal time for the phone calls to and from my attorney for it.

Chris Jette was assigned to represent me. Subsequent to the horrible ruling in the divorce trial and being without any money left to secure counsel, I contacted the Legal Aid Society of Palm Beach County. The director, Robert Bertisch, was not in a big hurry to help a man in family court, and he told me that. The Palm Beach County Legal Aid Society wanted to keep the "contributors" happy with the good work they were doing, and as Mr. Bertisch told me, getting a father more time with his child wasn't a priority of the program. After literally having an emotional breakdown on the phone with Mr. Bertisch, he scheduled me for an intake that yielded Christopher R. Jette as my pro bono attorney.

My first meeting with Mr. Jette was to decide whether we were going to take the route of my appeal that I filed on my divorce ruling or to petition the court for more time with Katie, subsequent to complying with all of the provisions set forth by the court prior to doing so. We decided to go forward with petitioning the court for more timesharing. This took in excess of two years before ever getting the opportunity. When we finally did, Maureen's attorney, Greg Burdick, found a way to convince the court to have me jump through even more proverbial hoops. This is what is done to generate more revenue for the court, therapists, attorneys, etc., feeding the industrial, family court machine.

Chris Jette talked a great game, as I learned the attorneys usually do when talking about what they could "conceivably" do. I recall a mediation when the opposition was being difficult, and Jette said, "I could bankrupt them." Strong words, but merely that. It became obvious to me that being represented pro bono meant I was mostly on the back burner, and it certainly became obvious to me that he wasn't putting forth the effort that a paying client would receive. Jette claimed he wasn't getting cooperation and funding from the Legal Aid Society for his expenses either.

Opposing counsel also took advantage of Jette's office working pro bono. Burdick inundated Jette's office with trivial notifications such as Maureen was going to be late or if Katie was ill. Something that could be achieved by merely texting me rather than going through attorneys. But Maureen had a war chest full of money, so wearing down Jette's enthusiasm to make the job more burdensome was one of their successful objectives.

Jette had been assigned the pro bono case on 4/27/2011 and was on and off the case for about four years. In an effort to deal with the overabundance of communications from Burdick, I suggested to Jette that I could submit all the filings, and he could just appear at the hearings. This worked for a while, until

Burdick complained to the judge that he never knew who to correspond with. This was malarkey because all he had to do was respond to whomever was acting counsel, either me or Jette. The whining worked however, and the judge informed Jette that he was either on or off the case and to make it known to opposing counsel. After that, Jette described his representation as "an epic pro bono representation." That was true for the duration of time that he was officially on the case. However, what was accomplished in those four years was absolutely nothing as far as making any progress whatsoever in getting me more time with Katie.

I am grateful for three things that Jette brought to the table in helping me during his pro bono representation. First, he told me to video record every child exchange. That suggestion saved me from a trumped up assault charge filed by Maureen that was ultimately sent to the States Attorney's Office; they determined that the state would not move forward with prosecution due to the content of the video. Second, Maureen contacted the Florida Department of Revenue whenever I fell one or two payments behind in child support and attempted to get my driver's license suspended. Jette or one of his protégés appeared to successfully explain reasonable circumstances so the court would not take my license. Third, and finally, Jette suggested that I could combat Maureen's repeated attempts at getting a no-contact order, by volunteering for one just to shut her up. I agreed to a limited no-contact order with an expiration date, and it was specifically a no-contact order with Maureen, not Katie. This actually worked. After this order expired, she never attempted to get one again. Jette described it as "consoling the screaming child."

Unfortunately, as far as the real objective, Jette was ineffective. One of his former paralegals described him to me as a slacker. That didn't really resonate with me until I hired Jette back on the case in 2018 after opposing counsel filed a 40-page Petition for Modification, which was to take away all of my parental rights. I paid Jette and alternated between waiting patiently and pestering him constantly for many months about getting together to prepare for the trial. Not once did we get together to compose questions for witnesses. I paid a process server thirty dollars directly to have each of the twenty witnesses served their subpoenas.

Jette twice asked the presiding judge for a continuance and was denied both times, but he still contacted all of the witnesses and canceled them. On the day of the trial, Jette asked a third time for a continuance. His request was again denied in open court, and the judge decided that we would have a Temporary Relief Hearing on the matter. It was basically the same argument, and there I was with all of my witnesses canceled and no trial preparation whatsoever. We lost miserably. I should have fired Jette right there in open court when his third request for a continuance was denied. Months later, when the trial actually began and I was pro se, Hanrahan, Maureen's attorney at the time, filed a Motion to Dismiss my Counter Petition for Modification, which was my attempt to gain more time with Katie. The grounds for his motion were that I had not complied with the order of the court in the Final Judgement for Dissolution of Marriage. It turned out that Chris Jette failed to file all of the documents with the Clerk of Courts. I connected with one of his former employees after she left his practice. She told me he was not crooked; he was just a slacker. I can see how right she was as I look through the court documents and review his lack of representation.

Steven Cripps was recommended to me by a coworker whose ex-wife used him to her advantage. I found Steven Cripps to be the poor man's attorney. His physical appearance resembled Kramer from Seinfeld. I saw him every single time that I went into the West Palm Beach County Courthouse. He was willing to represent me during a hearing for contempt from when I took Katie to Disney World after I picked her up from school two hours early, against the court order. This resulted in a multitude of professional people being called in to talk about it, many of them getting paid anywhere from $300 to $500 an hour. I remember Cripps saying to the magistrate as an argument, "This is like stepping on an ant with an elephant." His argument was ineffective, and I was found to be in contempt and was ordered to pay Maureen's legal fees for the hearing. What a waste of time and money.

Cripps was representing me at the time I sent a letter to Maureen's lawyer Hanrahan's first choice of guardian ad litem, Marina Pettilo. That letter, which you can read more about in a later chapter, caused Ms. Pettilo to refuse the court's appointment of guardian ad litem. Later in his office, Cripps told me that in 35 years of practicing law, he had never seen anything like my letter, and he proceeded to bang his head about five times in slow succession on his conference room table.

Don Pickett is the Department of Revenue attorney. He's the guy who tries to convince the court that your driver's license should be suspended for willfully not paying child support. I think Maureen had his cell number on speed dial and called him immediately if I missed a payment or two. At one point, Jette told me that attorney Pickett told him, "Mrs. Graves is a unique individual." Attorney Pickett was just doing his job in the halls of the courthouse. He was usually willing to make deals in open court. He comes off strong, but I found him to be reasonable.

Michael Hanrahan had been a criminal defense attorney, and that was how he was known in the judicial circuit. When I brought his name up to people within the Fifteenth Circuit Court of Palm Beach County and said that he was my former wife's counsel, they would often respond that he was a criminal defense attorney. I usually replied by saying he failed at that and is now cherry picking in family law. Years earlier, Hanrahan had been tapped for a high profile double murder case. His first defense argument for his client, Darnell Razz, was simply, "He wasn't there." He later flip-flopped to say, "Darnell Razz was not fully developed mentally and therefore can be rehabilitated into a functioning member of society." Hanrahan failed at defending his client, and Darnell Razz was sentenced to consecutive life sentences.

When Hanrahan took over the case to represent Maureen, he knew there was a war chest full of money. Hanrahan compiled and orchestrated the "Collusive Coercives" that I mentioned in an earlier chapter. With what I would consider a criminal defense approach, he gathered multiple experts to bring forth an argument to the court that there was imminent danger when it came to me being with Katie. He and his experts used words like "terrified," "abuse," "stalking," "dangerous," "threaten," "upset," "nervous," "alienating," and so on. I noticed during arguments in open court that Hanrahan would often use the word "surely" and would take about five seconds to say the word. He was attempting to imply that the judge would have to be an idiot not to see what a horrible person I was.

Before I realized that there don't seem to be any real consequences for contempt of a family court order, I was giving my argument as a pro se litigant about Maureen's refusal to bring Katie to court-ordered timesharing. I was looking down at my notes and saying unfavorable things about Maureen. Something came over me, and my eyes welled up with tears. As I looked down at my notes to continue, I couldn't read them because of the tears. Everyone was waiting for me, and the longer I took, the more overcome I became. Finally, I lifted my head, and the tears came down. I told the judge I needed a break and that I was sorry.

We took a break, and I went into the hall. Hanrahan and Alper came out. I told them I was having a problem saying these things about Maureen—that I felt I was throwing her under the bus. Hanrahan said, "You and your Google law degree aren't throwing anyone under the bus." That was the closest I ever came to punching an officer of the court in the face.

I ended up prevailing on the matter, and Maureen was found to be in contempt. This was when I learned that there are no consequences for contempt in family court with the exception of a document saying it happened, and there were no other consequences for Maureen in the matter.

On January 25, 2019, with Judge Sarah Willis presiding, I lost my daughter to a well-prepared Hanrahan who orchestrated the Collusive Coercives, while my attorney, Christopher R. Jette, had not one plan to implement or execute to prevent this from happening. It was the last time I was ever represented by counsel. One day, outside the courtroom, Hanrahan said to me after one of my self-representing hearings, "It's nothing personal, I just have to do the best job for my client's interests." I'm not really sure what he meant by that. All I could think of was how much I'd love to tell him what a low life scum he was for destroying a relationship between a father and a daughter.

Instead, I just turned around and continued on my way.

Dodger Arp and **Al Marten** were two attorneys that were referred to me by Chris Jette's former paralegal, Emily, through Facebook Messenger. Upon guardian ad litem, Anne Alper's March 28, 2022 Motion For Voluntary Withdrawal and Replacement of the Guardian ad Litem, which will be detailed in the next chapter, I needed to get ahead of the part of the motion that dealt specifically with the "replacement" aspect. The hearing was set by Judge Renatha Francis for April 6, 2022. My contact with the office of Dodger Arp yielded an answer that stated that he didn't refuse the case, just that he couldn't do the hearing on April 6th. When I attempted to get clarification on that answer, his office finally sent me an email, one day before the hearing, refusing the case. They should have sent that answer first or at least sooner than one day before the hearing.

I quickly contacted Al Marten's office. He reviewed the case history, told me that any attorney who looked at this extensive case history would not want to take this case on. Nevertheless, he accepted the case verbally, and we agreed on a $500.00 charge for his limited appearance at the hearing the next morning. At 3 P.M. that same day, he called me back and declined the case— literally two business hours before the start of the hearing.

As I had, figuratively speaking, been "left out in the cold" by these two attorneys, I had to appear at that hearing pro se. The results of that fifteen-minute hearing were incredibly complicated, and the details are written in Chapter 10, The Judges, under Judge Renatha Francis' entry.

The Judges

> *"Cameras should be the norm everywhere. It should be in every courtroom so that the proceedings are taken down and recorded just like stenography."*
>
> Judge Judy

The Honorable Judge Catherine Brunson had been a Superior Court Judge since 1994. She was appointed judge by Governor Lawton Chiles. What I learned about Judge Brunson early on, when I first entered her courtroom in 2009, was that she kept her hearings moving along. She kept a minute meter and wound it to the time allowed for any attorney or litigant to give their arguments. At first I thought this method was kind of ridiculous, but she had probably had her fill of grandstanding 15 years prior to my ever walking into her courtroom. When the "Ding" from the minute meter sounded, attorneys were to stop talking. Additionally, I saw other judge's courtrooms over the years that repeatedly lost control of time and, frankly, the cases themselves. In retrospect, I found Judge Brunson's method ingenious and efficient.

Judge Brunson wasn't my favorite judge but pretty close to it. She presided over our case the longest, and lucky for me, she was onto Maureen's false allegations in attempts to obtain three separate no-contact orders. My attorney, Eric Cheshire, made it obvious that the only reason Maureen attempted to get the no-contact orders was for custody reasons, and I believe Judge Brunson saw that. On every attempt, Judge Brunson denied Maureen from obtaining a no-contact order and cited insufficient evidence in her rulings.

As you may remember from the first chapter of this book, Judge Brunson presided over the divorce trial. I will always believe that her hands were tied because of Eric Cheshire's idea to involve the Office of Court Psychology. The flip-flopped testimony of Dr. Michaelanne Marie on Day 2 of the trial got me the unfavorable ruling, and even with all of her own first-hand knowledge of Maureen's dishonesty about the case in her courtroom, Judge Brunson put a lot of weight on Dr. Marie's testimony in her Final Judgement of Divorce. Judge Brunson was our first judge from 2009 until 2012 and then came around into a rotation to preside over our case again in 2017. She retired in 2018, at which time we ended up with the newly elected Judge Sarah Willis, who took my daughter away from me. This came after Maureen "forum shopped" for twelve years, with nine judges, in three states to achieve her objective of parental alienation, largely by accusing me of her own abusive actions.

The Honorable Judge Thomas Barkdull III presided over our case after the rotation of judges in 2012. The very first time Judge Barkdull entered the courtroom for a hearing in which I was petitioning for more time with Katie, I was absolutely enamored with his knowledge of the history of the case. He spoke at great length and was visibly annoyed with the amount of conflict of it. In that first hearing, Maureen's attorney, Greg Burdick, took some paperwork to the bench and handed it to Judge Barkdull. Within moments of receiving those documents, Judge Barkdull held up photos of unknown battered women that were included in what Burdick gave him. The judge furiously asked Maureen's lawyer, "Mr. Burdick, are you trying to dump oil down the well?"

Our hearing was continued, but I felt that I had a judge who was not going to stand for any type of nonsense in his courtroom. I spoke to my new attorney, Christopher Jette, about how good I felt about Judge Barkdull. He discounted the judge by saying, "He is far from the best." I thought this was a rather childish remark.

Unfortunately, we didn't have Judge Barkdull for very long. He may simply have been rotated out of our case, but I strongly believe that it was because of a case in 2013 on which he didn't act swiftly enough and inadvertently brought about the murder of a ten-year-old girl at the hands of her own mother. According to the Palm Beach Post, the former husband, Bradley Brooks, repeatedly pleaded with Judge Barkdull to take his daughter, Alexandra, away from the mother because he feared for Alexandra's life. Judge Barkdull only ordered a breathalyzer to be installed in the mother, Pamela's, car to prevent drunk driving with the child in the car. Unfortunately, Pamela Brooks stabbed her 10-year-old daughter Alexandra to death on September 12, 2013 before turning the knife on herself to complete her murder-suicide. I truly believe that Judge Barkdull simply couldn't walk into the courthouse knowing that he ignored the pleas of Alexandra's father, Bradley Brooks. That must indeed be a terrible thing to live with. Truly, my heart goes out to all of the people involved, except, of course, Pamela Brook's attorney, Phillip Chopin, who obviously knew about her substance abuse and had at least some idea of how mentally ill she was. Years later, I wrote a letter to Judge Barkdull to his address listed in public tax records and thanked him for his thoroughness in my case.

The Honorable Judge Charles Burton took over as presiding judge in our case in 2014. Chris Jette was representing me at this time. Jette's task at hand was to get me more time with Katie.

That never happened with him representing me for a number of reasons, which I'll get into later and again in another chapter. We all appeared in front of Judge Burton on Maureen's motion to have me re-evaluated by Dr. Michaelanne Marie of the Office of Court Psychology prior to me getting more time with Katie. And why not after Dr. Marie's damaging flip-flopped testimony at the divorce trial?

When Chris Jette and I were in preparation of the hearing, I mentioned to him that the Office of Court Psychology was overseen by the Palm Beach County Commissioners. Maureen's attorney Greg Burdick's wife, Paulette Burdick, was a County Commissioner, and I told Jette that I felt it was a conflict of interest. He responded that we were not going to attempt that avenue because we would sound stupid.

On my own accord, I texted Maureen and told her that we were going to get Dr. Marie off the case because it was a conflict of interest. I knew she would tell her attorney, and she did. So, while I sat on the witness stand being questioned by Burdick, he asked me about the text and if I thought that he and his wife talked about me and the case in bed at night. I told him that while I had no idea what he and his wife talked about in their bed, I did feel it was a conflict of interest since his wife signs the paychecks of the very psychologist he was asking the court to appoint, yet again, to evaluate me. While I was addressing the court, I looked at Jette. I knew what I had done. I got my concerns on the record by goading my ex-wife's lawyer to bring it up. Because of my end run, Judge Burton denied Dr. Marie's involvement due to a possible conflict of interest.

At the conclusion of the hearing, Judge Burton spoke of a psychologist that worked on a case that he presided over and stated in open court that this particular psychologist fooled everyone with the way she evaluated a particular litigant contrarily to the way everyone thought she would and that he found that interesting. The psychologist was Dr. Kristin Tolbert, and Judge Burton ended his story with his decision to use her services in our case. In short, and for the purposes of this segment, Judge Burton never was part of the evaluation findings because Dr. Tolbert took over six months to submit her evaluation report to the court. By that time, Judge Burton had rotated out and was no longer presiding. Our new judge was Judge Suskauer in 2015.

The Honorable Judge Scott Suskauer was appointed judge by Governor Rick Scott on June 18, 2015 and was immediately assigned to our case. I got the impression that the lawyers didn't like him, and I liked that. The reputation I heard was that he yelled at them. That is exactly what happened to Maureen's attorney, Michael Hanrahan, when he attempted to get a guardian ad litem assigned to our case on what's known as the Uniform Motion Calendar. The UMC hears cases that are agreed upon or are uncontested. They begin at 8:45 A.M. and are often referred to as 8:45s. They are to take no more than 10 minutes and are non-evidentiary hearings. While Hanrahan was developing his panel of experts or the "Cavalcade of Collusive Coercives," as I refer to them, the guardian ad litem was to play a big part in him surrounding himself with so-called experts. We all entered Judge Suskauer's courtroom on the matter. Once the judge put together that this was more of an argument to be heard on a normal hearing, he actually lost his temper at Hanrahan and berated him on him not knowing proper procedure and protocol. The judge slammed Hanrahan by saying he had deliberately attempted to get the matter through on a Uniform Motion Calendar hearing, which are easy to get swiftly in what is an extremely busy court schedule. All Hanrahan kept saying was "I'm sorry, I'm sorry." It was absolutely hysterical to me. When the judge was finally finished chewing Hanrahan up into cud, we all walked out of the courtroom. I exited first, took about ten steps, turned around, and asked Hanrahan if he needed to know protocol on how to properly file a motion. He told me, "Get away, or I'll file an injunction against you!" I turned walked away, looked back, and said, "Do you need me to draft it?"

This was about the time that Maureen started to really ignore the orders of the court by simply not bring Katie to court-ordered timesharing and not providing medical conditions or medical insurance cards. Hanrahan inundated Chris Jette's office with trivial communications such as Maureen would be 20 minutes late dropping her off and other matters of the like that could have easily been texted to me. This was undoubtedly done to run up my legal costs. Subsequently, I could not keep Jette as counsel and began a long period of being pro se. This was all part of their plan to erase me from Katie's life.

Judge Suskauer got annoyed with me at one point. When any hearing is set, it initially goes to the magistrate who basically takes some of the workload off the judge. However, there is always the option to object to this, and the judge is then required to hear the matter. I objected on every occasion. Judge Suskauer asked me if I had a problem with having the magistrate hear cases. My answer was that I wanted him, as our judge, to hear the matters. He was visibly angry about my answer.

In April of 2016, Maureen began to pick Katie up at school an hour before I was scheduled and ordered by the court to do so for our weekends together. She did this two weeks in a row before I decided that I would simply do the same. On my scheduled day, I picked Katie up from school two hours early, and because I was Katie's father, the school couldn't deny me. I knew it would be a shit storm, but since I knew it would take four months for the matter to be heard in any case, I figured I might as well make it a party. I took Katie to Disney World in Orlando. She was very upset at first because there's no telling what Maureen told her about why I hadn't seen her in weeks. Once I showed her the tickets, told her about our hotel, went to Red Robin, and ate while playing the trivia game, we were all good. She wanted to call her mom, and she did after Red Robin. I heard Maureen say to her, "Be strong!" as if kidnappers had her, and Maureen was getting the ransom money together.

Katie and I went back to the hotel room and started to wind it down by watching television while getting unpacked and ready to hit Universal Studio Park in the morning. The phone rang with a "private number." I answered, and it was a Palm Beach County Sherriff's deputy. I stepped outside the room to take the call. The deputy told me that I was to bring my daughter back immediately. First of all, I told him, I wasn't late in any way, shape, or form. It was my court-ordered time with Katie. The deputy stumbled and asked when I was bringing her back. I proceeded to tell him of the wonderful plans that we had for the weekend in Disney. My over-exuberance annoyed him, and he told me that I needed to bring her back. I asked him, "Deputy, has a crime been committed? You police officers always tell me this is a civil matter and that I should file a motion in family court. So fill out your report, and with all due respect, go fuck yourself!"

After a short return of Judge Brunson presiding over our case, **Judge Sarah Willis** was elected to the bench on the Fifteenth Circuit Court of Palm Beach County in November of 2018. The vacancy was created by Judge Brunson's retirement, so I was certain that whoever won that election would be our presiding judge. The candidates were Michael McAuliffe, Henry Quinn Johnson, and Sarah Willis. I voted for Henry Johnson. To me, he seemed to have the least self-interest, had the experience of having been a court martial judge in the Army, and served in the Army for 27 years. I thought he'd be the most pragmatic and impartial of the candidates.

Judge Willis's experience was with the Special Victim's Unit at the State Attorney's Office, the same agency that allowed Jeffery Epstein special privileges to leave his jail cell every day as a "work release" and to conceivably continue his sexual trafficking of young women in Palm Beach. Judge Willis's seat on the bench began on January 22, 2019 after being sworn in by Chief Judge Krista Marx, the one who refused to open the Jeffery Epstein files for an investigation until the Miami Herald ran a series of articles that prompted the governor to insist on an investigation. Unsurprisingly, the investigation showed "no wrongdoing."

The hearing that lost me my right to visit Katie was conducted on Judge Willis' third day on the job.

Ironically, I had represented myself numerous times as a pro se litigant. During my self-representation I managed to get overnight visitation with Katie, got Dr. Marie removed as the evaluating psychologist due to the conflict of interest that I mentioned in an earlier chapter, and kept my timesharing with Katie for ten years. The only times that I lost time with Katie or was not granted any time at all was when I was represented by counsel. This was no exception.

When Maureen's attorney filed the 40-page Petition for Modification (Filing #64282640) on November 16, 2017, I felt it was too overwhelming and insurmountable a task to take on as a pro se litigant. However, my now-hired attorney Christopher Jette's complete and utter "slacking" (a term used by one of his former paralegals) had us in front of Judge Willis, who had already denied Jette's request for a continuance twice, without any preparation. Jette was so confident that he would be granted the continuance on his third try that he told all twenty-six of my witnesses not to come in. This was after I had paid a process server over $1,000 to have each of them served. The judge did not grant the continuance, which left Jette with no questions ready and the two of us holding pens, writing pads, and our proverbial dicks in our hands. The Petition for Modification claimed twelve times that I was an offender of parental alienation syndrome.

Judge Willis decided that we would have a Temporary Relief Hearing as opposed to a trial, and we moved forward with testimony from Anne Alper, the $100K attorney—paid by Maureen—serving as the guardian ad litem for Katie. She professed to be working for the best interest of the child and was permitted to give hearsay testimony. The court heard testimony from disgraced psychologist Dr. Kristin Tolbert, who had been a contracted entity for the Fifteenth Circuit Court but had lost that privileged position by her negligence and mishandling of cases for which she had been successfully sued in civil court. My attorney floundered. He had nothing prepared, had deposed no witnesses, had canceled all of my witnesses, and had prepared no questions for any of the participants who testified in this hearing. At one point in the middle of the hearing, Chris Jette leaned down to me and asked me to "jot down some questions" for him to ask. Surely, a much better preparation for that would have been in his office prior to being smack dab in the middle of the hearing, in the courtroom.

So, on January 26, 2019, a Saturday, Judge Sarah Willis e-filed her Order on Temporary Relief. By filing her order on a Saturday, she prevented my attorney from having the opportunity to object to any part of it.

I had a meeting with Chris Jette immediately following the Temporary Relief Hearing and told him that he was responsible for the horrible showing at the hearing. He responded that he was going to slam my face into the table for saying so. Obviously, this conversation wasn't going to motivate him any more than any of our previous conversations in which I had tried to prevent this disaster.

In one hearing, Judge Sarah Willis took away all of my time-sharing with Katie, and her decision was based on three things: 1. Anne Alper's testimony, 2. Katie's alleged stomachaches, and 3. Katie allegedly biting her fingernails. The only time I was given with my daughter was with supervised visitation with Randi Shapiro or one of her trained supervisors. Of course, Ms. Shapiro was recommended to the court by the $100K paid attorney, Anne Alper. It was further stipulated that my therapist, Dr. Michael Rathjens, shall consult with any and all therapists who are or would be involved in "family therapy." The term "family therapy" was later changed to "reunification therapy" since Maureen refused to be a part of getting therapy herself.

An important notation about this hearing is that the trial itself was still pending. The 40-page Petition for Modification (Filing #64282640) on November 16, 2017 was still on the docket to be heard. Maureen had me erased from Katie's life without a proper trial. It certainly wasn't important to her to have that trial proceed at this point. She had already achieved her objective, after all.

After paying Chris Jette for his ridiculously sub-par representation, I knew I'd be pro se at the four-day trial when it did commence. I bought three used suits on eBay, compiled a 3-ring binder with all potential exhibits to be entered as evidence, composed questions, wrote subpoenas, had them served, again, at thirty dollars each, and bought a small, flat-screen monitor to show my videos of Maureen's public displays of lunacy.

I found Judge Willis to have little control of her courtroom and to have a habit of displaying an utter disrespect for her own position and the entity for a hall of justice. For example, she set the trial for four days, but five days into the trial proceedings, Hanrahan was still talking. Unlike Judge Brunson's minute meter approach, Judge Willis allowed grandstanding, so counsel could just go on speaking indefinitely with no deadline or time limit; she simply extended the hearings to accommodate the lawyers going over the time she allocated. The hearing could just continue indefinitely or until counsel passes out from lack of oxygen due to filibustering.

The proceedings were halted for the COVID-19 pandemic before I had my chance to speak. As of the winter of 2022, we had been in recess for over a year. We had one subsequent hearing when I brought up that Katie and I had not spoken on the phone as we should have per the order of the court. Hanrahan stated that the order only stated that I could physically *call* on those days and times. Judge Willis angrily said to Hanrahan that she hoped that she didn't have to specify the difference between me calling and a conversation actually taking place. Indeed she did but was apparently too much of a coward to address it directly and clearly. She knew this absolutely, and it showed literally in the words she spoke on the record, but by doing nothing, she ensured that Maureen could continue to refuse to accept my calls with impunity.

We had a few hearings that took place via Zoom. As a pro se litigant, I did some research on Judge Willis's campaign promises. As I prepared, I found her closing pitch for votes at a candidate debate in which she said:

> I have the experience both as a quasi-judicial officer presiding over cases and ensuring that litigants are heard in court, as well as...extensive trial experience as an assistant state attorney and as a statewide prosecutor. So I bring practical experience in the courtroom. Where I've been in the courtroom day in, day out. I understand that to be heard is to be empowered, and I want to empower the citizens of Palm Beach County.

I used a portion of her campaign promise in a hearing, verbally referencing her campaign promise of "empowering litigants in the courtroom by being heard." She knew exactly what I was referring to, and she had already enabled the alienation of me from Katie's life. At that point, I didn't really care about decorum. I cared about making it a point to show Judge Willis that I saw that her campaign promise to voters was hogwash.

Just eight months after Judge Willis took Katie from me, a biographical summary by William B. Lewis showed up online. As I read the piece, I couldn't help thinking how the understanding she gave to the children who gave her the teddy bear gift wasn't granted to a single one of Jeffrey Epstein's victims. I also could not help but wonder if, like the children in the story below, Katie thought *she* did something wrong to cause her life to be surrounded by conflict.

> As she reflects on her time at the State Attorney's Office, Judge Willis mentions a teddy bear that sits on a shelf in her chambers. The toy was a gift from the victims of a case involving the sexual abuse of four siblings, the youngest of whom was only five years old, by their uncle. Judge Willis recalls how the victims struggled to understand the judicial process and the heartbreaking conversations she had when the victims questioned whether they had done something wrong. Ultimately, after much hard work, Judge Willis secured guilty verdicts and a life sentence against the perpetrator. It takes a special kind of person to have the compassion to connect with the victims of such horrific crimes, yet also the strength and skill to prosecute the abuser.

The only experience that I found Judge Willis brought to the table in our case was inexperience and disrespect to the entity of the court itself. She would rule as either a matter of law or a matter of fact and in the best interest of the child, but she would only consider ruling when Hanrahan or Alper made the argument, which they only did when it suited their objectives.

One example was when I argued the point that Maureen had Katie on the Stay Well kids low-income medical insurance. I told the judge that I want her to immediately rule that Katie be on my medical insurance that was offered by my employer at no cost to my former wife, which, among other criteria, was one that disqualified our child from being on the program in the first place. Judge Willis could have ruled in the best interest of the child right then and there. I was told to file a motion, which is the "matter of law" ruling.

As another example, Judge Willis would not allow me to show a video of Maureen telling the manager of the soccer team that Katie was not to leave the soccer game even though she had what was later revealed to be a broken toe. In the video, Maureen contradicts my concerns to the point of raising her voice. Opposing counsel objected that the video could not be used as evidence because its audio content was protected under Florida privacy statutes and that I should be charged with a third degree felony. I argued that because the situations happened in public, there was no expectation of privacy. My plan was to follow the viewing of that video with the documentation from the hospital that validated my concerns that Katie's toe was broken. Judge Willis allowed the video to be played but without audio or narration. I wonder if she felt as stupid as she looked while the video played. How does refusing to view information pertinent to the health and well-being of the child not relate to the "best interest of the child"? Judge Willis refused to listen to the story that the mother was putting the child at risk for the sole purpose of undermining an ex-spouse.

When I tried to refute Dr. Kristin Tolbert's testimony, Judge Willis would not allow impeachment witnesses. She would not allow me to introduce a certified copy of the financial affidavit from Dr. Kristin Tolbert's divorce, in which Tolbert claimed under oath that she earned only $800 a month as a psychologist, thus proving that she lies in court. When I attempted to introduce the document in cross-examination, Judge Willis totally lost control of her courtroom. Tolbert shouted at me from the witness stand that I ascertained her personal information. I argued directly back to Tolbert that the document is public record with the Clerk of Courts. It was a moment best described as courtroom mayhem. The document's inclusion into evidence was objected to and the objection was sustained by Judge Willis.

Judge Willis would not allow screenshots of Facebook pages from witnesses showing content that included things from a meme stating that "a good cop is a dead cop" to a testifying psychologist who publicly said that Florida State University's "Tomahawk Chop" resembles someone "forcefully shoving cock down your throat."

I asked Judge Willis to interview Katie privately. Opposing counsel objected and would only concede to "testimony of the minor child" if it was simulcast into the courtroom and that Katie be made aware that everything she said was being heard by both her mother and father. Can you imagine a 12-year-old girl trying to testify honestly all the while knowing both of her parents and some strangers are listening to every word she says? Alper also insisted that she should be in the judge's chambers with Katie for "support." Alper being there was more likely to serve as an uncomfortable reminder that everyone was listening. The judge could have done the right thing and made the conversation private for Katie's sake, but she caved to opposing counsel's insistence. Since no one else was willing to consider Katie's needs in this case, I retracted my request to have her testify.

With just a little effort, Judge Willis could have gotten to the bottom of the case and ruled fairly, but since she'd only been a judge for five minutes, she couldn't see her way clear to rule on the side of a pro se litigant and surely not in Katie's best interest. Judge Willis was like a deer in headlights and should not have been allowed to bluster her way through a job she was not qualified for. She risked family relationships because she failed to grow a backbone to gain control of what she was elected to do. So as Sarah Willis campaigned by saying that "to be heard in court is to be empowered" and that she wanted to "empower the citizens of Palm Beach County," did she mean all citizens but me? No, she simply said whatever she had to say in order to get votes. When judges come up for re-election in Florida, the ballot simply states, "Shall Sarah Willis of the Fifteenth Circuit be retained in office?" I ask that voters do their homework. If you care about justice and having judges who respect the title of judge, when it's time to vote, vote "No" on Sarah Willis.

I finally got Judge Willis disqualified on June 5, 2020. I wrote her a letter on May 28, 2020 and filed it on the record. In the letter, I told her how I felt about her handling of our case. She had enough of me, and my letter finally got her off the case. I was trouble for her. The order stated,

> The standard for viewing the legal sufficiency of a motion to disqualify is whether the facts alleged, which must be assumed to be true, would cause the movant to have a well-founded fear that he or she will not receive a fair trial at the hands of that judge.

I filed my letter, the order, and other pertinent documents in one filing to the Palm Beach County Clerk of Courts, Case#200910788, Docket Entry #1204 regarding how she, as a superior court judge, failed to act in the interests of a child in a case assigned to her.

Magistrate Damary Stokes presided over one hearing. What I really liked about Magistrate Stokes was that she simply ignored stupidity or nonsense. She did not even address it; she just ignored it. For example, when Hanrahan filed a Motion to Dismiss my motion, Magistrate Stokes didn't even address the filing. She simply moved on with my motion. I said something about the Motion to Dismiss, and she even ignored my bringing it up. She ruled in my favor on my motion, and the hearing was over in no time. Hanrahan tried to grandstand, but the hearing moved on to its end without any continuance. I found her to be efficient and not willing to be distracted.

Magistrate Thomas Baker presided over an unsuccessful attempt by Maureen and the Department of Revenue to suspend my driver's license. The feeling I got from Magistrate Baker was that of a regular guy. He walked the public halls of the courthouse. As I saw him walking through one day, I spoke and said hello to him. He was extremely cordial by returning my greeting with a smile and asking how I was doing.

Magistrate James Williams presided over my Motion for Contempt. Here's another justice who cannot control the time or content in his courtroom. Magistrate Williams continued the Motion for Contempt of Maureen not seeing to it that Katie and I spoke on the phone per the court order. The calls either happened or they didn't. One point I made was that we certainly weren't going to bring a 13-year-old child into court and hold her accountable, were we? Williams stupidly answered my rhetorical question as though it were a serious question rather than recognizing the point of the order that states Maureen has an "Affirmative Duty" to abide by the order. The hearing was continued two times, equating to three separate times we had to meet to determine what was originally allocated one hour for the matter to be heard.

When Maureen left Rhode Island for Florida in the middle of the night with Katie, **Judge Howard Lipsey** of Rhode Island ordered the "IMMEDIATE RETURN OF THE MINOR CHILD TO RHODE ISLAND" on December 29, 2008. The Judge's Order included that we were to reconvene on January 5, 2009 before Magistrate John J. O'Brien. Katie was to have been brought back to Rhode Island by that hearing.

When we reconvened on January 5th, with **Magistrate John J. O'Brien** presiding, he called for a meeting in chambers for the attorneys only. When they emerged, I could see on the face of my attorney that it did not go well. When court was officially back in session, Magistrate O'Brien spoke from the bench, and my paraphrase of what he said was that he was aware of what Judge Lipsey ordered, but O'Brien contrarily felt and ordered that Florida should handle the case. I look back at the incident as a legal kidnapping.

I found an interesting history on Magistrate John J. O'Brien for multiple misconduct allegations at https://law.justia.com/cases/rhode-island/supreme-court/1994/650-a-2d-134.html. It is interesting how judicial behavior is sometimes handled.

Judge Renatha S. Francis was our newest presiding judge in the 15th Circuit. Judge Francis had recently returned to the bench at the Fifteenth Circuit after being appointed by Governor Ron DeSantis to the Florida State Supreme Court and being denied that appointment by Congresswoman Geraldine Thompson due to not having been a member of the bar for the required time for that judicial appointment.

I filed two motions for contempt against Maureen in October 2021. I had not been able to get a hearing date after five months of asking for one. I repeatedly called Judge Francis's judicial assistant who finally told me that she would ask the judge how to proceed. When I still did not hear back, I left a message on the judge's assistant's voicemail stating that I would instead contact Governor DeSantis' office regarding my inability to get a hearing date after so many requests. Before I could make that call, I was given an appointment for a hearing on March 28, 2022. Included in that hearing date notification were the judge's instructions on submitting exhibits. I dropped off a copy of my exhibits to the judge's mailbox at the courthouse and sent a link to the exhibits on the cloud to attorney Hanrahan's email because the file was too large to attach to an email. When the hearing started, attorney Hanrahan requested to address the court and stated that he had not gotten copies of my exhibits. It was a coy attempt, and he actually put on a bewildered act for the judge.

The judge denied both of my motions on Hanrahan's

statement within the first five minutes of the hearing. At the conclusion, Anne Alper stated that she had filed a Motion for Voluntary Withdrawal and Replacement of the Guardian ad Litem, citing that she had been threatened by me multiple times during her tenure in the case. She actually wrote it in her filing as "borderline" threatened her. Let's face it, if I had actually threatened an officer of the court, there would have been consequences. Within her filing, she named attorneys Kim Nutter, and C. Debra Welch as replacements and stated that she "has not discussed this case with either potential successor guardian ad litem" as if she pulled them from the phone book. Judge Francis immediately scheduled the ten-minute hearing on the Uniform Motion Calendar (UMC) for Tuesday, April 6, 2022.

I filed an objection the next afternoon, Docket #146618499 at 12:43 P.M., citing Administrative Order 5.201-6/19* It states that the purpose of the UMC is to provide a forum in which to resolve non-evidentiary procedural motions and uncontested family division proceedings, such as dissolution of marriage actions, within the framework of hearings that do not exceed 10 minutes. My intention was to contest Alper's motion mainly on the fact that she had "hand selected" her successor. The objection was denied without a hearing. I assumed Judge Francis was certainly getting her fill of me, and I'm pretty sure Hanrahan was feeling that I was digging myself into a hole with her.

I contacted the Legal Aid Society of Palm Beach County and requested to speak to the Executive Director, Mr. Robert Bertisch. Mr. Bertisch called me back, and I told him of the situation. He informed me that the organization would provide an attorney ad litem to represent the minor child and that I would certainly be at risk in losing my daughter further if my daughter did not want to have a relationship with me. I replied that if someone who was familiar with parental alienation syndrome were appointed, the truth of the matter would render favorability for my daughter and me to reunite. This was sounding like a long shot, but it certainly had a better chance than Maureen's father's money buying another attorney's testimony that supported estrangement. Mr. Bertisch and the organization were on board as an option for the court's decision. All I had to do now was get the option into open court in a ten-minute hearing. That was when I knew that I would have to get an attorney to get this option in for an allocated five minutes of a ten-minute hearing. That's where Dodger Arp and Al Marten from the previous chapter came in. Mr. Marten even contacted Robert Bertisch to confirm his commitment to the cause before he decided to refuse the case at 3 P.M. the day before the hearing. I was on my own to get this option into open court.

I found it incredibly ironic that Judge Francis was still holding Zoom court hearings, especially since Governor DeSantis was holding back school funding to the schools who refused to lift the mask mandates for Covid-19. Yet, his appointed judge to the State Supreme Court was still not holding court in person due to the Covid-19 pandemic. Nevertheless, I sat in front of my tablet on April 6, 2022 as the hearing began. Anne Alper spoke at length about how threatened she was by the many threatening things that I had done to her and that she needed to withdraw from the case. Judge Francis stated the motion was granted as she looked down at a document and began to write. I started to speak, and the judge interrupted me by saying that she made her decision. I began to ask permission to address the court. The judge stopped, looked at me, and interrupted me again by saying; "Let me caution you Mr. Graves!" I stopped talking, and the hearing ended. I immediately called Robert Bertisch and asked him to call the judge stating his commitment for being an option for the best interest of the minor child. This took a lot of pleading. He asked me if Al Marten was there to represent me, why I would need him. When I told him that Marten declined the case at 3 P.M. yesterday and that I was not allowed to bring up the option in open court, he agreed to call the judge.

That same day I filed a Motion for Rehearing and Disqualification of the Presiding Judge. That motion was denied two days later. I had my fill of Judge Renatha Francis, and I wasn't done yet. The next day I filed a formal, written complaint with the State of Florida Judicial Qualifications Commission in Tallahassee, Florida. I listed Hanrahan as a witness. What could anybody do? UMC hearings are audio recorded. The statement of facts on the complaint read as follows:

> On Case# 200910788, guardian ad litem's (attorney Anne Alper) Motion to Withdraw was heard in Judge Francis' courtroom via Zoom on April 6, 2022 at 8:45am on the Uniform Motion Calendar docket. The current guardian ad litem had two (2) candidates that she suggested in her filing to replace her. Anne Alper has been paid by the former wife in excess of two hundred thousand dollars in this case. This fact has arguably created a major conflict of interest. At the conclusion of Anne Alper's testimony, Judge Francis immediately granted the Motion to Withdraw and began to sign a document in front of her. I asked to address the court, as I had already had the Legal Aid Society of Palm Beach County's Executive Director, Robert Bertisch promise to provide an unbiased attorney, free of charge, for consideration to be appointed to the role of Guardian ad Litem for the minor child. Judge Francis forbade me from speaking and threatened me by saying, "Let me caution you, Mr. Graves!" The judge gave no time to present a viable opportunity for consideration in the best interest of the minor child at this hearing.

I filed the complaint on the case docket, Filing # 147215957. In addition to opposing counsel (Hanrahan), I sent copies to the following people:

- The Honorable Governor Ron DeSantis

- The Honorable Congresswoman Geraldine F. Thompson (denied judge's appointment)
- The Honorable Glenn Kelly (Chief Judge, 15th Circuit)
- County Commissioner, Maria Sachs

If my proverbial goose wasn't cooked with Judge Francis prior to this point, I'm sure everyone, including myself was undoubtedly sure it was now. Then the court order came in my email.

IN THE CIRCUIT COURT OF THE FIFTEENTH JUDICIAL CIRCUIT IN AND FOR PALM BEACH COUNTY, FLORIDA

IN THE FORMER MARRIAGE OF

DAVID GRAVES,   CASE NO: 2009-DR-010788

Petitioner/Former Husband,

vs.

MAUREEN GRAVES,

Respondent/Former Wife

IN THE INTEREST OF:

/ Minor Child

ORDER APPOINTING THE JUVENILE ADVOCACY PROJECT OF THE LEGAL AID SOCIETY OF PALM BEACH COUNTY, INC.

THIS CAUSE came before the Court, sua sponte, upon review of the Court's docket. On April 6, 2022, the Court discharged the Guardian Ad Litem at a UMC hearing based on a motion to withdraw.

It is clear to the Court given the history of the litigation in this cause that it is in the best interest of the child for the Court to appoint an Attorney Ad Litem in this matter. As of this writing, there are 1242 docket entries in this matter, most of which are various motions, not actual orders. The issues that necessitated an appointment of a Guardian Ad Litem do not appear to have abated, and if anything, may have increased.

Therefore, it is ORDERED:

1. The Legal Aid Society of Palm Beach County's Juvenile Advocacy Project, 423 Fern Street, Suite 200, West Palm Beach, FL 33401, Telephone: XXX-XXX-XXXX, is appointed as attorney for the child.

2. The Attorney ad Litem, including staff and agents of the Juvenile Advocacy Project, shall be granted access to the child/ren upon presentation of this order.

3. The Legal Aid Society of Palm Beach County's Juvenile Advocacy Project shall be entitled to copies of any and all records pertaining to the minor child/ren, including those that are deemed confidential. This order authorizes the Attorney to access information and/or records from any hospital, doctor, or any health care provider; therapist, psychiatrist, psychologist, counselor, or any mental health provider; or other social or human services agency, without the necessity of written consent by the child through his/her parent or legal guardian.

4. The Attorney is authorized to use and/or disclose the entire medical record or complete patient file for the purpose of this appointment. These records include but are not limited to HIV test results and records; school records; medical and mental health records and/or substance abuse records regarding the minor child that otherwise would be confidential or protected under state and federal law.

5. The Attorney ad Litem is further authorized to retain co-counsel or separate counsel to represent the legal rights and interest of the minor child/ren who is/are the subject

of these proceedings. The Attorney ad Litem may further serve as next friend on behalf of the child/ren.

6. This authorization shall terminate upon discharge of the Attorney, or by separate court order.

DONE AND ORDERED this April 11, 2022, in West Palm Beach, Palm Beach County, Florida.

Honorable Renatha Francis

Circuit Court Judge

What accomplished this? Was it every effort I put forth? Was it being the tenacious asshole that I became with my actions up to filing a formal complaint? Was it merely Robert Bertisch's phone call? As blown away as I was when I read the order, it couldn't be anywhere near the surprise Hanrahan and Maureen got. What about Anne Alper? How flabbergasted was she when she read the order? All I could think of was "The power of the pen is mighty." With that thought in my head, I immediately drafted the following letter to the judge, copied Robert Bertisch, Hanrahan, and filed it on the case docket:

Dear Judge Francis:

I am in receipt of your Order dated April 11, 2022. I would like to take this opportunity to thank you for obviously looking into the extensive case history in order to have it weigh in on your decision to appoint the Legal Aid Society's Juvenile Advocacy Project to represent mine and Mrs. Graves' daughter in this matter.

While it has never been about winning, my objective has/ and continues to remain fighting for our daughter's right to a loving relationship with both of her parents, against an extremely well-financed estrangement/alienation campaign. I am propitious that in the capable hands of the Juvenile

Advocacy Project that Robert Bertisch has so kindly committed to this case, that those involved will uncover the contemptuous environment of the estrangement campaign that our daughter has endured for over 14 years and will give her some relief after such a long and exhausting time of it and perhaps may know that it is okay to love her dad as opposed to aligning herself with the objectives of the campaign because it is just easier.

I would like to ask that those involved include former teachers and school guidance counselors of our daughter in their investigation. Thank you again for taking such a close examination into this case.

Sincerely,

David Graves

That letter was deliberately written to contain the double intention of giving testimony, and there wasn't a thing Hanrahan could do about it.

At the time of the publishing of this book, four months later, there is still no Attorney ad litem assigned to this case.

CHAPTER 11

The Guardian ad Litems

" The virtues are lost in self-interest as rivers are lost in the sea. "
Franklin D. Roosevelt

Family Law attorney, **Marina Petillo,** was Mr. Hanrahan's first attempt at a court appointed, paid guardian ad litem. The estrangement campaign had been pretty much spinning its wheels with attorney Burdick for years now, and with an endless war chest full of money, attorney Michael Hanrahan went right to work when he took the case to represent Maureen starting on May 19, 2016. He began by compiling a team of hired guns to assist with his client's objective of an estrangement campaign. With the availability of an endless supply of financial backing, Hanrahan dug in and recruited a paid guardian ad litem and a forensic psychiatrist that specializes in expert court testimony. I was a pro se litigant at this point and still had scheduled times with Katie, including overnights.

On May 19, 2016, Mr. Hanrahan filed a Motion to Enjoin Former Husband from Interfering with Minor Child's Therapy. This motion laid the groundwork for forensic psychiatrist, Michael O'Hara to begin his hired gun "Kids for Cash" involvement culminating in his testimony at a future hearing as an expert witness.

The first attempt at a guardian ad litem was in Maureen's Motion to Appoint Guardian ad Litem, filed by her attorney on May 24, 2016. The attorney selected for the appointment of guardian ad litem was Marina Petillo. After a failed attempt by Mr. Hanrahan to manipulate the court's scheduling system— and being reprimanded by Judge Suskauer on July 13, 2016 for doing so—the motion to appoint Ms. Petillo was later granted by the court as the minor child's guardian ad litem on July 28, 2016.

I made multiple attempts to set an appointment to meet with Ms. Petillo, but was unable to get on the schedule. On August 19, 2016, I finally sent Petillo a letter with the intention of introducing myself and giving my accounts of the circumstances of the case *(Fig 1)*. To maintain transparency, I copied the following people:

- Honorable Judge Scott Suskauer, 15th Circuit Superior Court Judge
- Senator Maria Sachs, Florida State Senator District 34
- Senator Jeff Clemens, Florida State Senator District 27
- Dennis Miles, Southeast Regional Managing Director, Florida Dept. of Children and Families
- Honorable Governor Rick Scott
- Dr. Richard A. Warshak
- Ryan Thomas, Adult child of Parental Alienation
- Terri Parker, Investigative Reporter, ABC News, West Palm Beach, FL

On September 4, 2016, Ms. Petillo declined her appointment by the court *(Fig 2)*. This infuriated Hanrahan. He immediately contacted my newly hired attorney, Steven Cripps, and contended that I harassed Ms. Petillo *(Fig 3)*. My attorney forwarded Hanrahan's email to me. The next time I saw Mr. Cripps, he told me that in 35 years he had never seen anything done by a client like my letter to Marina Petillo. A letter. Yes, a letter that is available as a public filing and can be accessed and read by anyone with a computer—or a copy of this book. This letter had such an effect that Ms. Petillo walked away from tens of thousands of dollars because of it (Filing #664 and read by Judge Suskauer on 08/19/2016). The email from Hanrahan to my attorney, Steven Cripps, on September 6, 2016 stated:

> As you know, Marina Petillo has declined to accept the appointment as GAL on this case. Ms. Petillo called me last week to tell me that her decision was made subsequent to her receiving a rather disturbing letter from your client, David Graves.

David A.

August 6, 2016

Marina D. Petillo

Re:
      Case No. 502009DR010788XXXXMBFC

Dear Attorney Petillo:

As you are surely aware by now, my former wife's (⬛⬛⬛⬛) counsel, Mr. Michael Hanrahan, has motioned the court for your inclusion as Guardian ad Litem in our now eight year litigation involving timesharing of our daughter, ⬛⬛. It is my understanding that you will be reviewing the circumstances and looking for solutions to suggest to The Court, moving forward. Please find this letter for information purposes for your research.

I would like to start with myself. Though I made contributions to the demise of our marriage, my role as a father to my daughter has been nothing of what Mrs. ⬛⬛ has, and continues to spend tens of thousands of dollars to attempt to discredit.

After three attempts at in-vetro fertilization and one miscarriage, ⬛⬛⬛⬛ and I have a beautiful daughter, ⬛⬛ Mrs. ⬛⬛ knew that I would be a good father or she never would have gone through with what we did to have a child with me. After the miscarriage and the third attempt, I pushed my wife in a wheelchair for full term, nine months. I love my daughter and Mrs. ⬛⬛ knows it. In spite of what she maliciously does to hurt our relationship, when the day comes that ⬛⬛ shares her resentment for being used to hurt me, I have told Mrs. ⬛⬛ that I will not be a part of having peace with a daughter in society that resents her mother and I will stand by that.

I am a certified Little League umpire by their official standards of their Williamsport, Pennsylvania organization headquarters and oversee hundreds of children in Little League Baseball play. I assure you that organization headquarters and oversee hundreds of children in Little League Baseball play. I assure you that my leadership skills, team building, and fair play qualifications are that of children first. In my second year (2014), I am extremely proud to say that I was asked to umpire the regional finals in East Boynton Beach. Home of the 2003 Little League World Series Champions. My actions on the field, often times with challenges of coaches and parents who sometimes lose the focus on what is important can be attested to by any board member of the West Boynton Beach Little League, where I am based. I am able to furnish those contacts if you are interested.

████ and I have been attending church for the eight years since the divorce. She has a Christian foundation with our membership at church. It is the only regimented, religious foundation that she is exposed to.

I have coached girls' softball. I have coached girls' basketball. I have played team sports every year since the age of eight, and I know the importance of bringing a team together, to achieve a common goal. That includes knowing how to lose as well as win as a team and do both graciously. You see, I find it incredibly ironic that I am found to be qualified to oversee hundreds of children, yet in the murky waters of family court, I have such a challenge taking a vacation with my own daughter.

In the unlikely event that DCF ever finds itself with a low caseload, I can assure you that they may find evidence for new ones at any local children's sporting event, but I digress.

Speaking on our own daughter's participation in sports, my former wife has publically behaved in a less than appropriate fashion that can be attested by many people. One of which was a complete stranger and she literally walked up to me and handed me her number and said, "Call me," "I saw the whole thing." That woman was Lynn Lester, who was deposed by counsel on May 24, 2013 and is in our case file, as well as attached.

I am able to furnish you with other people's contact information if you are in fact interested in actual accounts of actual events and circumstances, with actual people who stood to gain nothing by way of revenue or "professional findings", but by their eyewitness accounts of my former wife's inappropriate public displays. All of which have occurred in front of our daughter, as well as other children.

Please be advised of the one that took place two months after the divorce at a baseball field on February 14, 2011. I was in attendance, as was Mrs.████'s mother at████'s tee ball practice. It took her a long time to realize that I was there, but when she saw me, Mrs.████'s mother called 911 and a sheriff's deputy arrived shortly thereafter. The deputy came over to me and told me of the situation and told me that everything was fine and to just stay away from my former mother in law.

Obviously not pleased with the outcome, about fifteen minutes later, Mrs.████ arrived with a copy of the divorce decree and proceeded to read it at the top of her lungs to a bleacher full of parents. The display not only got the attention of the parents, but the coaches and children as well. Mrs.████ closed her presentation with "He goes to AA." "Do you want him around your children?" I can't imagine what was going on in our daughter's mind.

In the eight years since our divorce, my former wife has attempted five (5) No Contact Orders on me, three (3) Department of Children and Family investigations, and one (1) formal charge of assault.

- Not one, No Contact Order was found to have evidence and all were dismissed.
- In spite of the obvious over time coercion by Mrs.████ of our daughter found within her statements while being interviewed by investigators, not one DCF investigation has yielded me being a danger to our daughter or Mrs.████.

Thankfully they were able to see the obvious. One DCF investigator told me that my former wife isn't in his report. He told me that he wasn't allowed to. I have asked that the DCF investigation reports be included in court proceedings, but I have been told that they are "hearsay". I would venture to say that they would have made their way to the courtroom if the findings were contrary.

- Thankfully by the advice of my attorney and countless allegations by my former wife, I was video recording every child exchange when Mrs.████ accused me of hitting her in August of 2013. That video file was sent to State's Attorney, Dave Aronberg and the assault charge was dropped.

I am certain you will be provided a copy of a final psychological report by Dr. Kristin Tolbert. What you will not be provided is the "rough draft" that took the better part of six months for Dr. Tolbert to complete before sending her "rough draft" with mistakes and inaccuracies, including my name (Mr. Bean), who I was married to, and text message references from my former wife to me, that Dr. Tolbert referred to as me sending them to Mrs. ███. What Dr. Tolbert was able to accomplish by doing this was that she was able to have her report proofread by any of the recipients (including Mrs. ███) and correct her erroneous mistakes before sending "her" final report to the court. Text messages that she referred to as being inappropriate by me simply vanished from her report subsequent to the opportunity for proofreaders to correct her rough draft. I am certainly able to provide you with this chain of emails with their attachments to validate this fact.

I have asked my former wife to provide me with a copy of the medical insurance card that covers our daughter in the event of a medical emergency while in my care. This is not the first time that this has occurred, but her former attorney was able to provide my former attorney with the (now expired) card. She and current counsel, Mr. Hanrahan have chosen to go a different route subsequent to my request for our daughter's current proof of insurance. This time the response to asking for an insurance card and what doctors our daughter is seeing, is a Motion to Enjoin Former Husband from Interfering from Minor Child's Therapy. I'd like to address the "interfering" example, specifically mentioned in that motion.

In December of 2011, my daughter, ███ told me that her mom was taking her to see "Miss Ashley" who "just wants to know my business." I looked for a child psychologist in Wellington by the first name of "Ashley" and found Ashlee Comeau, Counselor, MS, LMHC. I called her on January 3, 2012. During that lengthy phone conversation, Ms Comeau told me that she was "having trouble getting through to ███." I asked her if she thought co-parenting counselling would help. After Ms Comeau contacted my former wife, Mrs. ███ voluntarily agreed to go. We continued to go weekly until May 2012 with positive steps forward to some civility. That's five months of weekly co-parenting therapy. The sessions abruptly ceased after Ms Comeau suggested in session that Mrs. ███'s parents be included in some future sessions.

In spite of licensing laws for length of time to keep patient records, I have in writing from Ms Comeau that she does not have ours, as well as five months' worth of email correspondence with her during the co-parenting counseling period.

Medically speaking, I'd like to address our daughter's prescription eyeglasses.

It was just before all communications between Mrs. ███ and myself came to a complete stop in 2014. Mrs. ███ called me and told me that ███ needed prescription eyeglasses. My first thought was that I was sad that our daughter needed glasses. My second thought was that I heard our daughter say numerous times that she wished that she had eyeglasses. Similarly, she has expressed her intrigue for a cast and crutches as well. I suggested that Mrs. ███ a second opinion. She refused and told me how competent she was to make this decision on her own. Although ultimately getting the eyeglasses and refusing to allow our daughter to bring them to my home, claiming to our daughter that I would "steal them", I now know from my daughter that she lied about what she could see during the exam to acquire the glasses in the first place that she thought she wanted. I'm not sure of what the truth is at this point. I am curious if our daughter required medication if Mrs. ███ would allow it to come to my home after refusing to allow the prescription eyeglasses to be at my home. If you are interested, our daughter's third grade teacher, Mrs. Moore could be of assistance with a better understanding of that particular eyeglass issue as Mrs. ███ verbally assaulted her in an email regarding her opinion on the matter.

Also medically speaking, I'd like to bring up a dentist appointment that our daughter asked me to go to while she had a procedure done. She wanted me to be there because she was "afraid". Mrs. ███ refused to tell me the name of the dentist in spite of the court order of my having access to our daughter's medical providers. My daughter told me that the office had a lot of "trains" in it. I found the "Train Dentist" and went to the office after they told me the appointment time. After I arrived at the dentist, the office called Mrs. ███ to inform her that I was there for our daughter. Mrs. ███ called her father who was literally in route to taking ███ to the dentist. He turned the car around with our anxious daughter on board and didn't go to the appointment.

In my research, I have found the term for what the claim of me being an alienator is, while the contrary is reality. It is called "Freudian Projection". It is the opposite defense mechanism to identification and my former wife finds it imperative to maintain it.

Thank you for your time in reading my letter. I hope you are able and willing to use all resources available to you for a full comprehensive understanding of the circumstances. Please feel free to contact me regarding any information for contacts or otherwise.

Respectfully,

David ▉▉▉▉▉

Copies:

Honorable Judge Scott Suskauer, 15th Circuit Superior Court Judge
Senator Maria Sachs, Florida State Senator District 34
Senator Jeff Clemens, Florida State Senator District 27
Dennis Miles, Southeast Regional Managing Director, Florida Dept. of Children and Families
Honorable Governor Rick Scott
Dr. Richard A. Warshak
Ryan Thomas, Adult child of Parental Alienation
Terri Parker, Investigative Reporter, ABC News, West Palm Beach, FL

Filing # 46048281 E-Filed 09/04/2016 01:01:49 PM

IN THE CIRCUIT COURT OF THE FIFTEENTH JUDICIAL CIRCUIT, IN AND FOR PALM BEACH COUNTY, FLORIDA

IN RE: THE FORMER MARRIAGE OF

DAVID ▉▉▉

    Former Husband,

CASE NO.2009 DR-010788 MB FC

Family Law Division

and

▉▉▉▉▉▉,

    Former WIFE.
_____/

NOTICE OF NON-ACCEPTANCE

PLEASE TAKE NOTICE that MARINA D. PETILLO, the undersigned, was appointed as Guardian ad Litem for the minor child in this matter. MARINA D. PETILLO is declining the appointment as Guardian ad Litem.

CERTIFICATE OF SERVICE

I HEREBY CERTIFY that a true and correct copy of the foregoing is being furnished by e-portal to everyone on the service list on the 4th day of September 2016.

MARINAD. PETILLO, ESQ
▉▉▉▉▉▉▉▉

BY: /s/
MARINA D. PETILLO
Florida Bar ▉▉▉▉

From: Michael Hanrahan [mailto:██████████████████]
Sent: Tuesday, September 06, 2016 10:46 AM
To: Steven Cripps
Cc: ██████████
Subject: ████████████

Mr. Cripps

As you know, Marina Petillo has declined to accept the appointment as GAL on this case. Ms. Petillo called me last week to tell me that her decision was made subsequent to her receiving a rather disturbing letter from your client, David ████████ In addition to this letter sent to Ms. Petillo, your client send disturbing text messages to my client on Sunday immediately after Ms. Petillo filed her notice of not accepting the appointment which can only be interpreted as harassment and designed to place undue influence and anguish on my client.

Please immediately forward to me a copy of the letter that your client sent to Ms. Petillo. This letter is discoverable and by not providing it immediately, you and your client are simply requiring us to incur additional attorney fees and costs to obtain this document. I will be filing a Request to Produce and a Motion to Shorten Time to Respond to the Request today but will wait until tomorrow to set the matter for a hearing, giving you adequate time to send the letter to me without the need to set a court hearing.

Finally, I will be filing a Motion to Enjoin your client from harassing my client through text messages, or any other means. Your client's actions are unnecessary, disturbing and must stop immediately.

Michael R. Hanrahan, Esq.
Michael R. Hanrahan, P.A.
████████████████
West Palm Beach, FL 33401
███████████

So when reading the letter, in what sense is it "rather disturbing"? Did I threaten Ms. Petillo, make her accountable, draw too much attention to her inclusion as a paid guardian ad litem making it easier to simply walk away from the case, or something else? Petillo gave no reason for declining the appointment in her filed submission to the court on September 4, 2016. My guess is that she felt she would be held accountable; she didn't run from my letter; she ran from the implied accountability because of the people I copied.

Additionally, notice that, according to his email, Mr. Hanrahan received a phone call from Ms. Petillo prior to her declining the appointment. Why? Why would one attorney receive a phone call and not the other as well? It's a simple show of collusion. A posse. A "Dream Team" focused on the objective of achieving the common goal of alienating me from my child. This is the remarkable—yet never addressed—truth that makes any hearing the "hired gun" scenario that it is. When the "Dream Team" was finally coordinated and the players were ultimately in place, I referred to them as "The Collusive Coercives."

Remarkably, 11-year-old Katie came to me after Ms. Petillo declined the appointment by the court. She told me that she wanted an attorney of her own and asked me why I would keep that from happening. Obviously, she had been told by her mother that what I did resulted in attorney Petillo's declining. This indicated that Katie continued to be informed of the process as circumstances unfolded, but that she was getting a very skewed version of events. My problem then, as now and possibly always, is to correct the misinformation without implying that her mother lied to her on purpose. This is the difficulty divorced or divorcing parents must struggle with every day: How to convey the truth without confusing the child or setting the child up to choose between her parents.

Anne Alper was next. Lilith, according to Jewish scholars, was the first creation of God, first wife of Adam, and now rules beside Satan. She is known as sheer evil that walks among us, "Stealing the lives of children represents a certain madness that accompanies her solitude and exclusion." I believe Lilith channels strongly through attorney Anne Alper. Lilith is most recently depicted in our popular culture as Mary Wardwell in "Chilling Adventures of Sabrina." Anne Alper was Michael Hanrahan's second, more successful attempt to get the court to appoint a guardian ad litem after his embarrassment in front of Judge Suskauer and my letter to Marina Petillo.

Subsequent to Ms. Petillo declining her appointment, Mr. Hanrahan filed another motion #703 Motion for Appointment of New Guardian ad Litem [filed by respondent] on March 21, 2017, requesting Ms. Anne Alper from Fort Lauderdale to be appointed. The appointment was cleared on August 23, 2018. One of the absolute paramount stipulations of this court-ordered appointment was that Ms. Alper would be permitted to use hearsay testimony. It was, basically, a license to lie.

My first encounter with the new guardian ad litem was at a scheduled first meeting at Panera Bread. After the initial hellos, I sat down, and Ms. Alper began to tell me about herself, including that she was previously a psychologist. She said that her friends convinced her to go for a law degree later on. She also claimed on her website to have been a psychologist. I then told Ms. Alper that I wanted to audio record our initial conversation and asked her if she minded me doing so. She asked why I would want to record our conversation, and I told her that I did not want my words to be manipulated as had happened with this case over the last ten years. Ms. Alper replied that she would not give her permission for me to record our conversation because she had previously been the victim of someone who only played a portion of a recording, which gave a poor impression of her. She suggested that if I insisted on having a record of our conversation that I have a court reporter present. I agreed to this, even though it would result in having to spend more money! After all, we must get as many of the people in the system paid as possible. At this point, Ms. Alper excused herself and left Panera Bread. I stayed behind and ordered my dinner.

A week later, we met at a court reporting agency and had our official initial interview. Anne Alper speaks in a high-pitched, melodic tone, as if she has developed a type of delivery that conveys sincerity along with an easy listening tone. She portrayed a "kids first" intent and referenced her dedication and her years of service in doing so. A real master of "the interview" is Ms. Anne Alper. As I listened to her well-practiced introduction, I heard more evidence of an attorney speaking rather than an advocate for children. I realized I was already anticipating what I would be dealing with regarding Anne Alper's inclusion in our case. I wasn't wrong.

I did a web search on Anne Alper. I found the usual praises and complaints. Basically, the parental winners and losers during her tenure as the "Kids for Cash" hired gun that she is. Most remarkably, I found an article written by Bob Whitby, titled "Guardian ad Chargem," in which Ms. Alper was featured as the hired gun that I suspected. The specific case referenced in the article was Gumberg vs. Gumberg, referenced as "The grand-daddy of all guardian ad litem bills." To date, and per her sub-poenaed invoices, Anne Alper has been paid over $200,000.00 for her services in our court case.

Next, there was Anne Alper's public Facebook page. It was all about the wonderful do-gooder that Anne Alper works hard to convey. In going through her Facebook "Likes," Ms. Alper includes, "Dear God, please help me from slapping an idiot today, Amen." I printed a screenshot of this and other examples of what I found to be behavior unbecoming an officer of the court. I later showed these to Judge Sarah Willis and stated that Facebook Likes and posts are in the sole control of the account holder. Ms. Alper subsequently wrote and filed a Status Update on June 25, 2019 (Filing #91600896) stating "Father hacked into the guardian ad litem's Facebook private account" and referred to me as a "potential danger" when I questioned such behavior of hers needing to pray in order to not slap an idiot today. Keep in mind that Ms. Alper's Facebook page was public.

She immediately removed the controversial "Like" and then made her entire Facebook page private. I suppose I assisted her in cleaning up her public profile. I also filed a Rip-off Report including the screen shot as well posting it to her claimed Yelp page, accompanied by a review, which are both currently still accessible online.

Katie and I had been having daily phone calls on the days

that I didn't see her. This all started when she was in first grade after an incident in which Katie got out of her chair in class and went out into the hallway to see what was going on. She wasn't a bad kid, just curious. Nevertheless, her actions disrupted the class, so the school called for a parent-teacher meeting. Maureen did not attend. It was suggested by Katie's teacher that Katie speak with me daily to go over the day's events. This kept Katie accountable to me, and she never really had any more behavior issues like that again.

It was great that we spoke every day, and Judge Suskauer praised the fact that we spoke daily when it came up in open court. Anne Alper didn't appear at any hearing until after Judge Suskauer was no longer presiding over our case. Alper contended in one of her "Status Reports" that I bullied Katie and imposed "consequences" on her if we did not speak. What she didn't include was what those consequences were to be. They were no desert if we didn't speak one day, no television if we didn't speak for two consecutive days, and grounded for the weekend if we didn't speak for three consecutive days. We never went past one day of not speaking, and I listened to her reason, which was usually the same reasonable explanation for a child, "I forgot. I'm sorry." No consequences of any kind were ever enforced.

Alper habitually contended, "the minor child was very upset." She would begin any story of what she had found by utilizing the alarming remark of Katie being upset. Some stood out to me more than others simply because they were so completely erroneous. The absolute favorite of mine was when I gave Katie a Saint Michael pendant in a velvet jewelry pouch with a drawstring. The pouch was three inches square. Alper testified under oath to Judge Willis, that Katie was extremely upset because her father gave her the pendant in a gun pouch. Yes, a gun pouch. As in a gun that shoots bullets. I stood up in open court, pointed at Alper, and addressed the court, saying, "She's lying!" Judge

Willis told me that I would have the opportunity to cross-examine, but how do you "un-hear" that? You don't. All one remembers is the word "gun." It's even more ridiculous than a judge instructing a jury to, "disregard the last remark." Put simply, Alper is a paid liar and knows it.

In my hearing before Magistrate Williams for Maureen being in contempt, Alper referenced a comic strip that I texted to Katie. The single strip was an alleyway with Mr. Clean and Scrubbing Bubbles facing Pigpen from Peanuts fame. Alper visibly struggled to understand whether I was trying to convey a joke to Katie. She claimed Katie was upset over the comic strip that said under the cartoon, "Mr. Clean and Scrubbing Bubbles knew this was no ordinary opponent." As if I was implying support of alleyway violence or something. Alper spoke at what I thought to be a great length of time over this comic strip. At one point, I objected on relevance. The objection was overruled. I followed up with telling the magistrate on record that if Alper found my text messages to be inappropriate to my daughter, there was a procedure for filing a motion to change the order. I further pointed out that we were here on the matter of contempt for phone calls not taking place, and this testimony and argument in no way purges my former wife of that claim. On her website, she claimed to be a "former psychologist." So, under my cross-examination, I asked Ms. Alper if she was ever a licensed psychologist in any state in the country. Her answer was "No because she was a psychologist before a license was required." Sometime after I posed that question in open court, her claim of being a psychologist was removed from her website.

The court appointed Laura Melvin as family therapist, later renamed as reunification therapist because of Maureen's insistence of non-involvement. Laura Melvin stressed in her testimony to the court full transparency for all parties if she were appointed. In support of that, she notified me of an upcoming meeting with Anne Alper. I sat in the waiting room with Alper to attend the meeting. Ms. Melvin seemed to be a great candidate for the position, but when Alper got up from her waiting room chair, she informed me that I was not to attend. That meeting Alper had with Laura Melvin completely changed Melvin's demeanor and her attitude towards me. This shows that Alper is indeed a manipulator. She filed a status report and included my presence as if it were a threat that left her feeling endangered. I knew she would pull some sort of stunt and report something dishonest to the court, so I went right back to my office, punched my time clock to show the duration of time that had elapsed from the time I left the building to my drive back to work.

On December 18, 2019, I received an email from Alper. She wanted to speak with Dr. Rathjens. The exact content of the letter was:

Hi David,

I hope all is well with you during this holiday season!

As you know, I plan to submit the Guardian ad Litem Report at the end of the month.

Would you please send the name and phone number of your therapist and sign a release of information so I may ask the following:

- Do you attend the sessions on a consistent basis, and when you began to use his services?

- Does he think that you follow through with his recommendations?

- Does he see any reason to believe that you are presently a danger to your daughter, emotionally or physically?

From that email, I assumed that was all Alper intended to

accomplish from the phone call. Following his favorable answers of me to her questions, Dr. Rathjens told me that Alper said, "I have concerns…" and proceeded to talk for 40 minutes. The next time I had a session with him, Dr. Rathjens spoke to me as if I had been lying to him in sessions for years. I was dumbfounded and felt betrayed. I suppose that he felt lied to because of whatever it was that Alper said to him. I decided that if he didn't trust what I had talked to him about and believed that I had been dishonest with him, then I wouldn't see him as my therapist any longer. In retrospect, I believe that is exactly what Alper intended. After a short break, I went back to sessions with Dr. Rathjens, and I continue to see him today. The fact that Alper even duped my own therapist shows that she is an expert at what she actually does for a living, which is only to lie and manipulate on behalf of whoever is paying her check.

As I prepared for the trial on Maureen's Petition for Modification, I subpoenaed the videos that she had been taking of me at Katie's soccer games. She would display the obvious by holding her cellphone with her outstretched arm so I could see that she was either video recording me or just pretending to. This was also clearly visible to anyone else who looked at her. I wondered how it didn't embarrass her to act this way in public.

The only video that was produced in response to that subpoena came from Alper. The video was taken immediately after Katie's team lost a tournament championship on a penalty kick with only a couple of minutes remaining in the game. It was a heartbreaking loss for the girls. Maureen videoed Katie and I walking from the game to my car; she used the same obvious and obnoxious pose of holding her phone out with her outstretched arm. I think that was the only video I spoke in. As we got to Maureen, I stopped and told her to put the phone away and asked if she thought Katie wanted to endure this kind of nonsense at her soccer games. She didn't stop. In fact, as we passed her, she followed us, continuing to record us walking. Noticing that she was following us, I turned around and Katie followed. The look on Katie's face when she looked at her mother told me how irritated she was at this behavior.

I incorporated the incident within Alper's segment because this video-recorded incident never made it on any of Alper's status reports, and I knew perfectly well that she saw it because she was the one who sent it to me. Alper also never reported the incident in which Katie broke her toe at the Orlando tournament but Maureen refused to take Katie to the hospital for an x-ray. One would think that seeking a medical diagnosis and treatment subsequent to sustaining an injury was in Katie's best interest. I sent Alper the video of Maureen insisting Katie remain in the game prior to getting an x-ray just to undermine me. That incident never appeared in any of Alper's reports either. Alper's modus operandi was simple. She was paid by Maureen to depict me as a monster, so she simply stated multiple times that Katie was "terrified" of me.

Alper filed a Motion to Withdraw and Replace Guardian ad Litem on March 28, 2022, citing that I threatened her repeatedly and it was the advice of the bar that she withdraw from the case. Within her filing, she named two specific attorneys to be her successor. The details of that motion are written in the previous chapter, *The Judges, Judge Renatha Francis.*

CHAPTER 12

The Incidentals

66 *For evil to flourish,*
it only requires good men to do nothing. 99
Simon Wiesenthal

Patrick Zoete is the director of coaching of the Wellington Wave Soccer Club in Wellington, Florida. Katie had taken to the sport of soccer after a year of recreational soccer, and while she and I were at the fields one day, someone who was affiliated with the Wave Soccer Club offered her a tryout. I was a little worried since the offer came while Katie was with me. This, historically, was a sure way for Maureen not to support it. Nevertheless, Katie got her tryout. Of course, Maureen didn't let me know when the tryout was; I ascertained the information from the club's website.

It was quite a large event with dozens of kids from around eight to eighteen years old. I hung in the background and watched from afar. The website had a sign-in for parents to follow practice and game schedules. I asked a man wearing a Wave shirt how I could get information on scheduling without a sign-in account. The man pointed to a group of four men walking between the fields holding the tryouts and told me to talk with Patrick. I walked over to the group of men, introduced myself, and asked which one was Patrick. Patrick Zoete spoke up with a European accent. I told him that I wanted to obtain a parental sign-in ability on the website. Patrick Zoete's next words were a loud exclamation, "Oh! You're the guy!" This put together the pieces of a prejudice I've observed in people many times. I knew that Maureen had already planted the proverbial land mines before Katie even made the team; the fix was in against dad, and negative attention was already drawn to Katie.

Patrick spoke extensively about how my ex-wife instructed club personnel not to divulge any information to me, whatsoever. "Would you like to see the court orders that state otherwise?" I asked the group of men. They agreed to look at the documents, and this is why I keep copies on my cell phone for just such situations.

Once they understood the situation, Patrick gave me an email address for a woman who would furnish me with the instructions on how to get into the website for practice and game schedules.

Regardless of the negative attention it brought to Katie, Maureen continued to work on anyone who would buy into her side of our over-a-decade-ago divorce story. Maureen's philosophy is simple: You are either "with her" or "against her." If you choose to be friendly towards me, she takes that as a sure sign that you are against her. Since she had the power to remove Katie from any particular program, which meant revenue loss for any particular proprietor, people tended to side with her, that is, to keep the revenue rather than risk losing it. While this is a cunning and calculated approach, I'm sure it has to be exhausting. Parental alienation can be quite time consuming, and the family court enables the process and ignores the results.

As expected, Patrick started to show signs of his favoritism towards Maureen. He had a talk with me about my cheering and claimed that I was coaching from the sidelines. Since I knew that I never gave direction to any team or player, I could see where this would lead. I told Patrick that moving forward I would wear an audio recording device during each game, and if he thought that I was being inappropriate in my behavior at any game, he could let me know exactly when it happened so I could refer back to the recording at the section in which it occurred. I further told him that all of our future conversations would be recorded as well, and he could take this notice as an agreement.

As promised, I used the recording application on my cell phone and kept my phone in my shirt pocket during games. After a game, I uploaded the audio file to my computer, dated it, and deleted it from my phone to save storage space. At no time afterwards did Patrick Zoete claim that my cheering was inappropriate, nor were there any further "talks." My daughter just wanted to play soccer, and this mania continued the whole time.

Craig Mullings was a parent of a player on Katie's Wellington Wave Soccer team, and he was also the team manager. His managerial duties included bringing the shade cover for the team bench, sending text messages to parents for any game or practice schedule changes, and planning team bonding get-togethers during far away tournaments. While Katie was participating in the Wellington Soccer program, the team registered for a huge tournament in Walt Disney World. The block of housing rentals for the girls and their families were 2- and 3-bedroom townhouses. This was an exorbitant affair. Playing at the ESPN Wide World of Sports facility, the fanfare was quite the scene. Thousands of players and their families from around the world came together for this event.

Unfortunately, Katie injured her big toe during her first game and limped off the field as the game ended. The tournament had trainers everywhere for injured players, so I took Katie to a trainer's table for advice and treatment. Instead of examining her toe, the trainer told us to see how it feels in the morning and to go for x-rays if it is still bad then.

I realize now that I should have taken her to the emergency

room immediately. Katie went back to her mother at 6 P.M., per the timesharing order, so the morning decision was up to Maureen. Maureen decided Katie could play with her team as scheduled the next morning.

I was watching the game through my binoculars and saw Katie limping all over the field. She was obviously injured and in pain. I watched as she was removed from the contest and taken to the team manager, Craig Mullings, and he taped her toe. When Craig came over to address some parents' concerns, I approached him about what I had seen. The conversation did not go well, so I turned on my video recording device. The transcript conveys an awkward sounding conversation, but it was a tense situation, which was not helped when Craig just kept repeating himself over and over. The video dialogue from May 27, 2018 is verbatim as follows and ends with Maureen's remarkable objective at the end to simply undermine me regardless of Katie's well-being:

Mr. Mullings: You knew there was an issue before she got on the field, right?

Mr. Graves: I didn't have her last night. My question to you is clear. Do you have a degree in sports medicine to tape athletes?

Mr. Mullings: When you ask me that question, my question for you is, I can have a trainer go over there and look at her foot. Is that what you prefer?

Mr. Graves: There you go!

Mr. Mullings: Is that what you prefer?

Mr. Graves: There you go!

Mr. Mullings: Is that what you prefer?

Mr. Graves: Yes, yes.

Mr. Mullings: Is that what you prefer? You want me to take her out of the game and have a trainer look at her right now?

Mr. Graves: A trainer is to come over and see her foot right now.

Mr. Mullings: Would you prefer that right now?

Mr. Graves: That's what *has* to be done. You can't...

Mr. Mullings: No, no, would you prefer that? That's what I'm asking you. You're saying that's what *has* to be done.

Mr. Graves to Mrs. Graves: He's taping up players, and he's not qualified to do so.

Mr. Mullings: Hold on a second, you're walking away, and we're having a conversation.

Mr. Graves: I'm done with the conversation, Craig. You have no qualifications to tape up any player.

Mr. Mullings: She's not injured to the point where she's coming out of the game.

Mr. Graves: You still have no qualifications to tape any athlete, Craig. You don't.

Mr. Mullings: We're not even having a conversation.

Mr. Graves: You don't.

Mr. Mullings: We're not even having a conversation.

Mr. Graves: You don't. You're going to put yourself liable for taping up players. That's not your call. They have trainers out here.

Mr. Mullings to Mrs. Graves: Let me have a conversation with you. Your daughter was not injured to the point where she's coming out of the game. All I did was offer to put tape on it to reduce the (@ Mr. Graves) *sensitivity*, because for...

Mr. Graves: You're opening yourself up to liability for taping ANY athlete up. I'm telling you that as...

Mr. Mullings: Ok, fair enough, but just for your information, ok, she wasn't complaining about coming out of the game. She said her big toe is sensitive. I asked, I offered to put tape on it…

Mr. Graves: I understand that Craig.

Mr. Mullings: …so it's not as sensitive.

Mr. Graves: I understand that Craig. The point is, you can't be treating any athlete, not just my kid…*any* athlete.

Mr. Mullings: If you don't want her in the game, and you don't want…

Mr. Graves: That's not what I said. They have trainers here to take care of that. We paid money to come here to get these services.

Mr. Mullings: That's why I'm asking you, do you want a trainer to go look at her?

Mr. Graves: I said yes twice already.

Mr. Mullings: No, you didn't answer my question clearly, that why I was asking.

Mr. Graves: YES! Is that clear?

Mr. Mullings: Ok, good enough. I will have the coach remove her and have a trainer come and look at her.

Mrs. Graves: No, no, no, no, no, no, no, no she is not getting removed from the game.

Mr. Graves: He's making it something…

Mr. Mullings: No, you're making it something that it isn't, and I want to make sure we're clear since you're recording this conversation without my consent and my permission and my knowledge, we'll make it very simple. Thank you.

Mr. Graves: You're welcome.

Craig Mullings walks away. Mrs. Graves follows him to team bench. Katie is seen by a trainer, and it is advised that she be removed pending an x-ray.

I saw the Wellington Wave director of coaches, Patrick Zoete, and Mario Rodrigues, vice president of the Wellington Wave girls program, walking together at the event. I told them about what happened with Katie's injury. Patrick asked me what I wanted them to do. I answered that I wanted them to do whatever it was that they felt appropriate as officials of the league.

Later in the day, an x-ray confirmed Katie's big toe was indeed broken.

Mario Rodrigues was the vice president of the Wellington Wave girl's program. The way Patrick and Mario walked around together at the fields reminded me of Scut Farkus and his "toady" pal Grover Dill from *A Christmas Story*. Mario became a victim to Maureen's manipulation techniques; she was like a magpie landing on his shoulder and repeatedly squawking into his ear. The two of them were seen together talking at games multiple times prior to the day Mario approached me to say that Katie is welcome to continue in the program, but I was not.

Thirteen days after the incident of the big toe, on June 9, 2018, I received the following in an email from Mario Rodrigues:

> The only way for Katie to continue with our club is without your involvement. If you are willing to not be in attendance for her games or practices, we can provide a place for Katie to continue her promising playing career at Wellington.

My response was:

> No. Not agreed. Your program is below the standards of what I find to be in the development and safety of my daughter. In addition, as you know, Katie was treated medically by Craig Mullings and sent back into play with a fractured big toe.

Katie and I were still relatively close at this time, so Katie was no happier about this than I was. In addition to the drama her mother was creating, Katie had trouble with her coach Mike

Plummer who actually grabbed her head and squeezed it during a practice. So, when Coach Maria invited her to join the Royal Palm Beach Strikers Soccer Club, Katie was glad to accept. Coach Maria approached me at a tournament they hosted and asked if I was "#88's dad." It was nice to hear from an opposing coach that they thought so much of my daughter's abilities. This is why, thanks mostly to her mother's efforts, Katie left the Wellington Wave Soccer Program.

Colin Beneby is truly a trifling participant, yet his non-actions as a process server contribute to the corruption within the system. Mr. Beneby is listed as a certified process server for the Fifteenth Circuit of Palm Beach County Courts. His father had passed away, and Colin somehow went through a process to carry on his father's business. I used both Colin and his father for serving my subpoenas, so I knew the difference between the two as far as integrity goes. Colin's father actually served the documents in a timely manner, while Colin once took three weeks to unsuccessfully serve one document for me. Ironically, opposing counsel (Hanrahan) also used Colin Beneby. I had never been served a Petition for Modification, and I testified to that at a court hearing. Opposing counsel returned later with a "Proof of Service" signed by Colin Beneby, falsely claiming that I was served. Mr. Beneby's forgery of service should not be overlooked when speaking of a corrupt system, no matter how trivial it may seem to be. He is part of the problem, but it would take an immense peeling back of an onion in order to make this dishonest process server accountable. I wouldn't even know where to start.

Susan "Sam" DeFiglio was the name of a supervisor of visitation. Immediately following the judge's decision to order supervised visitation on January 25, 2019, Alper had her business card—already filled out with the supervisor's name and phone number—pulled out and ready for me. We hadn't even gotten up from our chairs to rise for the judge's departure from the courtroom. While tears streamed down my face, she handed me the card.

I received the first texts from Susan DeFiglio, starting at 1:54 P.M. on January 26.

Susan DeFiglio: This is Sam. Sam is my nickname. My name is Susan DeFiglio. That is what you will find in Zelle. Everyone at work calls me Fig. I'm from Jersey where everyone has a nickname. What's your daughter's name?

Me: Katie.

Susan DeFiglio: Maybe 4 hours instead of 6. Looking into indoor activities.

It had been raining very hard with no end in sight, including the next day when the supervised visitation was to occur. The next day was also Katie's birthday; I swear the rain was the tears of God.

Me: Great. She has to go easy on her ankle.

Susan DeFiglio: Could go bowling and a movie and eat all at the same place. Frank's Cinebowl.

I was beginning to get impatient, but I held onto my temper. I had learned that she is also an investigator for Child Protective Services, but how could she think that bowling was a good idea for a kid with an injured ankle?

Me: She shouldn't be bowling. No sports per the orthopedic.

Susan DeFiglio: What's the orthopedic issue? Ankle?

Me: *replied by sending a copy of the doctor prognosis document without comment*

After a few more of her suggestions, I decided that we go to Steak and Shake and a movie.

On Katie's 13th birthday, I prepared for our visit by going to Walmart. I bought five ankle bracelets that came in a little package together and a card. I had been on the verge of crying all morning. When I found a birthday card that started playing the song, "Just the Way You Are" by Bruno Mars, I broke down. That song had reminded me of Katie ever since the first time I heard it. I stood there in Walmart just sobbing from the depths of my soul. Yellow-vested Walmart employees gathered and stood together watching me. I had to call a friend to help me. My friend talked with me on the phone while I walked around pushing an empty cart. I can't imagine what those Walmart employees must have been thinking. I finally pulled myself together and was able to pay for the gift and the card and get on my way to meet Katie and Ms. DeFiglio at Steak and Shake.

I was the first to arrive. It was still pouring rain. I had $260.00 in cash to pay the fee to DeFiglio for the four hours of supervised time with Katie at $65.00 an hour, not including any food or other expenses she might incur while supervising our visit. These and other rules for this compulsory service were sent to me by DeFiglio's boss Randi Shapiro. Maureen and Katie pulled up. DeFiglio waited in her vehicle until Maureen and Katie got out of their car, and then the three of them stood in the parking lot talking under umbrellas. I went inside and picked a table.

Katie and DeFiglio came in together and sat at the table with me. When we met, I immediately paid the initial hourly fee, I asked her to text me to confirm my payment since she did not carry a receipt book. My guess would be that she doesn't claim this income either, but that's just a suspicious guess. I expected her to go to her own table at this point and observe from a distance, but she settled in as if she were part of our party. It was an extremely awkward situation for me, and I'm sure Katie wasn't feeling exactly fluid with the whole scenario either. Katie and I ordered food. DeFiglio declined to eat, which did not make it any less awkward.

Katie sat across from me on the same side as DeFiglio. Katie began to lightly but repeatedly kick me under the table to get my attention. I was pretty sure I knew what she wanted. I kept my head down as if looking at my plate of food and then looked up at her with my eyes as far up as the muscles would allow. Katie mouthed the words, "Is that a man?" referring to DeFiglio. I lightly shook my head, no.

Katie and I discussed what we would do next since I was unable to reach her on the phone the day before. The many moving parts of this whole scenario made the entire situation more difficult. Katie was not allowed to ride in my car, we had to go somewhere close, we had a time limit, and it was pouring rain. Katie decided that she wanted to watch the movie *The Escape Room* that was playing just down the street. The next show started in two hours, so we had some time to spend together.

We finished our lunch and the cake from Steak and Shake was brought out. As I sang "Happy Birthday," it took every molecule of strength not to cry. I did my best to show a smile and appear celebratory. A few minutes after the singing, I excused myself and went to the restroom to gather myself before I blew an emotional gasket. I came back to the table and ate my cake. We started talking about the movie that coincidentally was rated PG-13 on Katie's 13th birthday. I thought, *That's a good thing because otherwise I'd be answering to taking my daughter to a movie that wasn't age appropriate with a visitation supervisor present.* Just as that thought crossed my mind, DeFiglio decided to engage in conversation after being silent the whole time to this point. She asked Katie if she liked "horror movies." Katie said that she did. DeFiglio then took out her cell phone to show pictures of the Stanley Hotel that was the inspiration for the movie, "The Shining," by Steven King. I was flabbergasted. All of a sudden,

I felt like the supervisor of visitation while she talked about the one movie I find to be the absolute scariest of all movies. Every time I see it, I get scared even though I know what happens next. I sat there, speechless, as DeFiglio commandeered the conversation, showing pictures of everything, including Room 217's door, while Katie's questions started rolling in including, "What happens in Room 217?"

The phrase, "You just can't make this stuff up" comes to mind.

When we got to the movie theater, I got out of my car and hurried over to DeFiglio's vehicle with my umbrella. The rain on that January day was like no other rain I had ever seen outside the summer rainy season in my twenty years living in Florida. As we all walked to the theater from the parking lot, I did my best to keep the three of us under my umbrella; as far as I could tell, DeFiglio did not have an umbrella of her own. I especially want Katie to see that a good man does this for others, especially for women. I believe that a daughter learns from the actions of her father what qualities she should look for in a boyfriend or husband.

When we got inside the theater, Katie appeared to have become a bit withdrawn. I wondered if the car ride with DeFiglio had anything to do with it or if she realized that the whole situation just sucked. The theater had a huge game room with video games, but Katie didn't want to play. She and I had been to this particular theater several times and she always wanted to play, even after a movie. She was showing general signs of being out of sorts. I told her that I had her laptop in my car and suggested that I could use my phone as a hotspot if she wanted to use it. She liked that plan. I started to lead us all back to my car when DeFiglio declared that Katie was going to stay with her. Something in this situation wasn't sitting right with me, but I could not put my finger on it. I told DeFiglio that I was Katie's father, and I would not leave her in the theater lobby by herself.

I pointed out that I didn't know her well enough to leave Katie alone with her. I said that if she wanted to supervise a walk to my car and back, then she should come along with us.

The situation deteriorated from there. DeFiglio then threatened to end the visit immediately. I refused and said that I would be informing the judge of her behavior to that point, so she wouldn't have to be concerned about ever supervising another visit between Katie and me. With that, I looked at Katie and said, "I promise you, I will never put you through this again."

I motioned to Katie to walk with me and held the umbrella over her as we walked to my car and back. DeFiglio did not get the same umbrella coverage she got on the initial walk from the parking lot. To be honest, I'm very surprised she didn't end it right there.

Once we were back in the theater and Katie was set up with the laptop, DeFiglio informed me that she would be sitting between Katie and me in the theater. She said that she couldn't supervise visitation if Katie and I sat together. I asked her if Katie could sit in the middle. DeFiglio threatened me again with ending the "visit."

DeFiglio sat in her chair during the movie with her bright cell phone light on as she texted in the dark movie theater. It was very embarrassing. After this went on for some time, I asked, "Who are you texting? I paid for this time, and I find it unprofessional, rude, and inappropriate." She replied, "I'm texting with your ex-wife."

She just took unprofessional to a whole new level. I was dumbfounded into silence.

Since the movie's conclusion was past the scheduled time for Katie and my time together on this occasion of her 13th birthday, I left, ending the worst birthday of her life, without question. They remained at the theater to finish watching the movie. I still don't know how "Escape Room" ends.

After this entire debacle of a day concluded, I posted on my Facebook page, "Tears of God fall from the sky today."

As I look at the chronological list of events, I'm not sure how Chris Jette was still my attorney when we filed Former Husband's Motion to Appoint New Timesharing Supervisor on February 1, 2019. I had already ripped him a new asshole for his not so stellar performance the prior week. I *do* believe this was the last thing he did on my case, and I did represent myself at the hearing. The reasons given were, basically, that it was a financial hardship. That wasn't the real main reason for wanting to get rid of what we had. The real main reason was Anne Alper's purposeful sabotage with a woman who had clear preconceived notions about who I was. Susan "Sam" DeFiglio obviously had been told something very derogatory about me. Then she decided not to bother to try to make my daughter's birthday a pleasant experience. In spite of what she had heard, she should have approached the job with a sense of professional detachment and based her own behavior upon what she saw for herself rather than what she heard before she met me. At the very least, she should have tried to make the day as pleasant as possible for Katie, and she should never have been texting with my ex-wife during our visit. Whatever her issue is, her behavior was extremely unprofessional, and she should not be allowed to work with children if she cannot control her own behavior.

In an effort to have her face consequences for her behavior, I had DeFiglio served with a subpoena on March 20, 2019 for the hearing to replace her. On March 21, 2019, the following commenced via text:

DeFiglio: As an expert witness, my fee is $75 per hour, which includes travel and prep time. I will be requesting payment prior to any testimony. The Judge will be made aware.

Me: Who is this?

I knew who it was.

DeFiglio: Susan DeFiglio. You sent me a subpoena yester-
                 day. Thank you for acknowledging you got this
                 information.

Me: You are not being called as an expert witness.

She was being called for her inappropriate behavior during
the timesharing.

DeFiglio: My estimate is approx. 4 hours including 2 hours of
                 travel.

Me: You are not being paid a cent by me, and if you think
                 you're exempt from the law, we'll see how that goes
                 for you

Me: Do not ever contact me again.

So, DeFiglio showed up in court without being paid a cent.
If she had failed to show because I would not pay her for her testimony, I would have asked the judge for a bench warrant.

I was able to question DeFiglio with almost no objections.
Opposing counsel had no interest in cross-examination. When
I finished, DeFiglio reached into her back pocket, unfolded a
yellow paper, and said that she "had notes" I told her no one
seemed to be interested.

The judge said, "Please state your name for the record, sir." I
thought, *Did I just hear what I think I heard?*

After Defiglio left the courtroom, I addressed the judge
to say, "Judge Willis, you just referred to the witness, Susan
DeFiglio as "sir" when asking her to state her name."

The look of seething anger on the face of Judge Willis was
immensely obvious as she sneered at me in my place in the room.
She said nothing.

The entity of Susan "Sam" DeFiglio was never to be heard from in our case again, but I'm sure she continues to adversely affect other families with her completely unprofessional behavior.

In the Order for Temporary Relief, the court appointed **"Randi Shapiro**, or one of her trained supervisors" to oversee timesharing. The truth of the matter was the only other person in Ms. Shapiro's operation was Susan DeFiglio. Since Ms. DeFiglio was now disqualified from supervising this case, it had to be Randi Shapiro.

After the hearing, I tried to contact Randi Shapiro directly to set an appointment for her to oversee timesharing. She did not answer or return my calls or respond to text messages.

On 5/26/19, I submitted Filing #90129247, Motion for Contempt and Enforcement of Order on Temporary Relief with Sanctions. Randi Shapiro was personally served at her home on June 14, 2019. The pleading has yet to see the light of a courtroom as of late April 2022.

My first suggestion in a series of attempts to find a reasonable timesharing supervisor was a woman by the name of Ashna Wallace. She mysteriously retracted her name for consideration after being contacted by Anne Alper.

Joe Nullet is the Executive Director of the Supervised Visitation Network with the closest local chapter, which is located in Jacksonville, Florida. This non-profit organization has a board of directors. On their website, they have a Code of Ethics page, an About Us page, board member bios, by laws, and even a history page. I reached out to Joe Nullet about my experience with Randi Shapiro and her trained supervisor, Susan "Sam" DeFiglio. I included screenshots of text messages, copies of emails, and a description of my daughter's and my experience with Randi Shapiro, who was a listed member of the Supervised Visitation Network of which Joe Nullet sat as Executive Director. I included the demeanor, attitude, appearance, and everything that I felt was remarkable to report to someone I thought would be able to not only address the issues, but perhaps also help us find a new person to supervise our visitation. The written answer I received from Joe "JJ" Nullet, the Supervised Visitation Network Executive Director was:

> David,
>
> I received your letter today. I would be willing to discuss via telephone why there is not anything we can act on. We are not a governing agency of our members. Good luck in resolving your situation. Please visit the parent's resources on our website which may offer helpful guidance.
>
> Thanks, Joe

This is a national organization, but they don't govern their members? This is apparently just a place for members to advertise their overpriced, glorified babysitting. The Board of Directors, Code of Ethics, and Mission Statement are apparently just for show. I tossed it away in disgust.

Vanessa Donadio is the current Competitive Program Coordinator for the Royal Palm Beach Strikers Soccer Club. Katie was in the program for two years before Vanessa Donadio was appointed as the program coordinator. This is remarkable because as I have established, Maureen searches for people who will support her parental alienation objective, but she had not been successful with the Royal Palm Beach Strikers Soccer Club until Vanessa was appointed to an authoritative role. Suddenly I was not allowed to be included in the TeamSnap application that informed parents and fans of upcoming games, practices, schedule changes, etc. When I contacted Vanessa about this, she informed me that my former wife would have to give permission for me to be included in the app notifications. I told her that I could be listed as a fan. Vanessa refused to allow that. I went to the president of the program, Mal Hasen, and he said, "I thought you were already on there. You should be."

Mal came up to me one day, and we were talking about just how bad things were with Maureen and me. Within that conversation, Mal said to me, "You must have done something."

That was the sole inspiration for the title of this book. It encompasses the demeanor of the people who look down their noses at me because I *must* be the bad guy. I don't hammer Mal in my story because, as president of the soccer club, he really does look out for the kids in general. That means a lot these days. However, when it comes to standing up for the right thing against his staff's behavior—especially against Vanessa Donadio—when it comes to doing the right thing, and when it comes to my involvement with my daughter's sports life, he fails.

As far as getting information on Katie's soccer games, Coach John and our team manager, Anne, send me texts. If they had continued to refuse, I would have probably filed a suit against the club and likely would have won. My treatment from team staff after Ms. Donadio was appointed was very different from how other parents were treated, even at games.

On one occasion, Katie got hurt and was carried off the field. I went over to ask her how she was. Maureen saw me speaking with Katie on the bench and caused an absolute maniacal scene, screaming and yelling at the top of her lungs. I walked back over to my Nikon camera on the ground where I had been taking pictures of the game. Maureen continued her tirade. Coach John turned around to watch Maureen in awe, as did many players, parents, and referees, basically almost all of the around 70 people who were in attendance. The team manager and the coach's wife came to stand next to me as if they were keeping me from returning to my daughter's side. All I had done was to ask my daughter if she was ok after an injury; Maureen screamed like a banshee, but I was the one who was treated as if I were unstable.

I wonder how Katie felt about all of this negative attention in front of her coaches, peers, teammates, and their parents.

John and Veronica Solek Coach John Solek had always been someone I could go to and chat with about Katie's progress. He would usually give me updates on her overall demeanor and attitude towards soccer and her social life. I often gave him Katie's gifts from me for him to pass on to her. Until the beginning of the 2021-22 competitive soccer season, he felt like an ally in that he considered Katie's best interest.

That relationship changed dramatically when he included his wife Veronica on the team sideline as assistant coach. His interactions with me abruptly became standoffish. For example, I had spent the last four years providing, setting up, and taking down the team bench shelter that protected the girls from the hot Florida sun and tropical downpours. Suddenly, that service was not wanted, and that message was delivered to me in front of Coach John by Veronica. The reason given to me was that the shelter did not have any airflow through it, in spite of the fact that the shelter had five screened openings on the back and sides, and the front was completely open air. As this new contemptuous situation continued to unfold, I noticed Veronica and Maureen were frequently together at other social events besides competitive soccer. The relationship has gotten to the point where Coach John sent out an email for a two-day tournament to 86 email addresses (parents) but not to me. I only found out about the tournament and email when one of the parents posted a team picture on social media. I made it to the tournament on the second day. Another example of what had become the new ongoing pattern by Coach John was the new Trace Team (traceup.com) video link access to view the team's game footage that was emailed to team parents, but not me. Coach John told me in a text message that he "was working on it", "trying to figure it out", and "not everyone can see it". The next morning,

I contacted Trace and I was added by a company support team member with absolutely no issue whatsoever through the administrator's (Veronica Solek's) sign in . Within 24 hours John had me removed and told me that he was filing suit against Trace for privacy infringement.

Deputy Jennifer Baker was a local sheriff's deputy who enjoyed working closely with local kids. I heard about Deputy Baker from some local residents. She was well known throughout the community. I contacted her and told her I would like my daughter to get a better feeling for police officers than the one she was getting since the only time she saw the police was during conflicts between my former wife and me. With all of the drama that often included police standby when exchanging Katie, Katie couldn't help but have a negative view of police.

Deputy Baker agreed to meet with Katie and me and showed up in uniform. Deputy Baker was a warm person with a big smile. Katie enjoyed talking with her. I enjoyed the relaxed atmosphere that emanated from her. We kicked the soccer ball around, had water ice at Rita's Italian Ice, and it was going great. It showed Katie how nice it could be to just hang with a police officer.

Of course, this was too good an idea, and it needed to be stopped. I filed a motion with the court proposing that Deputy Baker could be the supervisor for visitation. I happened to walk out of the courtroom prior to the hearing, and opposing counsel was there, talking with my witness, Deputy Baker. I looked him in the eye and asked, "Having a little deposition in the hall, counselor?" In his short chat, he got the one element that he needed. He asked Deputy Baker on the stand if she would need to leave a visitation in order to answer a call to duty. This should have been moot since she would already be on a call with Katie and me, but it would be an unlikely yet still possible scenario. Based on that one unlikely possibility, the judge denied my request for Deputy Baker to be our visitation supervisor.

Tina Bigiotti is a long-time family friend. Tina was one of the only people that Maureen would allow to babysit when Katie was a baby and toddler. We moved away when Katie was two years old, and when Maureen returned to Florida, she reconnected with Tina. Tina fosters cats, sometimes up to twenty cats at one time, you would never know because her home was always so clean. Katie loved playing with the cats, and obviously, the kittens were always a big hit.

Tina is a lovely lady and always in favor of creating the best scenarios for harmonious living. This included our broken family being the best it could be. When I returned to Florida, Tina offered to let me stay in her mother-in-law suite that was detached from her main house. The moment I took residency there, Maureen stopped talking to Tina. You see with Maureen, you are either with her or against her. If you were merely on speaking terms with me, it was imminent that she would write you off and that you were dead to her. This divorce rule of Maureen's remains in full effect to this day.

Since I was staying at Tina's, I was able to get a job quickly. This gave me the money to pay her board while I was there. Katie didn't suffer from this because she still got to see the cats and Tina while I was living there. It didn't take long before I was able to get my own place again. It was 2011, and Katie was four years old at this time. The divorce had only recently concluded. Tina was a great witness at the divorce. She never went into any mudslinging or spoke discouraging words about either party of the divorce. It wasn't her style. She only gave testimony on the strengths of each parent and her opinion for a healthy future. Of course, it would take the court to ensure that the two parents were kept to responsible standards and maintained a two-way respect for each other in order for the plan to work.

That never really happened.

As things got more and more contemptuous between

Maureen and me, Tina started to see just how rotten Maureen was being and how Maureen's behavior affected Katie's happiness and well-being. Tina changed from trying to be neutral in her testimony to being a witness for me. She was anxious to share with the court what she had witnessed.

Maureen constantly claimed to be in fear for her life. In 2017, well before the ruling for supervised visits and just two years before Maureen was able to convince the court to take Katie away from me because of how horrible and dangerous I was, Hurricane Irma, a category 4 hurricane, was barreling in on south Florida. It was my visitation time with Katie, and my hurricane plan was to stay with Tina. I chose to take Katie to Tina's house for several reasons, the first being that otherwise, Tina would be alone. Another powerful reason was that Tina was on the same electrical grid as the hospital, so she rarely lost power. Finally, I thought it would be good for Katie to help with the cats; that job would keep her happy and distracted. I packed freeze-dried food, tools, and provisions of all kinds to help make a bad situation as tolerable as possible.

Just as we were settling in to our plans, Maureen decided that she wanted to join us at Tina's house. In spite of her constant testimony in court that she was in fear for her life, she left her boyfriend at their house and stayed two days and three nights under the same roof with me. After years of being snubbed by her, Tina welcomed Maureen into her home and gave up her master bedroom for Maureen and Katie to share while she slept on her living room couch. At the end of their stay, eleven-year-old Katie pulled me aside and said, "Dad, thank you for this." Those five seconds made all the worry and discomfort worth it because Katie let me know I was her hero.

The testimony about this visit never saw the inside of a courtroom. When we were in court that last time, opposing counsel chose to grandstand for the first four days of what should have been a five-day trial. Before I had a chance to present my case, Covid-19 stopped everything. Continuation of that hearing has been postponed repeatedly ever since. Tina was present in court every day, waiting for her turn to tell the story of the four days Maureen spent at her house with Katie and me during that storm and its aftermath. She particularly wanted to tell the story about catching Maureen kissing me in the kitchen.

Arline Moore and Dr. Randi Schietz were on staff at Binks Forest Elementary School in Wellington, Florida. Mrs. Moore was Katie's third grade teacher, and Randi Schietz was the school counselor. Randi Schietz was with Katie from the very beginning and earned her doctorate while Katie was a student at Binks. Dr. Schietz led a class for children of divorce and told me that Katie gravitated to the group. I was pleased to know this. Randi showed an interest in the well-being of the kids, and I truly believe her objectives were in the right place.

Another noteworthy, remarkable feeling I had whenever speaking with Randi was that she treated me with respect. That's a hard thing to come by when your ex-wife tells tales of her imminent danger to anyone who will listen. Randi Schietz never seemed to buy the drama. She simply kept her sights on Katie's best interests the whole time Katie was in her care, and I will forever be grateful to her for that.

Unfortunately, that did not stand true for the school principal, Michella Levy, who seemed more interested in establishing her authority than in focusing on the best interests of the children.

I consolidated Mrs. Moore and Dr. Schietz together as an entry because they came together to dig in against what they found to be inappropriate actions by Maureen that ultimately had Katie suffering from those decisions. Maureen would not allow Katie to bring her prescription eyeglasses to my home and told her that I would steal them. Mrs. Moore was first to discover this in class. She noticed that Katie was leaving her glasses in her desk on the days I was picking Katie up after school to stay at my home for my timesharing. She also noticed that Katie would change her clothes at the end of the day on those same days. Some people pay attention to these types of things, and Mrs. Moore was indeed one of those people.

Mrs. Moore decided to contact both Maureen and myself regarding her concerns about the eyeglasses being left at school on the days that I picked Katie up. After all, Katie had homework to do when she was at my home too. Katie was nearsighted; without her glasses, she had to bring books and papers up to her face to see them.

Maureen lost her mind in a reply to Mrs. Moore because I hadn't had Maureen's email address, and with the email, I now did. That was her only concern. Absolutely nothing in her reply referred to the eyeglasses whatsoever. Mrs. Moore forwarded me Maureen's reply. I was flabbergasted. This then prompted a meeting between Mrs. Moore, Dr. Schietz, and myself to discuss the issues.

The conference took place on April 4, 2014. Mrs. Moore formally presented a copy of the email thread to Dr. Schietz. Dr. Schietz reiterated Katie's participation in the group for children of divorce. She stated that Katie is a willing and active participant and "seems to enjoy the experience and those peers." Stated in the minutes was another comment from Dr. Schietz:

Recently Katie has started to wear glasses, which her teacher (Mrs. Moore) has noted have been very helpful to her in class. There were days when she was not wearing glasses because her mother did not want them to go home when she was going home with her father at his house, where she often has to do her homework, and this is a concern. She also has to change out of her clothes to wear clothes that are often too small or inappropriate for school when she goes to aftercare on the days that her father will pick her up. This is something that seems to bother Katie.

In the "Conclusion and Recommendations," she wrote the following:

> The teacher and the school counselor feel that Katie is happy in both homes and presents as a happy child, but it would be in her best interest if the parents could communicate more effectively with one another, and this might only happen with a mediator or outside support in an effort to more peacefully and collectively co-parent Katie.

Both Mrs. Moore and Dr. Schietz were in court with the written record and waited for four days to testify. That is the trial I mentioned before that was stopped after four days of opposing counsel testimony and never concluded because of Covid-19 restrictions and the ultimate recusal of Judge Willis. A judge has never seen that document or heard Dr. Randi Schietz or Mrs. Arline Moore's supporting testimony.

DCF Investigator Melanie Hull was the investigator when Maureen called the Florida Department of Children and Families (DCF) on me on two separate occasions. The latter of the two were when I picked Katie up at aftercare three hours earlier than the court order stated because Maureen had been picking her up two hours early on my days, so Katie wasn't there when I arrived to pick her up. Katie and I went to Disney for the weekend. When she and I were in our hotel room, I received a call from DCF Investigator Melanie Hull informing me that I was to return with the minor child so that she could see that she was "alive." I told Ms. Hull that I had no intention of coming back until late Sunday night. I offered to have Katie talk to Ms. Hull on the phone, but she said that was not sufficient.

When Katie and I arrived back at my home on Sunday, Melanie Hull and a sheriff's deputy were waiting for us. I invited them in, and they asked me to wait outside while they spoke to

Katie privately. At the conclusion of their interview with Katie, they came outside and spoke to me very briefly. DCF Investigator Hull told me that Maureen told her that she is in fear of her own life. Ms. Hull then shared with me her opinion that Maureen's behavior indicates that she is not in fear at all; she is simply using that phrase for embellishment. I asked Ms. Hull if she could share that opinion in her report. She told me that she could not. The best she could do in the report was state, "Katie is safe living with the mother and while with the father."

I called Investigator Hull on a couple of occasions to let her know that I would be serving her with a subpoena so she could testify about her observations in court. She was apprehensive but told me the process necessary to do so. On October 2, 2019, my process server knocked on her door. A young man answered the door, and a woman in the background said Melanie Hull did not live there. The process server believed the woman was Melanie Hull and gave the subpoena to the young man to complete the service. On October 29, 2019, we served her at the office for the Department of Children and Families office in West Palm Beach. That subpoena was accepted by Thelma Green who indicated that she was authorized to accept service and confirmed that Melanie Hull was still employed with the department. Melanie Hull never showed up for court. Judge Willis did not charge her with contempt or issue a bench warrant. Nothing. We simply moved on as if Melanie Hull was excused from obeying a subpoena.

Dads and Donuts. I received an email that said, "You're Invited this Tuesday morning at 7:30 am in the media center. Enjoy donuts, coffee, and juice while shopping the last day of the book fair with your child." I accepted the invitation and attended the event that was a get-together to sell books at the book fair. All's fair in marketing, and I was prepared to browse and shop with Katie. Katie knew I was coming also knew what would happen if she told her mother about it in advance. Events with dad were always discouraged. My official sworn statement about the event read as follows:

At 7:10 A.M. on 4/25/17, I reported to the front reception area at Binks Forest Elementary School for the "Dads and Donuts" event scheduled for 7:30 to 8:00 A.M.. Knowing that my daughter, Katie was on Safety Patrol detail, I asked the receptionist if she thought it would be a problem to get my daughter relieved from her assignment. I was given a Visitor's Pass sticker and took a seat.

As I noticed a large number of dads collecting outside the front door of the school for the event, I still hadn't seen my daughter; I went outside too. I figured I would see my daughter sooner as she would be dropped off.

At 7:25, when the dads were led down the hall towards the Media Center for the event, I still hadn't seen my daughter. I asked Mr. McCormick (teacher) if he knew where I might find her. He told me that if I proceeded to the Media Center, I would probably see her on the way. I proceeded towards the Media Center.

Walking down the hall, I noticed a woman with a clipboard who appeared to be checking Safety Patrol kids and checking them off. I told her who I was and that I was looking for Katie. I asked her if she knew where she was.

She told me that her post was "right there, and she is not at her post." She pointed to a door six feet away from where we were standing. I saw the top of Katie's head coming down the hall and called her name. She walked towards me and the clipboard woman who was also her homeroom teacher, Mrs. Gouveia.

As soon as Katie got to us, Mrs. Gouveia asked her, in an elevated tone of voice, "Why are you late?! Why are you not at your post?!" In an effort to answer one question at a time, Katie told Mrs. Gouveia that she was studying for her science test and that she was sorry that she was late. Mrs. Gouveia interrupted her with "I am taking your belt, and you are getting a slip!" Mrs. Gouveia's tone was elevated, and her facial expression was that of fury. There were Katie's peers, parents, and school faculty walking up and down the hall in the early morning traffic.

I asked Mrs. Gouveia, "You're taking her belt for this? May I email you later?" She exclaimed, "There is no reason to email me regarding this." Then she fully turned to me with the continued fury." She said, "She doesn't want to go with you! I am not authorizing that she is going with you!" I told her, "Back off!" I took my daughter by the hand and proceeded to the Media Center.

I spotted the principal, Mrs. Levy. We went over to her. Katie explained what had just happened, and Mrs. Levy told her, "Your belt is not getting taken away, I run the program." Katie burst into tears.

The ripple effect of this 30-minute event to eat a donut and buy some books went on for weeks. Besides the school's report, I went to the Palm Beach County School Board and reported the incident. I received sympathy for what had happened, but Katie was the one who was severely traumatized in front of all of those people. It seems that two kinds of people emerge in this horrible set of circumstances. People like Randi Schietz and Arline Moore, who truly want peace for a child, and people like Gianna Gouveia, who went out of her way to incite the highest possible drama one could fathom.

In the mind of a child, it would seem reasonable to conclude that if I hadn't come to the "Dads and Donuts" event, she wouldn't have been yelled at in front of everyone just for being a little late for her patrol duties. In all that I've read from professionals, especially Dr. Richard Warshak, this is the one of the ways parental alienation syndrome manifests. The child starts to withdraw from the targeted parent because it's just easier for the child to not have to deal with what happens when that parent is included.

Florida State Senators Maria Sachs and Jeff Clemens are two of the politicians I talked with to try to get custody laws changed in Florida.

Senator Sachs was at an event to give free tickets to hear President Obama speak at the Delray Tennis complex some weeks later. To hear and see any sitting President of the United States in person is way cool, so I was excited about this event. Senator Sachs and I made eye contact from across the room; she walked towards me, not breaking that eye contact. When she got to me, she reached out to shake my hand. As I stood up from my chair, she said, "I'm Maria Sachs." I introduced myself. She said that she was looking for help with her re-election campaign for state senator. I told her that I would be glad to help, but that I actually needed help with a horrible situation in family court. She replied that family court was an issue she already wanted to make some changes in and that she and I should sit down and discuss what could be done with legislation.

So, I worked phones, knocked on doors, and went on a group beach cleanup wearing a Re-elect Senator Maria Sachs t-shirt. I took Katie to that one partly because I thought Senator Sachs would be there for the big photo opportunity, but Senator Sachs did not show up.

Senator Sachs won re-election, but we never had that conversation. Later, when I needed an attorney to help me when I was losing Katie, I asked her if she could tell me about anyone who would represent me in court for one hearing. I said that I could pay over time. Her exact words to me were, "No one knows your case better than you. You'll do fine in court." In other words, she completely abandoned me after promising to help me in exchange for my help to get her reelected.

Maria Sachs is no longer a state senator. She is now a County Commissioner.

Jeff Clemens is not a State Senator anymore because of his affair with a lobbyist; he ultimately resigned in total public humiliation.

Prior to his resignation, Senator Clemens and I were in a posting battle on Facebook. My stand was for changing the standard in Florida to 50/50 shared custody in divorce cases. Anyone who knows about Social Security Act IV-D knows that every dollar collected by each individual state for child support, pays a monetary incentive to each state from the federal government. This isn't just from payments for arrears; this is for every dollar collected, whether you owe back support or not. Senator Clemens stood firm against the premise of 50/50 custody. Senator Clemens's political demise at his own hands was a win for alienated parents in the state. Good riddance Jeff!

Mark Roseman is the founder of the Toby Center, located in Delray Beach, Florida. I have met with Mark Roseman on several occasions. The interactions that I have had with Mark do not ever gel into any kind of plan that would be capable of executing anything of substance that could make a difference in real lives. While the Toby Center website offers a multitude of services, supports equal shared parenting, and refers to parental alienation, its support comes at a monetary cost, which shows it is simply another cog in the wheel of the revenue generating system known as family court.

After the debacle with Randi Shapiro and her "team of qualified supervisors" that consisted of only one person, Susan "Sam" Defiglio, I filed a motion to have the Toby Center assigned as the supervisor of visitation. Judge Willis granted the order. I contacted Mark about the costs. He explained that I would be responsible for the intake costs for both Maureen and myself, but he wasn't clear about why I had to pay both costs. He stated that the Toby Center is a not-for-profit organization and not so ironically a member of the "unmonitored" Supervised Visitation Network. The costs for the actual supervised visitation ranged from $45 to $75 per hour.

After working through the fee schedules, I spoke with Rose Berkoff Basilio, the intake coordinator. I wanted to move forward with the process so I could see Katie again soon. I explained to Rose that she should complete the intake process with Maureen first because Maureen would be uncooperative with the process. I explained that anything that would facilitate my time-sharing with Katie was going to be blocked and delayed by her mother. When I was proved correct, I contacted Mark. He told me to file a motion and that his testimony would involve an additional cost.

No matter what the mission statements are, no matter how strenuously they claim to only be interested in doing good, it all comes down to how much money they can make.

I have never filed that motion.

CHAPTER 13

Best Interest of a Child?

> *And these children that you spit on, as they try to change their worlds, are immune to your consultations. They're quite aware of what they're going through.*
>
> David Bowie

Every one of the court actions of over a decade obviously affected how things went in the real world, and I consider this chapter to be the collateral damage result. Maureen endeavored to get the court to enable her to make everything as difficult as possible, even though it hurt our daughter more to witness the behavior and to be directly in the crossfire.

At extracurricular activities such as dance recitals, sporting events, etc., Maureen would not allow Katie to speak with me if it was not during my timesharing specifically designated by the court. She often said, "Katie, get over here. It is not your father's time."

Maureen was bothered by her inability to get a no contact order, which would have determined that Katie and I were *not* to have any contact. What she got instead was a timesharing order. The timesharing order doesn't state anywhere that Katie and I *must* speak. If my former wife isn't directly instructed that our daughter and I *must* speak, then she will forbid Katie from

221

having any communication; this is her own modification of the rules of her timesharing. In contrast, during my designated timesharing—knowing it was the right thing for Katie's peace of mind—I would instruct Katie to go over to her mother and say hello. Her mother was present to support her, and it's only polite for Katie to acknowledge her, talk about the event, or whatever.

Maureen never got on board with that. She went out of her way to have Katie ignore me as a rule. I missed some events simply because Maureen had not informed me of their exis-tence. One of Katie's dance recitals had tickets on sale for three weeks before I found out about it. I sat in the very last row, while Maureen and her parents enjoyed fourth row center seats. When I bought the ticket, the director of the dance school saw how disappointed I was and gave me a wristband that allowed me to attend dress rehearsal the night before, and I was able to see the show from the first row. The formal show was merely the opportunity for me to give Katie a bouquet of flowers after the performance—none of the six people in the fourth row thought enough to do that. The way I saw it, she and I both won, but only because of my tenacity.

Following the divorce judgment, we had our first pub-lic scene right out of the gate. Katie had a T-ball practice on Valentine's Day. I had her bag of equipment, went to the prac-tice, and gave Katie her bag. I kept the flowers I brought for afterwards. I sat behind the backstop and could see Maureen's mother in the stands, reading a book and eating a sandwich. She didn't see me until she went to the restroom and saw me on the way. She called for police. The officer approached me and asked me if there was a no-contact order. I told him that there wasn't. He told me to stay away from Maureen's mother and left.

It didn't end there.

About 20 minutes later, Maureen showed up. She walked in front of the bleachers where parents were sitting, and she began to read our divorce order at the top of her lungs. This was her first public scene, so her voice quivered while she read aloud. Parents, coaches, and 4-year-old children stopped what they were doing to look at this woman yelling as she read. To try to minimize Katie's embarrassment, I walked over to the dugout, gave Katie her flowers, kissed her, and left. After the incident, Maureen went to sit in her car and remained parked at the entrance to the field.

Katie was training in karate at Top Flight Martial Arts. I would go on occasion and watch. One time, Maureen's mother brought Katie. Katie came right up to me and wanted to show me her new gear. She opened her bag and excitedly took items out to show me. Maureen's mother attempted to grab the bag away. I grabbed her wrist and told her to let go of the bag. She let go and screamed, "Somebody tell him to give me the bag!"

This type of public scene was what Maureen incorporated into her world as a means to draw attention at any public place. It was a long time, mortifying experience for Katie. I had a meeting with the owner of the business, Scott Rusnack. He told me that because Maureen signed Katie up, I was not welcome at the school. I video recorded the entire meeting and posted it on YouTube. When Rusnack discovered the posted video, he reported it to YouTube for his likeness being broadcast, and it was removed. I have no doubt that the content of what he said in that video was bad for his business.

We also had the ongoing drama of the child exchanges. "No deviations from the court order" was her standard reply to every request for even the slightest change. If I couldn't make it on time, I would lose my time with Katie, even if I called or texted hours or days ahead of time due to work or other commitments. If Katie and I were going to be late getting her back to her mother, due to circumstances beyond my control, Katie would go into a panic. "Child exchanges," as they were called by the court, seemed to create the most opportunity for the most drama, so I could certainly understand why Katie would be nervous on the way to one. My attorney advised me to video record all child exchanges.

This habit of recording the exchanges actually saved me a great deal of trouble at least once when Maureen accused me of striking her during an exchange. I was arrested and spent the night in jail. During the arrest, as I sat handcuffed in the back seat of the police cruiser with the driver's door open, a police officer was looming over Katie, and she was crying. Despite holding her mother's hand, she called out to me, hysterically crying, and said, "Daddy, I'm scared!" I called back to her, "It's going to be okay, sweetheart!"

At that moment, Katie's hysterical, deeply emotional, distressed condition that was directly caused by her mother's actions tempted me to do something that would have justified my arrest. I suppose it was lucky that I was already handcuffed and in custody at that point.

One of the things that the police officer told me on the way to being processed was that my daughter was very upset that my mother would worry where I was. Can you imagine this seven-year-old little girl having more compassion for her fellow human beings than her forty-four-year-old mother? It literally nauseates me any time I think about it.

In addition to being arrested and spending the night in jail, I was under a temporary no contact order, which was later dropped after my attorney submitted my video of the incident to the State Attorney's office. The assault charges were dropped for the sum of a $5,000 retainer.

I asked the court numerous times to simply allow me to pick Katie up in front of her mother's home. This way, Katie only had to walk out the door to my car, and Maureen could video record the exchange to "monitor" a pickup or drop off. The court never changed the order despite the reasons that I gave to show that this would be in Katie's best interest. It honestly seemed as though the more drama that ensued, the better they liked it because it would generate more court hearings and subsequently more revenue.

Katie's mother would put Katie in the most ridiculous clothing for our visits. She would even go as far as putting flip-flops on her, then keeping the shoes and socks I sent back with Katie, perpetually causing me to buy new clothes and shoes for every visit just to keep Katie decently dressed. This issue was noted by Katie's teachers and guidance counselor. The report from a parent/teacher conference stated:

> Katie has to change out of her clothes to wear clothes that are often too small or inappropriate for school when she goes to aftercare on days that her father will pick her up. This is something that seems to bother Katie.

Against all suggestions from friends, attorneys, family members, I refused to put Katie back into the inappropriate clothing when I returned her to her mother. This was a matter of Katie's self-esteem, and I would not jeopardize that by stooping to Maureen's level. I got smart and bought lots of clothing from eBay.

Katie was eventually diagnosed with farsightedness and needed prescription eyeglasses to correct the problem. Maureen forbade Katie from bringing them to my home; she claimed that I would steal them. Katie was instructed to leave her glasses at school on days that I picked her up. Without her glasses, she was not able to do her homework at my home. This either caused her to not get it done at all or pressured her to try to rush through it in the short amount of time she had left before school when she got back to her mother's home. This was like a punishment for being at my residence and gave Katie a reason to not want to see me due to the consequences at school. You can see how Maureen did not violate the court order but instituted a methodical plan to inject unnecessary stress on a child.

It is perfectly clear that Maureen's objective was simply to make loving her dad an unpopular condition for Katie. The way in which Maureen went about this campaign ultimately hurt Katie the most. Katie eventually realized that she couldn't talk with her mother about her good times with me. Anything that Katie and I did together was downplayed or derided. One of my creative ideas for an activity that I knew Maureen couldn't physically interfere with was golf. Katie told me that her mother told her that golf was only for old men. I got Katie a scholarship at The First Tee in West Palm Beach, financed mostly by Jack Nicklaus. It turned out to be a futile effort because Maureen would not take her to the classes. So I let Katie drive a golf cart, hand me the club that I asked for, and paid her twenty dollars a round. I golfed, Katie had a blast driving the cart—which helped get her used to the feeling of driving, which helped later on when she got her driver's license—she earned a few dollars, and we had fun times together, outdoors.

Katie was only eight years old when she wrote on her Christmas Wish List, "A real phone so I can call my dad when I want." It was very sad because it showed that Katie wasn't able to call me when she wanted to talk to me. She felt if she had her own phone that she could. For some reason, I thought that would work too. I bought one, loaded it with an Ariel (the Little Mermaid) screensaver, wrapped it, and gave it to Santa Claus at the mall to give to Katie when she sat on his lap for pictures. I know what I was thinking, but I surely didn't realize that I had set her up for a great disappointment. During a later child exchange, Maureen called for police standby, placed the phone in the middle of the parking lot, walked away from it, got in her vehicle, and drove away. The police officer asked me, "What just happened?" I told him he just watched a mother disappoint her child, and I had unwittingly handed her the opportunity to do so.

On October 27, 2012, Katie and I went to the local park, called Scott's Place after a little Halloween event we attended at church. She was dressed as Supergirl, and I was in full Spiderman costume. When we got to the park, kids flocked to me as Spiderman. I posed for some pictures and then Katie and I played on the swings and ran around. I texted Maureen and asked if she would like to pick up Katie at the park and maybe they could just stay after I left and enjoy the rest of the event. The park was literally right next to the parking lot of the Chevron that the court designated as the exchange location. This is one example of how I looked for opportunities to make exchanges easier on Katie. In this situation, I would simply leave when Maureen showed up, cutting out a whole opportunity for drama. Katie and I still had an hour to be together and with both a Subway and an ice cream shop nearby, we had treats planned.

Instead, Maureen showed up almost immediately and called to Katie to leave. I walked over to Maureen, holding Katie, and Maureen proceeded to drag Katie from my arms. At this point, it was quickly turning into emotional drama, so I simply let Katie go free to the pulling of her mother. As Katie was leaving my arms, the look on her face was sheer terror. She was crying, and her face was scrunched in anguish. To see that little girl dressed in a Supergirl costume going from having a nice holiday to such misery was truly heartbreaking. I cry as I sit here and relive that vision by writing it. I will never forget that image of my daughter as long as I live.

I retreated to my vehicle and sat in the driver's seat. I held and looked at the plastic pumpkin that Katie had painted at the church event and just cried. Three people walked over to me and professed their willingness to speak up for what they just witnessed. This doesn't happen often, as people usually don't want to be involved. The man was on vacation and lived outside the United States. The other two were local residents, a woman by the name of Lynn Lester and her daughter. Lynn Lester was later deposed on May 24, 2013. This twenty-two page deposition has never seen the light of day in court as evidence. The closest I ever came to getting a judge to read the testimony of this atrocious event was when I submitted it as docket entry #594 to the clerk of court on October 28, 2015 and had it made into public record that can be viewed by anyone.

Katie took up gymnastics. On some days, the timesharing schedule for me overlapped as Katie was in her classes. I never did anything but enjoy watching her train. It was hard work, and she was a determined girl. I recall her tenacity to successfully do an aerial, which is a cartwheel without hands. One day she told me that she had six pack abs. I said, "No way!" She pulled up her tee shirt and that child had *six pack abs*. I don't believe I had ever seen six pack abs in person. She was so proud, and I was flabbergasted.

One particular day after gymnastics class, I made plans to have dinner with a friend who had a daughter that Katie knew and got on well with. Class was officially over at 6 P.M., but the girls often did some freelance exercises on their own when the coach was finished with a class. I told Katie that we were having dinner with these particular people, and she said she wanted to leave immediately, as the freelance training wasn't mandatory. We started walking towards the door to leave. Maureen was still there because she always acted as if she were a secret service agent sent to closely monitor the situation. When Maureen saw us leaving, she yelled, "Somebody call 911!"

The girl at the desk had no idea what was going on and made the call immediately. Maureen ran to the door and stood in front of it. She took Katie by the hand and marched away from the door. Now imagine this scene in front of parents, children, and staff inside a place of business where the foyer was approximately 10 x 20.

When the police arrived, I was outside with a man we'll call Adam. Adam was inside when the public scene unfolded. He heard everything. Police came back outside and asked me a few questions. I gave them my answers, which were not recorded accurately on their report. For example, I said we were going to have dinner with friends at six. The report said we were going to have a nice dinner. It may sound petty, but one is more time sensitive than the other. The police officer asked Adam if he saw the incident. He replied that he did, and the police asked him to step away from me so they could ask him a few questions.

Evidently, Maureen had told the officer that I threatened to kill her inside the gymnastics school. They asked Adam if he heard me say that. He told me that he told the officer that he never heard those words come out of my mouth. Of course he hadn't heard those words come out of my mouth; they didn't. I never said anything like that.

After all of this public mess was sorted out, Maureen actually had the audacity to ask the officer for a chance to speak to Katie once more as she and I were getting into my car. The police officer called to Katie to come back. Maureen said whatever she had to say, Katie came back, and we left. Katie was once again mortified by the public dramatics caused by her mother in front of her peers.

In the interim of the hiring of the "Collusive Coercives," Maureen began to utilize a new approach for denying me my court-ordered time with Katie. In the Final Judgement of Dissolution of Marriage, an entry within the Order stated:

It is in the best interest of the minor child for the parties to share parental responsibility of the minor child, with the wife being responsible for making all ultimate decisions.

Well, I thought, this was new. The emails or texts that I began to receive stated the following, depending on whether I received the notice from Maureen or her attorney.

"I am exercising my right as ultimate decision maker and have decided that I will be withholding timesharing at this time."

OR

"My client is exercising her right as ultimate decision maker and will be withholding timesharing at this time."

It would appear that this loophole was discovered by Maureen's new attorney, as this was never used as a method to withhold timesharing previously. If found to be in contempt, it would merely just generate a monetary fine to the court. Hence the term "Kids for Cash."

Katie had gotten to be quite a good soccer player. After playing one year in recreational, two years in middle school, and four years in competitive travel, she entered high school in 2020. Her freshman year, Katie chose not to play high school soccer. I was concerned that this might be a sign of positive activities losing way to not-so-positive choices, which is a danger as one enters into the new realm of peer pressure that high school can bring. Maureen's only notification to me about this was a text that said, "Katie doesn't want to play high school soccer." Of course, I replied right away to ask why. My reply rendered no response. So, I contacted her school counselor with my concerns.

Katie's counselor, Mr. Farley, was a great find. He truly seemed to care about kids. Over the years, I have learned to worry how I will be received by the people in Katie's circle because of the way Maureen lays down the negative groundwork. Speaking with Mr. Farley felt like a green light. He had been a pitcher in college, and he knew the importance of kids participating in clubs and sports teams in high school. He knew how keeping kids engaged in positive activities can help keep them from making bad choices during this vulnerable time in their lives.

Mr. Farley had been in contact with Katie and Maureen regarding changing Katie's curriculum. She was taking more advanced courses than was recommended. This had been her mother's influence because it was very important to Maureen to be able to speak to the court about what a great parent she was and then prove it by showing Katie being academically driven under her parenting. This strategy meant Katie often had to forsake being able to enjoy just being a kid. The amount of homework Katie had each night seemed absolutely insurmountable to me at times.

After our talk, Mr. Farley contacted Katie in a matter-of-fact way, telling her that he heard that she was quite a good soccer player. Katie replied to Mr. Farley that she regretted not going out for the team. Mr. Farley arranged for Katie to have a special opportunity to meet with the coach for a spot on the team. Katie was quite pleased, and I was certainly amazed that Mr. Farley and the coach would make such an exception for her. Unfortunately, Katie never made it to the special tryout. Her mother found out that I called Mr. Farley and sabotaged the opportunity, as she did for so many other things I arranged for Katie—solely because I was involved.

The travel soccer club that Katie played for had an app that the club staff used to inform parents of games, practices, and any sort of changes. That app was called "TeamSnap." I had access to this method of communication until a new staff member canceled my account. When I asked her why I no longer had access, she told me that Maureen had to approve my inclusion and that she would not do so. I thought of suing the soccer club for discrimination, but the negative attention would ultimately fall on Katie.

I went to the president of the soccer club and asked him to intervene. His entire response was, "I can't believe you're not on it." That response didn't sit well with me because all he had to do was tell the staff to include me. Instead, he simply expressed confusion. This is the same person who provided the inspiration for the title of this book. He came up to me one day and said, "You must have done something" referring to Maureen's behavior regarding me. His strength was in how he treated the kids, and I felt that made up for any shortcomings he had as president overseeing the organization, so I let it go. In the early days, Coach John and the team manager went out of their way to keep me informed of upcoming games by text messages. That changed, of course, after Maureen made best friends with Coach John's wife, Veronica.

The parents of the other girls on the team avoided me for the most part. Maureen goes through "planting of land mines" as soon as there is someone new involved. Whether people believe what she says or just do not want to get involved, the results are the same when it comes to the way they engage with me.

One of things that I like to do for the girls is to take pictures of the games, crop them, and post them on the Shutterfly website. From there, I share the game albums to each of the parents' email addresses. I wanted to be a sports photographer as a youngster, and by golly, I finally am one. Another thing I do to contribute involves a sports shelter and an accordion type bench that seats five players, which I bought from Premiere Sports Products. This is to protect the girls from the blazing Florida sun and rainy games. I set it up before each game. To avoid drama with Maureen, I am usually the first person there to set up, and I'm usually the last person there, taking it all down. A mother of one of the players walked up to me at one game and said, "I give you a lot of credit. You come out here to every game, set up, take down, take all of those pictures, and send them to us, and you aren't even able to talk with Katie because of the situation."

I was so blown away because this parent was one who often hung out with Maureen at the games. I thanked her for her kind words and said that I knew that it meant something to Katie for her dad to contribute to the team whether she could say it to me or not. Other parents started to speak to me, too. After three years of just doing what I do, they were finally forming their opinions based on what they saw of me and not on what my slanderous ex-wife trumpeted about. Having people formulate their own opinions was exactly what Maureen did not want to happen. Almost simultaneously, many of the parents began engaging with me at the games. It wasn't all of the parents, of course, just those who were willing to reconsider the situation and think for themselves.

On February 7, 2021, Katie was injured on the soccer field. It was her knee. She ran head on with an opponent and fell to the ground. She needed to be carried off the field by the coach and another member of the team's staff. Her face was writhing in pain as she was carried off, straight towards me. She was on the bench with ice on the knee. The game continued. I walked 30 feet over to her and asked her a couple of questions about how she was doing. Within 20 seconds, Maureen was almost running towards us, screaming at the top of her lungs, "No! No! No! No!"

I said to Katie, "Here comes the scene. I'm sorry, sweetheart."

In front of Katie's teammates, their parents, coaches, and referees—about 80 people or more—Maureen created another one of her public scenes. I honestly think that she thinks that I am embarrassed when she does this. I'm not. However, I can see that it mortifies Katie. Then, of course, I can see the opinions being formed based on what the other people actually see, which is Maureen acting like a lunatic.

At another tournament, Katie's ankle started acting up again. She went to the trainer's table, and I went along to hear what the trainer had to say about the injury. Katie got on the table to be examined, and Maureen told me to leave. I didn't speak; I was focused on Katie and the trainer. Maureen got louder and exclaimed, "You won't leave, so we will." With that, she took Katie by the hand and walked her away from the trainer's area without letting the evaluation continue. Maureen had actually begun to jeopardize Katie's well-being by having Katie walk on a bad ankle just to keep Katie away from me.

Our church had a program called Upward Basketball that Katie became involved in at my suggestion. They had a boys and a girls division. She made new friends, was eager to practice, even when it wasn't scheduled, and was given a weekly bible verse that was handed out in the form of a basketball card— that would be the Christian inclusion at the end of the weekly basketball practice. Katie played three years in the program. In the first two years, her team won three games. She learned how to lose sporting contests with dignity at an early age. I started coaching her team during her second year, and by her third year, her team went undefeated. I was so proud of how gracefully she won after losing so often her first two years.

The weekend of her birthday, I brought cupcakes for the whole team so Katie could celebrate both her birthday and their win with her team.

Maureen stormed into the classroom where we were having post game individual recognitions while the girls ate cupcakes. She began to raise her voice and became very animated at the other two coaches about a conversation she and I had had earlier about a conflict between something she had planned and an upcoming game. Katie was so upset that I walked her down to the water fountain just so she could get away from the mania that her mother started in that classroom.

Maureen came out of the classroom after us and yelled down the hall that Katie was to get back there and that it was *her* time-sharing time. Poor Katie didn't know what to do, so I said. "Go ahead." So she went back to hear her mother finish her tirade.

One of the other coaches said to Maureen, "You have our phone numbers. Why would you come in here and do this in front of these kids, especially your own daughter?"

That may have been the only time anyone ever stood up to her and stopped her in the middle of one of her public scenes. Sometime later, I asked the assistant coach to testify at a hearing. He refused, saying he didn't want to get involved.

At the conclusion of Katie's recreation league soccer game on February 25, 2017, Maureen approached me with Katie by the hand. I was still there because I had decided that remaining in the public eye and waiting for Maureen to leave before me at events reduced the opportunities for her to make credible false claims. As soon as she was close enough, Maureen started verbally assaulting me and saying that I had "keyed her car" in the parking lot. I just walked to my car and left the park. I wanted to go look at her car but decided to just leave without going anywhere near her vehicle.

Later that evening, I was to pick up Katie for my timesharing. Because of the earlier drama, I called for police standby—to keep the peace, as they say. I called early to let the officer know what happened earlier and why I thought a peacekeeper would be useful. When Deputy Sheriff Stephen Ferreira badge #7432 arrived, he told me that he was, ironically, the same officer that answered the call at the soccer field six and half hours earlier. He told me that he inspected the alleged damage to Maureen's vehicle, licked his thumb, and wiped off the dirt. He told her was time for a car wash. He also said my daughter "threw me under the bus" by telling him that she saw her father with "a sharp object behind his back in the parking lot" during the game. The distance from the middle of the soccer field to the parking space Maureen used was over 250 feet. Deputy Ferreira told me that he questioned Katie and verified that she really couldn't see that far and that during her game, she probably wasn't really watching the parking lot. I don't know why Katie agreed to corroborate her mother's story, but she was 11-years-old, and I can only suppose that her mother pressured her in some way.

Deputy Ferreira did not file an actual police report because no crime had been found. He only filed a "call report" to record that the event happened. Two years later, I had the opportunity to subpoena and question Deputy Ferreira at a family court hearing regarding this episode. He testified only to a vague recollection of the event.

At another game during the same season, I was watching the game next to another dad, when he said, "Look, it's Katie!" Katie was running across the field with her hand over her mouth while vomiting. I realized that she was suffering the effects of heat exhaustion and ran across the field toward her. I caught up to her just as she was entering the ladies' restroom. I knew that Maureen was behind us, and she was certainly not as fast as Katie and me. Knowing that Maureen would be more focused on having a confrontation in the restroom than in helping Katie, I locked the door behind us. I immediately soaked some paper towels with cold water and put them under Katie's arms, behind her neck, and on her head. I focused only on the effort to get her body temperature down. Maureen banged on the door the whole time, but I ignored the noise and did what I knew had to be done. At that moment, neither Katie nor I needed to know whose timesharing time it was. The whole process only took five minutes or so, and we came out as soon as she was feeling a little better. I told Katie to sit in the shade just outside the restroom while I went to get her some cold drinking water. A woman who had come to use the restroom herself informed me that this was a women's restroom. Maureen had probably coerced her to say that during the few minutes we were in there. After I sat Katie down, I sarcastically told the woman that I voted for democrats just so I could use any restroom I wanted.

As another example, Maureen sometimes texted me to say she would be late bringing Katie. The reasons were varied, but sometimes she stated it was because Katie was invited to birthday parties. Maureen knew that if she allowed me to be around the people she told her stories to, they would discover that I wasn't nearly as horrible as she said. This would put her coercive efforts at risk. Therefore, it was very important to Maureen that I stay away from those people.

I started to document her tardiness and her reasons why in the form of police reports. When she sent a text, I simply called the police and had them read the court order. This put a record of the incident on file. To avoid a whole dramatic scene with the police at a child exchange, I did this while I waited for them to arrive. Once I had a few reports filed, I forwarded the report numbers to Maureen so she would know what I was doing. Suddenly, I was able to take Katie to these events myself. I found out later that Katie had not even gone to some of the events Maureen claimed she was at because Maureen simply didn't tell her about them. Katie found out she missed parties when her friends told her about them later. So, once again, trying to get Maureen to do the right thing resulted in Katie being punished by not being told about parties because she was with me.

Maureen also did not allow Katie to bring her cell phone to my home, which caused her to be cut off from her friends while she was with me. The cell phone rule ultimately caused Katie to not want to come to my home. It was quite a cunning and calculated move by Maureen for parental alienation purposes.

The effect all of this had on Katie was a whole other issue and, frankly, the most important. Her relationships with others around her, including her mother and me, started to show signs of having had enough. This had been going on for thirteen of her fifteen years. Most recently and working backwards, Katie and I are currently pretty much estranged. Despite the current order by the court, she will not answer or return my calls. I see her at her soccer games, and she responds only after looking to see where her mother is first, and does so with just a nod or a smile. Being in an environment for thirteen years that revolves around disapproval and rejection for showing love for or enjoyment of your dad has shown her what she needs to do to survive peacefully. As a young child, Katie found that when she went back to her mother, she was ignored if she started talking about what she did while with me.

An extreme example of this was on the day Katie learned to ride a two-wheeler, and she wanted to show her mom at the child exchange. So, she rode toward her mom on the bike and yelled, "Watch me!" Her mother leaned into her vehicle and totally ignored Katie. When Katie reached her car, Maureen lifted her head from whatever she was pretending to do and said, "Cool."

Presents that I gave to Katie were not welcome in Maureen's home. On Christmas, when Katie was 12 years old, I got her a Google Chrome laptop. She was ecstatic. She brought the computer back the following weekend and said she "didn't need it." Katie and I would often bake pies, cakes, and cookies together, especially when she was little. Each time, Katie wanted to take some back for her mother, and every time she did, they were thrown out. One particularly memorable occasion, Katie brought home a plate of chocolate chip cookies, and Maureen purposely left them outside so that they never entered her home. Katie told me that ants got all over them, and her mother threw the whole plate into the trash the next morning. Can you imagine not tasting a cookie that your young daughter mixed and baked? Any normal person would taste the cookie simply to encourage the child and make her feel good. When I questioned Maureen on the witness stand about it, she testified under oath that it was my objective to make her fat.

Katy Perry was one of Katie's favorite singers. After specifically asking Maureen if it was ok to bring Katie home late, I got two first row club seats for the Katy Perry concert on July 2, 2014, at the BBT Center in Sunrise, Florida. Just a little after the court-ordered time to have Katie back to her mother, I felt my phone vibrate in my pocket. It was Maureen. I answered the first call to remind Maureen that we were at the concert. She lambasted me about "drug use at concerts," that she never agreed to "allowing Katie to go" or "allowing her to come back late." I hung up and put the phone back in my pocket after setting it to silent. Maureen called back many more times, but since the silenced phone was in my pocket, I had no idea at the time. Katie asked me who was on the phone. I told her that her mom forgot the concert was tonight. Katie felt we should go because her mom might be mad. I convinced her that it was ok because her mother now remembered about the concert and that we would be back soon.

The concert was cute. Katy Perry flew around on a trapeze and inflated a costume to emulate levitating like a hot air balloon, among other things. We both enjoyed the show.

When we got to the child exchange location, six Palm Beach County Sheriff's police cruisers were waiting for us. Katie was fast asleep when we arrived and woke up to this ensuing drama caused by her mother. Maureen could have simply reported the late return, had a police report, and filed a motion in family court, but she chose to make sure that Katie was exposed to the extreme drama of this police-involved event.

Katie has never mentioned Katy Perry to me since.

Police, church, school, sports, etc. It didn't matter the circumstances. Maureen was unrelenting. I really think she thought

I would give up and go away. That was never going to happen as long as I had love for my child and the tenacity to fight to be a part of her life. Maureen's father's money could not outlast me and never will. Maureen's father actually sent me an email stating that I would have to live forever to outlast the money that was being used to erase me from Katie's life.

The problem was that working on a child the way that they did was just too much for Katie to endure. It was so much more peaceful to show them that she wanted nothing to do with me. That is how parental alienation syndrome works.

The alienation wasn't limited to just me; it included my mother, too. Maureen would not allow Katie to speak with my mother, not even on the phone. When Katie was little, my mom and Katie would have what my mother called "Our Friday Tea Party." Katie would be in the bathtub, her grandmother would be on speakerphone, and they would have this fun time talking together on the phone. Maureen put an abrupt stop to it for no reason. My mother was so broken up about it, she called Maureen's father to ask for help. After that phone call, she called me, crying, because he also refused to allow the calls.

Ultimately, my mother moved to Florida so she could have the chance to spend time with her granddaughter. My mother was very ill with a plethora of ailments, and she shouldn't have had to go to such lengths, but she hadn't seen Katie in over four years. I convinced her to move so that she could have the experience of being with her granddaughter, even if it was only when Katie came to visit on my weekends.

My mother died three months after moving to Florida. The bright side was that before she left this earth, she was able to find the joy she came for by spending time with Katie during my weekends with her. I look back on it, and it is as if she lived a little longer than she was supposed to just so she could be given that gift before she died. For that, I am grateful.

CHAPTER 14

Family Court's Final Sword Thrust

> " *We hang the petty thieves and*
> *appoint the great ones to public office.* "
> Aesop

Maureen filed a Petition for Modification that was intended to remove all of my parental rights. After Chris Jette's second attempt at getting a continuance of the trial, he suggested to me to get the judge recused because her family attended the same church as his family. I declined, and Jette wanted me to send him an email stating such.

On the day of the trial, Mr. Jette showed up with a legal pad and two pens. No witnesses, no evidence, no questions prepared. Nothing! We sat in court before the Honorable Sarah Willis, and Mr. Jette made his last attempt to request a continuance. The judge told Mr. Jette that he had already been twice denied that request but "we have to be here for four days anyway, so let's have a Temporary Relief Hearing."

That was the moment I should have stood up and told the court that Mr. Jette was negligent in his preparation for the scheduled hearing and that he was immediately to be excused as my counsel. I thought, "*Sure judge, let's make certain that these fine experts and bar association members get some more money in their pockets because that's what family court is all about, isn't it?! What about my witnesses that Mr. Jette told not to come? We don't have questions for a hearing, much less a trial. Sure, why not move forward. What else do we have to do? We might as well look for reasons to separate a father and a daughter."*

The first hearing on August 13, 2019 was for my motion for contempt against Maureen for "Willfully Violating Order Dated June 28, 2019." The actual order stated that Katie and I were to speak on the phone four days a week (Sunday, Tuesday, Wednesday, and Thursday) between 7:30 and 9:00 P.M. The order also stated that we were supposed to have "one engaging text daily." The last time I had spoken with Katie on the phone was in October of 2019. I had filed a Request to Produce regarding Katie's cell phone. I felt that was important because I believed Maureen was forwarding my texts to another phone so that Katie never saw them. After three hours of the diversion of talking about 170 pages of unrelated text messages that did not, in the least, purge Maureen from the allegations set forth in my motion, I finally lost it on the court. I objected on relevance multiple times. Magistrate James Williams III overruled the objection saying I opened the door for text messages, which made no sense to me whatsoever. All I brought up about text messages was related to the motion.

Anne Alper's testimony in court had become so disgustingly evasive, that it wasn't even worth cross-examining her. When I did try, she spoke about something that did not even remotely resemble an answer to my question. One time, she began to read from one of her status reports for five minutes. At one point in her exposition, I picked up my phone and began to read emails. When she concluded, I asked her if she recalled the question. An objection was made by counsel that the question was in the record and answered.

What Maureen was able to accomplish was a casserole of small orders that ultimately were the equivalent to a no-contact order. After losing about a dozen no-contact order attempts over twelve years with nine judges in three states and having spent over two million dollars, Maureen and her "Cavalcade of Collusive Coercives" took small bites over a period of time from my rights as a father. until the only time I saw Katie was at her soccer games. The only time that I was allowed to speak with Katie was during the court-ordered telephone calls that were being blocked by her mother. I filed two motions for contempt because the calls were not occurring. The third time I filed a motion was with Eric Cheshire representing me. I met Eric in his office and hired him to ghost write the third motion for contempt. I suggested this method because I knew that opposing counsel would inundate his office with calls, emails, and letters as soon as they knew he was involved. I told Eric that if he announced his appearance, he would end up being my attorney for three days after Hanrahan hit him with a barrage of communications.

Right up to and including Katie's fifteenth birthday, my hands were tied to even get a gift to her. Maureen installed a camera in her driveway that would alert her of any Amazon deliveries while she was at work and Katie was at home attending virtual school due to the Covid-19 pandemic. I hated using Coach John for this, but I had few options, so he would sometimes be the intermediary by delivering gifts to Katie for me. Unfortunately, once Maureen duped Coach John's wife, Veronica, into a friendship, Coach John coincidentally did a 180-degree turn on me after Maureen befriended Veronica. He was actually verbally abusive with me during a phone call about him not informing me about game scheduling changes.

Katie was under constant scrutiny, and going against the regime of her "captors" would surely result in consequences.

You see, I am aware of the strings that are attached to anything that Maureen's father would do. Maureen herself had so many strings tied to her that she was a virtual puppet. The family court system enabled all of this. This was ultimately accomplished by the actions and rulings of Judge Sarah Willis, who was a green-horn judge at the time of her erroneous orders based on false testimony, mostly by Anne Alper.

People suggested calling or texting Katie to let her know I had a gift, but Maureen monitored Katie's phone data, both in and out. People suggested mailing gifts to Katie, but Maureen had USPS Informed Delivery, so she got scans of all mail coming in. The efforts that went into parental alienation are difficult to understand by anyone who has not gone through it. Can you imagine being a child and being monitored for any correspondence from your other parent? It must be terrifying, and it's certainly abuse.

As all of this took place over time, it became clear to me that the court wasn't in any way concerned with my daughter's best interest. How could it be? The court enabled continued opportunities for drama at child exchanges by having Maureen and I present at a gas station or a Burger King. It would have been much easier to simply have me toot my horn at their house and have Katie come out to my car. Maureen could look through the blinds all she wanted, but that wouldn't create the engaging efforts offered at a location that had all three of us vulnerable to anything that could keep us coming back to court for more appearances, to generate more revenue.

If you haven't figured out that kids are for sale in family court to the highest bidder, and that parental alienation syndrome is the main basis of this story, then perhaps you don't know anyone who has gone through it, and you most assuredly you haven't gone through it yourself. This is indeed what our society has become. I can assure you that if you know someone who has lost time with his or her children, there is a good chance it was to the highest bidder. As long as states continue to reap benefits of Social Security Act IV-D, the situation will never change. States generate no federal incentive money for equal, shared custody, and even if there were standard 50/50 custody in every state, an alienating parent who wanted to fight it would and would still make false allegations against the targeted parent. If 50/50 parenting were the default ruling, the law would need to include criminal consequences for false allegations against the other parent. Until all of these factors become law, there will be no change in family court corruption.

Time after time, after thinking I couldn't find the strength within me to fight for my daughter's right to have a relationship with both of her parents, I held on and somehow reached inside and found that strength. This was not without cost, of course. My ongoing collateral damage consisted of the inability to be emotionally available to have any kind of relationship with a woman. And frankly, what woman in her right mind—and in her fifties—would sign up for this situation? I resolved to be alone. I certainly wasn't going to abandon my daughter. She needed to know that despite the horrible situation we were trapped in, I was not going to give up, ever. I could never compete with the millions of dollars spent to erase me, but I could be tenacious. I could be there—as close as I was able to be.

However, I often got tired, lonely, depressed, and heartbroken.

After the January 26, 2019 Temporary Relief Hearing that lasted four days with a completely unprepared Chris Jette as my attorney, who went in with the hopes of a continuance after unsuccessfully trying twice already, after that four day hearing, for all intents and purposes, I was erased. The only contact I had with Katie allowed by the court was four phone calls a week and seeing her at her soccer games with the inability to speak with her. Not even a high five after the game. With the exception of contempt motions filed against Maureen for not abiding by the phone calls ordered by the court, it would take an attorney costing another exorbitant amount of money to even make a dent in undoing what Judge Sarah Willis allowed. Even if I did, the war chest full of never ending money would out-finance me. After twelve years of fighting with and without legal counsel, I succumbed to defeat at the hands of the Kids for Cash Family Court system.

With the twelve-year fight basically over, I was still emotionally unavailable for any deserving partner. I found escape, relief, and partnership in very wrong choices. I sat in my home, sobbing from the depths of my soul. I can't even say it was daily; it was constant. This went on for months, affecting my self-esteem and health. I never abused the prescribed Xanax, but I needed one with coffee in the morning to get in the car and drive to the office. I continued to take the photos of Katie's soccer games, post them on Shutterfly, and send the album links to all of the parents. This made me feel like I was contributing something to Katie's life. One day on the way to work, the song "Pictures of You" by The Cure came on my Pandora channel. As I listened to the words of the song, I couldn't see the road through the tears while driving.

I was losing the will to live. Never for a moment, though, did I entertain taking my own life. What I chose to do was find relief from the emotional pain that I had previously been able to fight through on my own—with support of friends and sessions with Dr. Rathjens.

I lacked companionship, any form of bliss, or even contentment for that matter. So, I signed up for a dating app called Plenty of Fish and met a woman there who I thought I understood.

She used cocaine.

I thought I understood addiction from the stories I'd heard from people who went through it and expressed it to me over the years. It wasn't until I could not keep myself from getting out of my living room chair and walking out of my door to get rid of my sorrow that I really knew the grip that addiction has.

My approach to what I knew was a bad choice was going to be a one-day-a-month user. Kind of like a binge drinking night because "I deserve it," as I have heard it said. I found that cocaine use does not come with a hangover or residual effect mentally or physically to interfere with my ability to perform my duties at work.

This method lasted a while, but of course, it manifested into two weekend nights a month, and then I started on a Tuesday and missed work on Wednesday because the run wasn't over. Risky sexual behavior also accompanied using.

So much for what I later heard was my attempt to "use as a gentleman," I now had a whole new fight on my hands. This new addiction at fifty-eight years of age, had just affected the last part of my life that had any positive purpose: my job.

I called some addiction recovery facilities in the area and went through the process of applying for the federal FMLA program. I ended up at Banyan Treatment Center in Boca Raton, Florida for an inpatient program.

I know now why I will always need to consider myself an addict. This is not a choice. All reasonable thinking escaped me while in the grip of using. I could not believe that as a rational, responsible grown, human being that this could ever happen, but it did. I am sober today, and that's all I have is today.

When I hear the phrase, "Kids are resilient," I reply with "What choice do they have?" Katie has been victimized here and, just like millions of other children caught up in the Kids for Cash Family Court, her best interest is absolutely the last thing that the revenue-generating machine is concerned with. When I lost her to the millions dumped into this campaign, I victimized myself by trying to fill the emptiness in my life with self-medicating behaviors. I've literally worried myself sick over how Katie will fare as an adult in her relationships and the statistical factors that are associated with enduring this high conflict situation.

If there is one thing that I would want her to remember it's that this situation was never, is not, and will never be her fault and that it is okay for her to forgive those close to her for what they have done to erase her father from her life. What's important is that Katie finds her way in life knowing that even inside scars are stories and she cannot allow herself to be bitter over any aspect of what was her childhood.

I know that it's fantasy, and without the eye rolling reaction to the dramatics of it, I tell you: If someone could have guaranteed me that every one of Katie's tears from the conflict she endured in her childhood could have been replaced with smiles from a mother and father who did what was truly in her best interest for happiness, I would have allowed any one of my limbs to be surgically removed if it was possible for that exchange, without a second thought.

> I love you and miss you, and I am here for you. Know that even though you weren't here physically, you were always here in my heart. I am so sorry for what you have been through, sweetheart. Forgive, but do not forget so that you don't unconsciously repeat this behavior on your own children or their father. Be happy and spread the goodness that I know is in your heart.

On February 28, 2021, Katie's travel soccer team played in the championship. The game was at their home field, and they played Parkland, who was a very good team. Katie's team suffered a loss by a score of 3-0. Being the team photographer, I walked from taking the individual pictures of the girls receiving their 2nd place ribbons back to the field for team pictures. As I walked, Katie started walking right next to me. I put my arm around her, kissed her on her head, and told her that I was sorry they lost and that they played a good game. All of the stories of how she hated me, didn't want to be with me, was afraid of me, mostly coming from the $200,000.00, hired gun guardian ad litem, they weren't true. I didn't realize it until later that evening, but Katie didn't stiffen up or pull away from me. She leaned into me and took in my consoling of her. That may sound strange to someone who hasn't endured parental alienation, but when I realized what I received back from Katie in that moment was that over time she had simply succumbed to not showing love to her father because it was not allowed by those around her—people who were supposed to have loved her. But she showed that she did—absolutely—in that moment when no one was close enough to deliberately disrupt it.

I spoke in session with Dr. Rathjens as Katie approached 16 years old. I told him that I was considering going back to court with Eric Cheshire as my attorney to go for a third attempt at contempt against Maureen for having violated the court order that allowed me to speak to Katie on the phone. After the public scene that Maureen threw when I spoke with Katie at the soccer game, I felt Katie deserved one more fight for her rights to have both of her parents in her life, no matter how small.

CHAPTER 15

Epilogue: A Look Back and Forward

> *Life must be lived forward*
> *but only makes sense by looking backward.*
> *Only in retrospect do the pieces of the puzzle connect,*
> *revealing an intelligently orchestrated evolution.*
> *Our journey through life is in a way like walking blindfolded.*
>
> Dorit Brauer

From the moment that she was born, and right to the present day, Katie has brought me the happiest times of my life. In the process of clearing the proverbial jungle of drama that the court has enabled, I sit and remember those times. We had Rapids Water Park season passes. We were always the first ones there when the gates opened. The park had a front half and a back half. Getting there first, we did the entire front section. After completing the front half, we would eat our packed lunch in the picnic area while most of the other guests arrived to enjoy the front section of the park. After we ate our lunch, we would go to the back half of the park, which was still pretty much empty. By 2 p.m., we were exhausted, and we would leave before the noon guests got to the back half. One thing we liked to do was float on the Lazy River and yell things back and forth to each other. Katie was learning Spanish, and one day she yelled to me, "Daddy, no pee pee in aqua!" I laughed so hard. We kept it in our silly dialogue, and we yelled it back and forth during many future visits as we floated along, laughing.

We would go to the soccer field and she would rapid-fire soccer shots while I played goalkeeper. We went on the golf course behind my home so she could practice an aerial. I was there the day she finally nailed it. I was the one who let go of her the day she learned to ride a two-wheeler. One day she recognized a lost girl at a water park and brought it to my attention. I informed the mayor of Royal Palm Beach, who sent her a letter of proclamation in recognition of her outstanding civil duty. It was me who knew the importance of her battle with acne and took her to the cosmetic department of JC Penny. This was an amazing boost for her self-esteem. Letting her drive the golf cart was a thrill for both of us. She got acclimated with driving at 12 years old. I literally gave her driving lessons on the golf course. I introduced her to style and the world of fashion, starting with Justice. This manifested into H&M, Forever 21, and Hollister. All I do currently is secretly replenish a Visa debit card so she can enjoy products from Shein.com. Watching her spend that money online makes me think that she had to have been thinking about me even when she only treats herself to a pretzel at Auntie Anne's. Sometimes I cry even as I smile when I read her expenditures. We used to have our favorite television shows that we would watch together. I still know all the characters from Henry Danger, Gravity Falls, and Sam and Cat. We had enjoyable times laughing with those shows. I think our favorite character was Piper from Henry Danger. I coached her Upward Basketball team for two years. That had us very close. Katie learned how to lose gracefully first with no wins her first year and subsequently win gracefully being undefeated her last year. I almost never missed a soccer game. Taking and sharing the photos of Katie's soccer games was enjoyed by most, although few said so. I compile a photo album for Katie every Christmas from Shutterfly. The albums are really nice, and I keep the same cover, as if they represent yearly volumes.

I know that Katie knows how much I love her, and I know that she loves me. Things were made easier for her to simply conform to the hatred for her dad and join the alienation campaign of her mother. Having to live with that pressure as a little girl and over a course of 15 years, what would anyone expect? Many people, including close friends, people who have gone through similar, as well as professionals have told me that she will come around. The whole scenario will resonate in her, and I just hope that she will not resent her mother for this. I do not wish that for Maureen's sake. I wish that for Katie's sake. It is very important that Katie never take responsibility for joining the alienation campaign. This never was, isn't, and will never be her fault. I hope she gets the opportunity to play this out and manages to have a good life, especially in her relationships. In the meantime, I will not falter in my continued efforts to fight for my daughter's right to have a relationship with both of her parents. I didn't start this, but I will indeed finish it. They most assuredly messed with the wrong dad. I sometimes get tired and weary and need to take a break from the grueling fight that the court fuels for its own revenue generation, but I will never quit on my daughter. Never! The children of contemptuous divorces need to know that we are fighting for them for the right reasons. We do not fight for victory, not for revenge, not for ego, but for them. Be steadfast and unrelenting.

Recommended reading:
Divorce Poison by Dr. Richard Warshak

Made in the USA
Columbia, SC
25 July 2024

38787566R00157